PRAYERS

AFTER GOD'S OWN HEART

PRAYERS

AFTER GOD'S OWN HEART

*An invitation to enter into a deeper, more personal
relationship with your Heavenly Father*

A Daily Devotional

Robert Alan McArthur

ELM HILL

A Division of
HarperCollins Christian Publishing

www.elmhillbooks.com

Prayers after God's Own Heart
An invitation to enter into a deeper, more personal relationship with your Heavenly Father

Published in Nashville, Tennessee, by Elm Hill, an imprint of Thomas Nelson. Elm Hill and Thomas Nelson are registered trademarks of HarperCollins Christian Publishing, Inc.

Elm Hill titles may be purchased in bulk for educational, business, fund-raising, or sales promotional use. For information, please e-mail SpecialMarkets@ThomasNelson.com.

Library of Congress Cataloging-in-Publication Data

Library of Congress Control Number: 2019912032

ISBN 978-1-400327799 (Paperback)
ISBN 978-1-400327805 (Hardbound)
ISBN 978-1-400327812 (eBook)

DEDICATION

This devotional book is written and published all for the Glory of God and is lovingly dedicated to my wife, Jesse.

My dear and precious Jesse,

You are an amazing and beautiful woman inside and out. I can't even imagine what these last several years of my journey would have been like had you not been right here by my side—loving, learning, sharing, and growing along with me, as we have walked this path together toward a deeper and more personal relationship with God.

I love your zeal for Truth and your desire to search for the Truth of God's Word—as well as your heart to apply that Truth to your own life—so that you might please God in everything you think, say, and do.

I love watching God work in you, through you, and all around you as you make God the Father your first and best love. I admire how you faithfully follow the example of Christ, carefully listen for the voice of the Holy Spirit, and willingly act on His promptings in obedience to His plan and for His glory.

It is such a blessing to hear you speak of your own personal love relationship with your Heavenly Father—how He speaks to you, heals you, restores you to wholeness, and guides you gently and patiently along, calling you ever closer to Himself and showing you things you do not know in yourself.

You have been and continue to be one of God's greatest gifts to my life. Thank you for sharing this journey and believing in me. But even more so, thank you for believing with me, the God we believe in.

Thanks for marrying me—for being "one" with me—joined as one forever by the only true and living God!

Love always,
Robert

INTRODUCTION

This one-year daily devotional is the product of a choice that God brought me to in the fall of 2011. After stumbling through life for over fifty-seven years, I needed to decide if I was going to continue down the path I had been on or choose the better path that God had in mind for me.

Was I content to continue a life that had often lacked real meaning, purpose and direction, had produced much heartache, and had resulted in multiple broken relationships? Or was I ready to give up on doing life on my own terms and finally go "all in" with God's plan for me? Was I ready to learn to trust Him completely with my life? Was I willing to do whatever it took to stop living the lie that I had sold out to Jesus, when in truth I was still living a life of hypocrisy in many ways?

I was blessed to have been brought up in a Christian home and was saved when I was eleven years old. But my journey had been one of incomplete commitment to God's plan for my life, incomplete surrender of my will to His will, and a hidden and subtle selfishness that wanted things my way more than God's way. I was living much of my life in fear rather than in faith.

God had tried to get my attention on many occasions before. But this time, at this season of my life, something had changed in me. I was weary of not getting "life" right. I was tired of living a life of fear and uncertainty. I knew the answer would only be found in Him, and I was ready to make a change.

In Matthew, Jesus is quoted as saying, *"Your mistake is that you don't know the Scriptures, and you don't know the power of God."* (Matthew 22:29 – NLT). I know now that what Jesus said was certainly true of me at the time.

I had never actually read the whole Bible through—not even once! But if you had asked me then, I would have told you that I had a good grasp of the Bible. In truth, I had no idea of the vast richness of wisdom which it contains, nor a full understanding of its potential to bring change to my life.

And while I did know that God was a powerful God, I did not fully appreciate the power that is in the very pages of His written Word. I desperately needed to know the truth that it is alive with His power and His promises. I needed to experience personally how we are inevitably changed when we truly know and apply the Scripture to our lives!

It was at that time, and into those circumstances, that God invited me to join Him in a journey into His Word. He had me begin by writing a blog of prayers based on scripture passages from the Bible. The idea was for me to solidify the Truth of His Word within my heart and to apply that Truth, moment by moment, to every part of my life. He was inviting me to know Him in an intimate and personal way. At the same time, He was also inviting me to know myself through His eyes.

In order to ensure that I would remain consistent in reading and studying His Word, and writing these word-based prayers, I made a public commitment on the blog to make prayer posts every Monday, Wednesday, and Friday. Over 1,100 prayers later, I am continuing to write, God is continuing to reveal Himself, and He is continuing to grow me into the likeness of Christ.

My words are not enough to express the abundant life that I have stepped into as a result of God's gracious plan to give me a heart after His own heart. It is a life filled with His incredible peace, faithful protection, uninterrupted provision, enduring purpose, and unexplainable joy. All this because of His unrelenting, passionate, pursuing love for me. And along the way, I have learned that the healthiness of all my relationships is in direct correlation to the intimacy of my relationship with my Heavenly Father.

Still, at times it seems that I have only scratched the surface of all that He has for me. So, my daily prayer is that I will continue to grow and learn to become more like Christ for the rest of my life.

I made the decision to publish this devotional as an encouragement to others to join me on their own personal journey into intimate relationship with God. I trust that you will discover that there are great benefits to praying prayers that are drawn from the Word of God, because His Word *is* His will for your life, just as much as it is for mine.

My prayer is that you would come to know God as He wants to be known, as you embark on the journey of a lifetime to develop your own deeper, more personal, and intimate relationship with your Creator and Heavenly Father.

— Robert Alan McArthur

How to Get the Most Out of this Devotional

"So then faith comes by hearing, and hearing by the word of God."

— Romans 10:17 (NKJV)

I would very much encourage you to read aloud the scripture passage for each day. By doing this, you will hear yourself speak the Word and it will help you to focus on the truth found within it. As that truth is revealed, allow it to work in you, to change you into the person God intends for you to be.

I would further encourage you not only to read each prayer that follows the scripture passage, but also to *actually pray them* from your heart and allow them to lift you into His presence.

Lastly, I would encourage you to spend some time after each prayer to quiet your mind and allow God to speak to you.

I have found that doing these things allows the Spirit of God to work in me to deepen my personal relationship with my Heavenly Father.

May God richly bless you on your journey with Him!

In the Strength of Christ Alone,
Robert

To Know the Scriptures, To Know the Power of God

Jesus replied, "Your mistake is that you don't know the Scriptures, and you don't know the power of God."

— MATTHEW 22:29 (NLT)

Heavenly Father,

Give me that deep desire to know and understand the Scriptures—so I would no longer live my life in ignorance, but would walk fully in the power of Your Word.

Show me how my lack of knowledge of what Your Word says—and my lack of understanding as to how it relates to me personally in the particular circumstances of my life—leads me down paths of sin and error; how it leads me away from You.

Grant me an insatiable hunger and thirst to understand everything You have for me in Your Word, so my path might be made straight—as I submit myself to Your amazing plans and purposes for me.

Help my faith in Your power to be enlarged as You open the treasures of Your Word to me by Your Holy Spirit—as You pull back the dark veil of my ignorance and show me the glorious Truth of Your Word.

And grant that I might personally experience more of Your power at work in me, through me, and all around me—as I seek to deepen my relationship with You and come to know You more personally and intimately through Your Word.

Give me that deep desire to know and understand the Scriptures—so I would no longer live my life in ignorance, but would walk fully in the power of Your Word.

In the name of Jesus, Amen.

Let There Be Light

Then God said, "Let there be light," and there was light. And God saw that the light was good. Then he separated the light from the darkness.

— GENESIS 1:3–4 (NLT)

Creator of Light and Life,

Let every word I speak be birthed out of truth, seasoned with grace, spoken in faith and motivated by love—bringing light and life to anyone who has ears to hear.

You spoke, "Let there be light," and light came into being from nothing—forever demonstrating for us the creative power of Your spoken Word.

Knowing that You have made me in Your image, may I ever be mindful that the words I speak also contain a power to create—either something that is good or something that is evil.

Forgive me, LORD, for too often my careless words have created doubt instead of hope; resentment instead of respect; discouragement instead of encouragement; hurt instead of healing; darkness instead of light; and death instead of life.

Just as You saw that the light was good, help me to speak in such a way that I might see good things created from the words that You give me to speak—that with every word, I would represent Christ well and bring You glory.

Help me to walk fully in Your light—so I can be the messenger of light, that You created me to be, to those who are lost and separated from You by the evil darkness of this world.

Let every word I speak be birthed out of truth, seasoned with grace, spoken in faith and motivated by love—bringing light and life to anyone who has ears to hear.

In the name of Jesus, Amen.

Your Word Lights My Way

Your word is a lamp to guide my feet and a light for my path.

— PSALM 119:105 (NLT)

Heavenly Father,

Help me to take up the lamp of Your Word, discover the Truth that it holds, and let it light my way—through the perils of this world as I journey home to You.

You have given me Your Word that I might learn Truth from You—Truth about You, about myself, about right and wrong and good and evil, and about Your great plan for my life.

When I study Your Word, I discover things I would not know otherwise—because the light of Your Word illuminates the darkness for me—making it possible for me to see Your Truth.

You gave me Your Word to be a lamp to guide my feet, so that when I carry the lamp of Your Word within me, I can see clearly each step that I am taking and I do not have to fall—in my thoughts, words, or actions—as I move through this life.

You gave me Your Word to be a light for my path, so that as I move forward in faith—as I trust You illuminate before me the best path for me to walk—You will safely lead me all the way home to You.

Help me to take up the lamp of Your Word, discover the Truth that it holds, and let it light my way—through the perils of this world as I journey home to You.

In the name of Jesus, Amen.

To Keep on Asking, Seeking, Knocking

"Keep on asking, and you will receive what you ask for. Keep on seeking, and you will find. Keep on knocking, and the door will be opened to you. For everyone who asks, receives. Everyone who seeks, finds. And to everyone who knocks, the door will be opened."

— MATTHEW 7:7–8 (NLT)

Heavenly Father,

Help me to be persistent in my pursuit to learn more about You—so I can live in all the fullness of that close, personal, intimate relationship with You, which was made available to me through Christ.

Help me to keep asking You for good things—things that You want me to have—like knowledge and understanding of Your ways, wisdom to discern the truth in every situation, faith to believe, and mercy, love, and compassion for others.

Help me to keep on being intentional, purposeful, and relentless as I seek You with all my heart—and keep me from settling for a halfhearted, haphazard approach to discovering who You are, who I am in You, and understanding Your plans and purposes for my life.

Help me to keep knocking at the door of Your heart, knowing that You will always answer me and welcome me into Your Presence—when I come to You believing that You take great delight in showing me things I do not know.

Help me to be persistent in my pursuit to learn more about You—so I can live in all the fullness of that close, personal, intimate relationship with You, which was made available to me through Christ.

In the name of Jesus, Amen.

In Joy, in Peace

You will go out in joy
and be led forth in peace;
the mountains and hills
will burst into song before you,
and all the trees of the field
will clap their hands.

— Isaiah 55:12 (NIV)

Heavenly Father,

Help me to live in the joy and peace that You alone can provide for me as
I trust in the Truth of Your Word.

Your plan is that, as I accept the Gospel of Jesus Christ and as I allow Him to be Lord of my heart, I will go out from under the weight of sin, which has kept me from being who You intended me to be, and walk in the joyous freedom that You have purchased for me.

Your plan is for me to walk with You in obedience, so that I can keep the peace that only You can give—peace that is reserved for those who put their full confidence in You alone, no matter what circumstances they may face.

As I live in this joy and peace, I will see all creation join with me in praise to You, and be encouraged to move forward because of the transforming work You have done in my heart.

Help me to live in the joy and peace that You alone can provide for me as
I trust in the Truth of Your Word.

In the name of Jesus, Amen.

5

Blessed, Nourished, Strong, and Steadfast

Blessed is the man
Who walks not in the counsel of the ungodly,
Nor stands in the path of sinners,
Nor sits in the seat of the scornful;
But his delight is in the law of the LORD,
And in His law he meditates day and night.
He shall be like a tree
Planted by the rivers of water,
That brings forth its fruit in its season,
Whose leaf also shall not wither;
And whatever he does shall prosper.

— PSALM 1:1–3 (NKJV)

Heavenly Father,

Help me to delight in being faithfully obedient to Your law. Let it become
my habit to meditate on Your precepts, instructions, and teachings both
day and night.

Keep me from being a person who takes the advice of the ungodly to heart—or who follows after their example of bad behavior—only to find I have been led away from the Truth that can only be found in Your Word.

Keep me from being a person who stands around doing nothing, in the midst of evil people who continue in pursuing their sinful ways, when I should be declaring the Truth of Your Word—having been motivated to such boldness by my great love for others.

Keep me from being a person who sits down, joining company with those who would dare to ridicule You and defiantly reject You—mocking the blessings that are made available to all of us when we embrace the Truth of Your Word.

Let me be a person who has cultivated a desire to hold Your Word in his heart—whose best joy comes from considering, studying, and meditating on the Truth of Your Word at all times.

Let me be a person who is like a tree that was planted by the streams of water—nourished, strong, and steadfast—producing the kind of fruit that brings blessing to all those around me as I allow the Truth of Your Word to guide my life and bring glory to Your Name.

Help me to delight in being faithfully obedient to Your law. Let it become my habit to meditate on Your precepts, instructions, and teachings both day and night.

In the name of Jesus, Amen.

I Am Not Ashamed

For I am not ashamed of this Good News about Christ. It is the power of God at work, saving everyone who believes—the Jew first and also the Gentile. This Good News tells us how God makes us right in his sight. This is accomplished from start to finish by faith. As the Scriptures say, "It is through faith that a righteous person has life."

— ROMANS 1:16–17 (NLT)

Gracious God,

May I never shrink back from sharing the Good News about Christ with others—for it is a message of hope and salvation which carries life-changing power to everyone who believes.

Help me not to be embarrassed or ashamed of my own inadequate attempts to share the story of Your most amazing mercy and grace.
Instead, help me to focus my heart on You and trust Your Spirit to speak through me the message that You want heard.

Help me always to look for opportunities to share the Good News of how You make us right in Your sight—most importantly, of how it is accomplished from start to finish just by believing You.

Help me not to lose sight of the fact that this Good News about Christ is intended for everyone—that something this great simply must be shared.

Help me to express that this Good News about Christ brings life to all who believe—life for both the here and now, and for eternity.

May I never shrink back from sharing the Good News about Christ with others—for it is a message of hope and salvation which carries life-changing power to everyone who believes.

In the name of Jesus, Amen.

Listening to the Truth We Have Heard

*So we must listen very carefully to the truth we have heard, or we may
drift away from it.*

—HEBREWS 2:1 (NLT)

Heavenly Father,

*Don't allow me to drift away from the Truth—but cause me to listen very
carefully to the Truth that You speak into my life by Your Word and by
the witness of Your Spirit within me.*

Help me to hold onto the precious gift of Truth that I have been given—
Truth which continues to be revealed to me in proportion to my willingness
and obedience to continue to read and study Your Word.

Help me to be careful to remember the Truth I have heard—by regularly
meditating upon it—so that I would be ready to apply Your Truth to every situation or circumstance in which I find myself, as I mix my faith with Your Truth.

Help me to recognize and guard against the weakness of my mind. For
Your Truth is so quick to drain from my heart when I allow the enemy to speak
lies into my thoughts, or entertain the condemnation that he spews, as he tries
to move me from the Truth I find in You.

*Don't allow me to drift away from the Truth—but cause me to listen very
carefully to the Truth that You speak into my life by Your Word and by
the witness of Your Spirit within me.*

In the name of Jesus, Amen.

Like a Treasure

"The Kingdom of Heaven is like a treasure that a man discovered hidden in a field. In his excitement, he hid it again and sold everything he owned to get enough money to buy the field."

— MATTHEW 13:44 (NLT)

Heavenly Father,

Like an open field You have placed Your Word before me. Help me to diligently search within it for the treasure that You have hidden there for me and then make me willing to sacrifice everything in order to make that treasure my own.

Help me not to be satisfied to observe this field from a distance. Rather, help me to walk carefully through this field, searching its every corner, digging deep below the surface to find that which I might not readily see with a glance—so I will discover all of the treasure it holds for me.

Help me to understand that the treasure hidden there is Christ Himself—and that in fully discovering Him and making Him my own, I will experience the life that You have reserved for those who have received Him.

So help me more fully experience that abundant and forever life You have for me—as I receive Your mercy, grace, forgiveness, knowledge, wisdom, righteousness, joy, peace, provision, power, and unconditional love.

And as I search, help me to be careful to listen for the voice of Your Holy Spirit—speaking to me and instructing me through the words of Your love story to me—and help me to then be faithful to do all that You show me to do, with grateful obedience that flows from my love for You.

Like an open field, You have placed Your Word before me. Help me to diligently search within it for the treasure that You have hidden there for me and then make me willing to sacrifice everything in order to make that treasure my own.

In the name of Jesus, Amen.

The Path I Should Take

Trust in the LORD with all your heart;
do not depend on your own understanding.
Seek his will in all you do,
and he will show you which path to take.

— PROVERBS 3:5–6 (NLT)

Sovereign and Loving LORD,

Let me always trust You with all of my heart, so that I do not rely on my own understanding but seek Your will in all that I do—knowing You will show me the path I should take.

Help me to lean only on You—to trust You completely and to remain confident that You have great plans for me—as I commit my love and surrender my life to You.

Help me not to depend on my own limited insights or understanding of things, but rather to put my trust in Your unlimited wisdom and understanding—always confident that You love me and always want what is best for me.

Help me understand that as I choose to trust You—more than I trust myself—You will show me what I should do and will remove every obstacle from my path, in order to bring me to that place where You have called me to live in Christ.

Let me always trust You with all of my heart, so that I do not rely on my own understanding but seek Your will in all that I do—knowing You will show me the path I should take.

In the name of Jesus, Amen.

The One Who Rescues Me

The LORD is close to the brokenhearted;
he rescues those whose spirits are crushed.
The righteous person faces many troubles,
but the LORD comes to the rescue each time.

— PSALM 34:18–19 (NLT)

Heavenly Father,

Thank You that when my heart is broken, when my spirit is crushed, and when I face many troubles, You remain close to me and You never let me slip from Your rescuing grip.

Teach me to trust You—whether my troubles appear to be insurmountably huge in my own eyes, or are just a series of small frustrations that have piled up on me to wear me down and rob me of my strength. Remind me that You are always here to rescue me.

Thank You for all the times when You have sovereignly chosen to rescue me by either shielding me from the trouble I was facing or by entirely removing the trouble from me.

Thank You for all the times when You have chosen to rescue me by equipping me with the strength, courage, and discerning wisdom that enabled me to remain in Your peace and push through the trouble that came against me.

And even though I may face many troubles—because I have chosen to walk in the righteousness of Christ—let me not be afraid but only believe that I will see Your goodness through it all, as I look to You to rescue me.

Thank You that when my heart is broken, when my spirit is crushed, and when I face many troubles, You remain close to me and You never let me slip from Your rescuing grip.

In the name of Jesus, Amen.

Filled with Joy and Gladness in You

But may all who search for you
be filled with joy and gladness in you.
May those who love your salvation
repeatedly shout, "The LORD is great!"

— PSALM 40:16 (NLT)

Great and Glorious LORD God,

May I forever be filled with the joy and gladness of being in Your Presence—as I search to find You at work in every moment of each new day!

Help me to seek You first and seek You always:

- *In praise and worship*—as I boldly declare who You are and testify to the amazing things You have done for me, with joy and gladness.
- *In prayer*—as I pour out the depths of my heart before You.
- *In reading and studying Your Word*—as I search to know You more.
- And *in quietness before You*—so that I might hear Your Spirit speaking to my spirit.

Let me repeatedly shout, "The LORD is great!" when I see Your love at work:

- *In me*—as You change my heart and patiently mold me into who You designed me to be.
- *Through* me—as You use me to minister Your salvation to others, filling my mouth with words of Truth and Grace, and causing all of my actions to be a reflection of Christ's love for us all.
- *And all around* me—as You show me how I can be part of the work that You are doing in the lives of those You sovereignly place in my path.

May I forever be filled with the joy and gladness of being in Your Presence—as I search to find You at work in every moment of each new day!

In the name of Jesus, Amen.

The God Who Knows My Every Sorrow and Collects My Every Tear

You keep track of all my sorrows.
You have collected all my tears in your bottle.
You have recorded each one in your book.

— PSALM 56:8 (NLT)

Compassionate LORD God,

Down all the paths of sorrow, where my wanderings sometimes lead,
remind me that you see each tear and know my every need.

When I find myself in a place of great sorrow—when I start to waver between faith and fear—comfort me with the assurance that You see me, You completely understand what I am feeling, and You are right there with me to carry me through my sadness and bring me back to that place of joy.

You know the end of every problem and trouble that I face before it even comes, but still You feel the hurt of every pain that I suffer along the way. Nothing that happens to me goes unnoticed, unrecorded, or unremembered by You—for You are lovingly compassionate and just—my God and my Defender.

Quiet my heart and soothe my restless emotions, so I can live in the peaceful reassurance that You intimately know and care about every detail of my life and are actively working for good through everything that happens—as You draw me closer to You.

Down all the paths of sorrow, where my wanderings sometimes lead,
remind me that you see each tear and know my every need.

In the name of Jesus, Amen.

Servant Leadership

So Jesus called them together and said, "You know that the rulers in this world lord it over their people, and officials flaunt their authority over those under them. But among you it will be different. Whoever wants to be a leader among you must be your servant, and whoever wants to be first among you must be the slave of everyone else. For even the Son of Man came not to be served but to serve others and to give his life as a ransom for many."

— MARK 10:42–45 (NLT)

Heavenly Father,

Help me to understand that when I sense You prompting me to lead, You are really prompting me to serve.

Thank You for the leadership example of Christ, Who came not to be served but to serve others and to give His very life as a ransom for many.

Help me to remember what true leadership requires—remembering it has nothing to do with what I might receive from others and everything to do with what I can do for them.

Thank You for showing me that my greatest joy in leading comes as I discover the joy of humbly serving others.

Help me to understand that when I sense You prompting me to lead, You are really prompting me to serve.

In the name of Jesus, Amen.

The True and Right Paths of the LORD

Let those who are wise understand these things.
Let those with discernment listen carefully.
The paths of the LORD are true and right,
and righteous people live by walking in them.
But in those paths sinners stumble and fall.

— Hosea 14:9 (NLT)

LORD of Heaven and Earth,

Give me the wisdom to search Your Holy Scriptures that I might gain
understanding. And grant me the discernment to listen carefully to Your
Spirit and walk uprightly in Your paths—to faithfully apply the Truth of
Your Word to my life.

I know that all Your paths are true and right—and that because You chose
to make me righteous through the sacrifice of Christ, I will find the abundant
life that You promised me by faithfully walking in those paths.

I know that without Christ, I could not walk those paths without stumbling
and falling. So help my heart to swell with compassion for those who don't yet
have Your light within them, to illuminate the path before them.

And make me bold to share that precious hope that is mine in Christ—that
they, too, can walk in those true and right paths that lead to *abundant life* and
a *forever home* with You.

Give me the wisdom to search Your Holy Scriptures that I might gain
understanding. And grant me the discernment to listen carefully to Your
Spirit and walk uprightly in Your paths—to faithfully apply the Truth of
Your Word to my life.

In the name of Jesus, Amen.

Loving God with Wholehearted Obedience

And you must love the LORD your God with all your heart, all your soul, and all your strength. And you must commit yourselves wholeheartedly to these commands that I am giving you today.

— DEUTERONOMY 6:5–6 (NLT)

O LORD My God,

Help me to learn to live in that place where the love I have for You flows freely out of me—in wholehearted obedience to everything You have commanded me—that place where I truly love You with everything that I am.

Your Word shows me that it isn't enough just to say I love You and then go on my way—pouring my heart into my own pursuits and disregarding Your will, Your plans, and Your purposes for my life.

Your Word cries out for me to have a love relationship with You as it commands me to love You completely—with all that is within me—so that there is not anyone or anything that can take Your rightful place in my heart.

I want my love for You to burst from my spirit and flood my mind, will, and emotions—so completely saturating me that with every ounce of strength in me, I prove my love for You in my every thought, word, and action.

Help me commit to love You that way, so that I can fulfill all of Your commands and instructions—and experience the joy of living in Your peace under Your protection, because of Your provision for my every need.

Help me to learn to live in that place where the love I have for You flows freely out of me—in wholehearted obedience to everything You have commanded me—that place where I truly love You with everything that I am.

In the name of Jesus, Amen.

My Salvation, My Strength, and My Song

"Behold, God is my salvation,
I will trust and not be afraid;
For the LORD God is my strength and song,
And He has become my salvation."

— ISAIAH 12:2 (NASB)

LORD God Almighty,

You are my strength and song—the One who saves me in every way! I
choose to trust You and not be afraid!

With wide-eyed wonder and an ever grateful heart, I declare that You are my salvation—not only because of the saving work of grace that was accomplished through the sacrifice of Your Son, but also because of the place of perfect peace and safety You have reserved and called me to in Him.

Knowing what You did for me, how can I still be afraid? How can I *not* believe that You will take care of every temporal need while I am here—working all things for my good because of Your great love for me—until such time as I am forever there with You?

Help me to reflect Your faithfulness to me at all times—by my consistent obedience to Your Word and Your Spirit—as I put all of my hope and faith in You for the continuing salvation that You have promised to me.

Be my strength—flooding the void of my weakness with Your sustaining power—equipping me in every way for every battle of faith that comes along the path upon which You have set me.

Be my song—overwhelming my spirit with Your Holy Spirit—so that the music of my life would be one of continual praise and thanksgiving for all You have done and uninterrupted worship for all that You are.

You are my strength and song—the One who saves me in every way! I
choose to trust You and not be afraid!

In the name of Jesus, Amen.

A Wise Hunger for Knowledge

A wise person is hungry for knowledge,
while the fool feeds on trash.

— Proverbs 15:14 (NLT)

Heavenly Father,

Let my God-given appetite for more knowledge be expressed in my life by
my hunger for a deeper understanding of Your will and Your ways—as
I seek first to know You. For only in You can I find my way, discover the
truth, and fully live.

Don't ever allow me to think that I know more than I know, but keep me humble and hungry to know more about You—so I can experience You more completely and will recognize Your hand at work in every new thing that I learn.

And in discovering who You are, help me to see who I am to You and understand more fully all the things that You have done for me—so that I will continue to grow into that person who only searches after the Truth and doesn't just collect knowledge for knowledge's sake.

Save me from the foolishness of settling for feeding from this world's trash heap of lies in order to satisfy my heart's hunger to know more—when You have prepared an abundant feast of Truth for me in Your Word.

Let my God-given appetite for more knowledge be expressed in my life by
my hunger for a deeper understanding of Your will and Your ways—as
I seek first to know You. For only in You can I find my way, discover the
truth, and fully live.

In the name of Jesus, Amen.

Beautiful for Its Own Time

Yet God has made everything beautiful for its own time. He has planted eternity in the human heart, but even so, people cannot see the whole scope of God's work from beginning to end.

— ECCLESIASTES 3:11 (NLT)

Heavenly Father,

Oh that I would see the beauty of everything that You have created—of all things You have done—and rest in the comfort and assurance of Your sovereignty, mercy, grace, and love.

Help me to accept that I am not able to see the whole scope of the work You are doing from beginning to end—and that sometimes it will be hard for me to see the beauty of what You have done, because the work is not yet complete.

Thank You for that glimpse of the perfection of eternity that You have planted in my heart—a taste of what is yet to come that keeps me never quite satisfied with anything this world has to offer, but always yearning for the perfect world that will only come by Your perfect rule.

Thank You for making me in Your image—so that the longing and hungering of my heart can only be truly satisfied by more of You in my life.

Oh that I would see the beauty of everything that You have created—of all things You have done—and rest in the comfort and assurance of Your sovereignty, mercy, grace, and love.

In the name of Jesus, Amen.

Finding Freedom in Surrender

"So why do you keep calling me 'Lord, Lord!' when you don't do what I say?"

— LUKE 6:46 (NLT)

Heavenly Father,

Help me to fully realize that making Jesus Christ the Lord of my life involves so much more than merely calling out to Him, "Lord, Lord!"

Help me to understand and accept the truth that in order for Jesus to be my Lord, I must freely surrender the liberty of *my free will* over to *His will for me*—and then and only then find true freedom from the things that hold me captive.

Help me remember that my obedience to His commands and instructions is the best measurement of His Lordship over my life—and that the example of how He lived His life is the only standard of comparison by which I should examine my own life.

Keep me from the hypocrisy of claiming Christ as my Lord while choosing to go my own way—allowing my own fleshly desires to control me rather than living surrendered to the Spirit of Christ that lives in me.

Help me to fully realize that making Jesus Christ the Lord of my life involves so much more than merely calling out to Him, "Lord, Lord!"

In the name of Jesus, Amen.

Everything Working Together for My Good

And we know that God causes everything to work together for the good of those who love God and are called according to his purpose for them.

— ROMANS 8:28 (NLT)

Merciful and Gracious God,

Help me to walk my life path courageously—in the strength, joy, hope, and peace that come from truly believing that You are always working all things together for my good.

Sometimes it is easy for me to believe that You are at work to bring about Your perfect plan and purpose for my life—especially when it seems, from my viewpoint, as if everything is flowing smoothly and falling into place just as it should.

Sometimes it is hard for me to see Your hand at work for my good—when I am so consumed by the difficult things that I am facing at a particular moment, that I fail to trust that my present trials will take me to a place where You can ultimately use them for my good.

Help me to remember that it isn't about what I see—for *my sight* and *my insight* regarding what is really going on is so limited—but it is all about trusting in the truth that You are always demonstrating Your unfailing love for me in everything I experience.

Remind me that even when it isn't so obvious, You never stop working to use whatever I may face in this life to bring about good for me—because I have chosen to *love You back* and *walk in the calling* that You have placed on my life.

Help me to walk my life path courageously—in the strength, joy, hope, and peace that come from truly believing that You are always working all things together for my good.

In the name of Jesus, Amen.

The Sense to Follow Your Commands

You made me; you created me.
Now give me the sense to follow your commands.

— PSALM 119:73 (NLT)

Creator God,

Knowing how well You know me—and what is best for me—help me to
have the good sense to follow Your commands.

You are my Creator. You made me by Your own hands—You created me according to Your own design and set me in place for Your own particular plans and purposes.

You created me, You designed me, to best function according to the commands of Your Word—and for me to try to function in any other way would be a misuse of who I was created to be and a denial of what I was created for.

Now, grant me a teachable spirit and the wisdom to study Your commands—that I may understand and willingly apply Your commands to my life—knowing that I can only fulfill my purpose and find Your provision for me in obedience.

Knowing how well You know me—and what is best for me—help me to
have the good sense to follow Your commands.

In the name of Jesus, Amen.

The Foundation of Wisdom, the Path to Good Judgment

Fear of the LORD is the foundation of wisdom.
Knowledge of the Holy One results in good judgment.

— PROVERBS 9:10 (NLT)

Most Holy God,

Help me to live with the understanding that any true wisdom which I might gain can only be built upon the foundation of my reverential fear of You, and that an intimate knowledge of You—which comes through my experience of a personal relationship with You—results in my having good judgment.

Help me to stand in awe in Your Presence, overwhelmed by Your Holiness, Power, and Majesty—fearing Your wrath yet trusting in Your mercy, grace and forgiveness, and completely dependent upon You to direct me according to Your unfailing love for me.

Don't allow me to stumble through life, carelessly making foolish decisions without taking time to consider Your will, plan, and purpose for me—when You have made Your paths of wisdom available for me to walk down.

Help me to know You more—more deeply, more completely, more intimately—so that my knowledge of Your ways would help me to make wise choices which reflect good judgment and bring glory and honor to You.

Help me to live with the understanding that any true wisdom which I might gain can only be built upon the foundation of my reverential fear of You, and that an intimate knowledge of You—which comes through my experience of a personal relationship with You—results in my having good judgment.

In the name of Jesus, Amen.

My Hope, My Help, My Strength, My Victory

Don't be afraid, for I am with you.
Don't be discouraged, for I am your God.
I will strengthen you and help you.
I will hold you up with my victorious right hand.

— ISAIAH 41:10 (NLT)

Heavenly Father,

Help me boldly move forward into this day with You—with confidence, with courage, and with great strength—upheld in every way by Your ever-victorious right hand!

Help me to see that there is nothing to fear, because You are actively present with me at all times to protect and deliver me from all the attacks of the enemy—whether they be attacks against my body, my mind, or my spirit. Thank You that You never leave me!

Keep discouragement far from me by helping me to find my courage in You, knowing You—the Creator and Sustainer of all things—are my loving Heavenly Father and the all-powerful LORD God. Thank You for being my God!

Help me to receive Your strength—as by Your Spirit You show me Your power at work within me to help me. Thank You that You help me according to Your unmatched strength!

Hold me up with Your victorious right hand—that I might not fall but rather accomplish everything that You have called me to do in service to You. Thank You for being my victory in all things!

Help me boldly move forward into this day with You—with confidence, with courage, and with great strength—upheld in every way, by Your ever-victorious right hand!

In the name of Jesus, Amen.

Just How Far True Love Will Go

For God so loved the world that He gave His only begotten Son, that whoever believes in Him should not perish but have everlasting life. For God did not send His Son into the world to condemn the world, but that the world through Him might be saved.

— John 3:16–17 (NKJV)

Heavenly Father,

Thank You!

Thank You for Your amazing love for us—a love which is ever reaching out to us to draw us into relationship with You.

Thank You for the amazing love that You freely gave in the form of Your only begotten Son—who You willingly sacrificed so we could know just how far true love will go.

Thank You for the freedom You bought for us and the path to joy and peace that You laid out before us—when Christ laid down His life for us.

Thank You for *not* sending Your Son to condemn us to die as we deserved—but to offer us life everlasting with You.

Thank You!

In the name of Jesus, Amen.

Secret Things and Things Revealed

The secret things belong to the LORD our God, but the things revealed belong to us and to our children forever, that we may follow all the words of this law.

— DEUTERONOMY 29:29 (NIV)

Infinite and All-knowing God,

Help me to use my time wisely, to become submitted and obedient to do those things that You have asked me to do—as revealed to me through Your Word and by Your Holy Spirit—trusting that You will show me everything I need to know in order to accomplish Your Will for me.

In Your infinite wisdom You have chosen to make me finite in my ability to comprehend and understand the secret wonders of all that You are—and of all that You have done, are doing, and have yet to bring to pass—so that my dependence would be on You alone.

Teach me that even though You have not revealed to me everything there is to know, I am responsible for everything that You *have* shown me—and that any disobedience in me is an act of my own rebellious will and *not* because I lack the knowledge I need to obey.

Help me to rest in the assurance that I serve an infinite and all-knowing God who loves and wants me—a God who is in control over everything and has revealed all the Truth that I will ever need in order to believe Him, to obey Him, and to see His salvation in my life.

Help me to use my time wisely, to become submitted and obedient to do those things that You have asked me to do—as revealed to me through Your Word and by Your Holy Spirit—trusting that You will show me everything I need to know, in order to accomplish Your Will for me.

In the name of Jesus, Amen.

Fixing Our Gaze on Things that Cannot be Seen

So we don't look at the troubles we can see now; rather, we fix our gaze on things that cannot be seen. For the things we see now will soon be gone, but the things we cannot see will last forever.

— 2 CORINTHIANS 4:18 (NLT)

Heavenly Father,

Help me look beyond any troubles that I see pressing in around me and help me to fix my gaze on the things that I cannot see—those things that will last forever but can only be known by faith.

Help me to remember that the troubles of this life that I face today are temporary and will soon pass away—just as everything that I now see with my eyes will one day be gone.

Help me to set the eyes of my heart on those things that I cannot see with my physical eyes—things which are timeless and deathless, which bring me eternal life and are *infinitely more real* than those things which I do see with my eyes.

Thank You that this life is not all there is—with its sickness, pain, suffering, persecution, and injustice—but that even while I am here You will use every hardship that I face for my ultimate good, and that in Your perfect timing, You will set all things right if I will surrender my will to Yours.

Keep me forward-thinking to that which awaits me—not as an escape from the troubles that I face but rather to keep them in perspective with the great plan that You have for my eternal destiny with You—as You keep me at peace and sustain me with Your strength through every hardship I face.

Help me look beyond any troubles that I see pressing in around me and help me to fix my gaze on the things that I cannot see—those things that will last forever but can only be known by faith.

In the name of Jesus, Amen.

What the LORD Requires of You

No, O people, the LORD has told you what is good,
and this is what he requires of you:
to do what is right, to love mercy,
and to walk humbly with your God.

— MICAH 6:8 (NLT)

Gracious and Loving LORD,

Thank You for giving me Your Word—for through Your Word I can learn
what is good and what You require of me.

Help me to do what is right. Reveal to me the Truth of Your Word and help me to fully believe it—knowing it flows from Your unfailing love for us all. Help me obediently apply that Truth to all my thoughts, words, and actions, as I choose Your ways over my own.

Help me to love mercy. Out of my overwhelming gratefulness to You for my own personal experience of Your continual mercy towards me—and an understanding that it is that same merciful love You offer to every one of us— let me be a loving vehicle of Your mercy to everyone around me.

Help me to walk humbly with You. Don't allow me to disobediently lag behind You or arrogantly run ahead of You, but let me walk submissively with You, intent on doing Your will.

Thank You for giving me Your Word—for through Your Word I can learn
what is good and what You require of me.

In the name of Jesus, Amen.

And You Will Find Rest for Your Souls

This is what the LORD says:
"Stop at the crossroads and look around.
Ask for the old, godly way, and walk in it.
Travel its path, and you will find rest for your souls.
But you reply, 'No, that's not the road we want!'"

— JEREMIAH 6:16 (NLT)

O LORD, My God,

Save me from any rebellious tendency of my heart to wander from Your
perfect path, the path that leads me to the very best that You have planned
for me—the only path where I will find rest for my soul! Let me never say,
"No, that's not the road I want!"

At every crossroads of life, help me to stop and look around—to take the time to carefully consider the ways that are set before me—and not just plow ahead following after my own fleshly desires or the ways of this world.

Remind me to ask, "What is the wise thing to do? The proven and godly way to go? The very best that You have for me?"—then grant me the faith to walk with You, my eyes fixed upon You, as You unfold Your plan before me one step at a time.

Help me choose to travel the best path, knowing that along that path I will find rest for my soul—I will remain at peace and be filled with joy—as you provide, protect, and keep me physically, mentally, emotionally, and spiritually whole.

Save me from any rebellious tendency of my heart to wander from Your
perfect path, the path that leads me to the very best that You have planned
for me—the only path where I will find rest for my soul! Let me never say,
"No, that's not the road I want!"

In the name of Jesus, Amen.

Being Believers,
United in Heart and Mind

All the believers were united in heart and mind. And they felt that what they owned was not their own, so they shared everything they had.

— Acts 4:32 (NLT)

Heavenly Father,

Grant that I would always do all I can to walk in unity of heart and mind with my brothers and sisters in Christ—and be willing and ready to share with them anything from that with which I have been blessed.

Remind me that no person was meant to live this life alone—that as a part of the greater body of Christ, we all must work together in unity for the same goals and purposes, in order to bring glory to You.

Help me to be a defender of unity—to make little of what sets us apart from one another and much of what unites us together, because of Your unfailing love for each of us.

Help me not to forget that what You have given me is as much intended for the benefit of others as it is for my benefit—that it is entrusted to me not to have, not call my own, but to be used for Your glory and honor.

Show me how I cannot fully experience the intended blessing of those things that I have been given until I choose to share them with others.

Grant that I would always do all I can to walk in unity of heart and mind with my brothers and sisters in Christ—and be willing and ready to share with them anything from that with which I have been blessed.

In the name of Jesus, Amen.

The Infinite Reach of Your Thoughts and Your Ways

"My thoughts are nothing like your thoughts," says the LORD.
"And my ways are far beyond anything you could imagine."

— ISAIAH 55:8 (NLT)

Sovereign LORD,

How limited I am in my understanding and yet how gracious You are—
when I put my trust in You—to show me things I could never come to
understand on my own!

You are the Sovereign LORD—my infinitely powerful, infinitely present, infinitely wise, infinitely loving Heavenly Father. How foolish it would be for me to depend on my own understanding or presume Your thoughts do not reach infinitely farther than mine!

Show me how I am kept from fully understanding Your thoughts and Your ways by the finite limits of my mind and by sin's assault on Truth—which distorts my thinking—so that I might not forget how I am totally dependent on You.

Draw me close and teach me to pursue a more personal and intimate relationship with You—so I might learn to trust more completely in Your love for me and Your absolute knowledge of, and provision for, everything that I need to accomplish Your will and purpose for me.

How limited I am in my understanding and yet how gracious You are—
when I put my trust in You—to show me things I could never come to
understand on my own!

In the name of Jesus, Amen.

Joy in Every Storm

Dear brothers and sisters, when troubles come your way, consider it an opportunity for great joy. For you know that when your faith is tested, your endurance has a chance to grow. So let it grow, for when your endurance is fully developed, you will be perfect and complete, needing nothing.

— JAMES 1:2–4 (NLT)

Heavenly Father,

In every situation, in any storm that comes, help me never lose my joy!

I know that troubles will come my way, because no one is exempt. But help me look for the good that You will bring out of every situation.

Help me to consider troubles as opportunities for me to have great joy in You, knowing You will go with me, that You will teach me, and that You will help me to grow as I allow You to carry me through the midst of the trouble.

When the enemy comes against me with trials and temptations to try to steal my joy, help me to pass the testing of my faith.

Help me to trust You with patient endurance—not just pretending to be happy—but remaining truly joyful, looking to You to rescue me, so I can become the mature and complete person that You want me to be.

In every situation, in any storm that comes, help me never lose my joy!

In the name of Jesus, Amen.

Relationship Building Prayer

Before daybreak the next morning, Jesus got up and went out to an isolated place to pray.

— MARK 1:35 (NLT)

Heavenly Father,

Help me to follow after the example of Your Son, Jesus, and seek after You in prayer—before the busyness of life crowds out my time alone with You and robs me of that desperately needed refreshing I receive from simply being in Your presence.

Each and every day, help me to *first* go to You *alone* in prayer—before the concerns of the day have an opportunity to overrun my thoughts—so that through my time with You, all of the demands of my day can be viewed from Your divine perspective.

Help me to find a *quiet place* with You—removed from anything that would distract me from the quality time I need to devote to spending with You—so that I can *tell* You the things on my heart and *hear* those things that You would *speak into* my heart.

Help me be *consistent* in seeking You out in prayer, knowing that the development of my relationship with You—coming to more fully understand and live out Your divine plan for how You and I relate to each other—must be my greatest priority if I am to please You in everything that I do.

Help me to carry that *attitude of prayer* and *passion for Your presence* with me throughout the day—so that my communion with You might continue like a warm and open conversation, as I seek to follow Your leading in everything that I do.

Help me to follow after the example of Your Son, Jesus, and seek after You in prayer—before the busyness of life crowds out my time alone with You and robs me of that desperately needed refreshing I receive from simply being in Your presence.

In the name of Jesus, Amen.

Judge Fairly, Show Mercy, Be Kind

"This is what the LORD of Heaven's Armies says: Judge fairly, and show mercy and kindness to one another."

— ZECHARIAH 7:9 (NLT)

O LORD of Heaven's Armies,

May all my judgments be fair and let mercy and kindness flow from me to others—as I am reminded of the way You judge everything about me fairly, yet still lavish me with love and grace, pouring out Your mercy and kindness upon me.

Keep me from standing arrogantly in judgment of others—condemning people who do not know You for their actions. For only You can truly know and judge the motives and intents of the heart of a person—including my own heart.

So instead, give me the boldness to speak the Truth in love against that which is sin—as You have revealed it in Your Word—all the while showing the same mercy and kindness that You pour out upon us all, because of Your great love for each one of us.

Grant me the wisdom to fairly and truly judge between what is right and good, and what is wrong and evil—by correctly applying the Truth of Your Word to each situation and to every person's actions—so that I would live a life full of truth and grace and bring glory to You by all of my thoughts, words, and actions.

May all my judgments be fair and let mercy and kindness flow from me to others—as I am reminded of the way You judge everything about me fairly, yet still lavish me with love and grace, pouring out Your mercy and kindness upon me.

In the name of Jesus, Amen.

The Mercy, Compassion, and Unfailing Love of Our God

The LORD is merciful and compassionate,
slow to get angry and filled with unfailing love.
The LORD is good to everyone.
He showers compassion on all his creation.
All of your works will thank you, LORD,
and your faithful followers will praise you.

— Psalm 145:8–10 (NLT)

Merciful and Compassionate LORD,

Thank You for the mercy and compassion with which You show us Your unfailing love. Let my heart and voice forever join the chorus of all of Your creation in unending thanks and praise to You!

Thank You for the kindness and tenderheartedness that You pour out so generously upon us—the ones that do not deserve it and could never earn it on our own—and for the great patience You demonstrate for all of us who fail You.

Thank You that Your love is unfailing—like an ever-flowing fountain of kindness which floods the earth filling every part with the evidence of Your great and enduring love for that which You have created.

Thank You that Your goodness is not only poured out on those who love You back but that it is poured out on all of Your creation—so that Your glory would be seen and all Your works would come to offer up thanksgiving and praise to You, just as they were created to do.

Thank You for the mercy and compassion with which You show us Your unfailing love. Let my heart and voice forever join the chorus of all of Your creation in unending thanks and praise to You!

In the name of Jesus, Amen.

An Ambassador of Reconciliation

So we are Christ's ambassadors; God is making his appeal through us. We speak for Christ when we plead, "Come back to God!" For God made Christ, who never sinned, to be the offering for our sin, so that we could be made right with God through Christ.

— 2 CORINTHIANS 5:20–21 (NLT)

Heavenly Father,

Help me not to take lightly the responsibility I have to speak to others about the reconciliation that You have made available to us through Your Son, Jesus Christ—making the most out of every opportunity You give me to declare Your amazing love for us.

As Your representative to a lost and dying world, grant me courage to boldly speak of the marvelous gift that Christ offers—as I plead with them, "Come back to God!"

Help me to share the wondrous exchange that Christ made for me when I invited Him to come into my life and be my Savior and Lord—how He took all of my sin and, in exchange, put me in right standing with You.

By Your Holy Spirit fill my mouth with Your words as I declare to them that this same exchange that was given to me, my sin for Christ's righteousness—as unbalanced in my favor as it was—can be theirs as well.

Prepare their hearts in advance to see and understand that once they accept Your Son into their hearts and lives, You will always look on them as pure and holy—as if they had lived the perfect life that Your Son, Jesus, did.

Out of my gratitude for what You have done, help me always willingly and obediently follow after Your plan for my life and in everything I do or say, represent my Lord and Savior well.

Help me not to take lightly the responsibility I have to speak to others about the reconciliation that You have made available to us through Your Son, Jesus Christ—making the most out of every opportunity You give me to declare Your amazing love for us.

In the name of Jesus, Amen.

I Am Yours and You Are Mine

*You are my flock, the sheep of my pasture. You are my people, and I am
your God. I, the Sovereign LORD, have spoken!*

— EZEKIEL 34:31 (NLT)

Sovereign LORD,

*What a joy it is to have been given the opportunity to live in this covenant
relationship with You—placing all of my life in Your hands, knowing that
I am Yours and You are mine!*

I am one of Your people, a sheep in Your pasture, and You expect me to listen for Your Voice and follow You obediently wherever You lead me—to place
all of my life in Your hands—for my own well-being.

You are the Good Shepherd, the One who continuously watches over me
to protect me in every way—the One who loves me with an unfailing love and
compassionately cares for my every need.

You are the Sovereign LORD, the One who created all things and the One
who holds all things in Your hands—the One who bends all things according
to Your will and the only One in whom I can confidently place all of my faith,
hope, and love!

*What a joy it is to have been given the opportunity to live in this covenant
relationship with You—placing all of my life in Your hands, knowing that
I am Yours and You are mine!*

In the name of Jesus, Amen.

The Gift of Grace and Peace

May God the Father and our Lord Jesus Christ give you grace and peace. Jesus gave his life for our sins, just as God our Father planned, in order to rescue us from this evil world in which we live. All glory to God forever and ever! Amen.

— GALATIANS 1:3–5 (NLT)

Heavenly Father,

No matter what might be happening in the world around me, help me to remain in the grace and peace that You have provided through the Lord Jesus Christ—in that assurance that Jesus gave His life to rescue us from this evil world in which we live.

I am so grateful that You always had a plan—even from before time began—for Jesus to give his life for my sins, so that I might be rescued from this evil world and no longer be crippled by the fear it brings.

Help me to remember that though I have not yet been rescued out of this present evil world, I have been rescued from its evil power over me—no longer bound by Satan's lies, which enslaved me to sin, but free to choose to live my life in Christ and for His glory, honor, and praise.

So let my life be a continual and ever-perfecting reflection of the One who saved me, a demonstration of my gratitude for all that He has done for me—as I live my life in the grace and peace of Christ and give You all the glory forever and ever!

No matter what might be happening in the world around me, help me to remain in the grace and peace that You have provided through the Lord Jesus Christ—in that assurance that Jesus gave His life to rescue us from this evil world in which we live.

In the name of Jesus, Amen.

Choose Carefully What You Search For

If you search for good, you will find favor;
but if you search for evil, it will find you!

— PROVERBS 11:27 (NLT)

Gracious LORD,

Grant this day that I would encounter the favor that comes when I set my heart to search only after that which is good.

Remind me that there is good to be found all around me, and help me to look for that good in every person I encounter and in each circumstance that I face. In searching for that good, let me not only receive the favor of man but all the more, receive Your gracious favor in my life.

Save me from the temptation to search for evil and don't let me walk away from Your sheltering protection—for I know that I will never find evil before it finds me, because it watches for every opportunity of catching me unprotected, in order to try to destroy me.

In everything help me keep my eyes fixed on You—the Author of all things good—so that all my thoughts, words, and actions can be lifted as a song of praise to Your glory and honor.

Grant this day that I would encounter the favor that comes when I set my heart to search only after that which is good.

In the name of Jesus, Amen.

To Choose to Rejoice and Be Glad

This is the day the LORD has made.
We will rejoice and be glad in it.

— PSALM 118:24 (NLT)

One and Only Creator God,

You have made this day! So I choose to rejoice and be glad in it!

Before You created everything there is—before You placed it all in order and set it all in motion—You knew this day would come, You knew the good plans You had for me today!

Today, I get to choose whether to embrace Your plans with joy and gladness or to resist Your plans—*as if to think that I would know better than You what is best for me*—and only reap a harvest of trouble and hardship for my efforts.

So help me open my eyes to all that You have done for me, to rejoice and gladly and obediently submit my will to Your sovereign plans for me. Help me to see that You have called me and saved me for such a time as this.

Grant me the faith to believe that You have already arranged to supply me with everything that I need to accomplish Your will for me today and that, in doing so, You have made it possible for me to live this day with deep peace and enduring joy!

You have made this day! So I choose to rejoice and be glad in it!

In the name of Jesus, Amen.

To Walk Humbly in the Blessings of My God

John replied, "No one can receive anything unless God gives it from heaven."

— JOHN 3:27 (NLT)

Heavenly Father,

Never allow me to forget that there is no talent that I have, no position I hold, no power I wield, and no possession I own that You haven't given to me—and help me to walk humbly before You in that understanding.

Keep me from the pride that comes when I am deceived into believing that the talents that I have are a result of my own striving—rather than the blessing of Your hand alone, which You intend to be used for Your glory and honor and praise.

Help me to represent Christ well in any position in which You have placed me—knowing that You have put me there in order to make me known, so that I would make You known to others.

Help me to use any power that You have entrusted to me with gentleness and kindness, to bring about good—as I reflect Your goodness in every thought I think, every decision I make, every word I speak, and every action I take.

And help me to hold any possession that You have given to me, with open hands lifted up to You—that You might use it, or take it from me, according to Your perfect plans and purposes, that Your will would be accomplished in me.

Never allow me to forget that there is no talent that I have, no position I hold, no power I wield, and no possession I own that You haven't given to me—and help me to walk humbly before You in that understanding.

In the name of Jesus, Amen.

Along the Riverbank

But blessed are those who trust in the LORD
and have made the LORD their hope and confidence.
They are like trees planted along a riverbank,
with roots that reach deep into the water.
Such trees are not bothered by the heat
or worried by long months of drought.
Their leaves stay green,
and they never stop producing fruit.

— JEREMIAH 17:7–8 (NLT)

Dear LORD,

Thank you for being an eternal river of life-giving water to me.

You, LORD, are my hope—and all my confidence is in You. Because You are trustworthy, I can place all my trust in You alone—and know that in doing so, I will be blessed.

As I trust You, You make me like a tree—intentionally planted along the banks of a river—which reaches down deeply and draws from that refreshing life-giving water of Your love.

Because I trust in Your love, I am able to remain strong and growing through the heat of adversity and with it, I can patiently endure any drought that might surround me.

As long as I remain in You, You not only keep me alive, strong, and growing, but You enable me to continually produce fruit for Your glory and honor.

Thank you for being an eternal river of life-giving water to me.

In the name of Jesus, Amen.

The Path Before Me

There is a path before each person that seems right,
but it ends in death.

— PROVERBS 14:12 (NLT)

Heavenly Father,

Lead me by Your Holy Spirit into all Truth, so that I might not be deceived
by the enemy into believing the path that I am on is right—only to find
out in the end that the path I have chosen has led me to self-destruction
and death.

Help me consciously, carefully, and continuously consider the path that I
have chosen, by first examining my heart to be sure that I have not fallen into
self-deception and hypocrisy—where I find myself *playing at religion* instead of
walking in true faith and obedience to You.

Help me to be careful to listen for, hear, and obey the promptings of Your
Spirit—making the choice *not* to follow after the lusts of my own flesh—so that
my path will be a path of life, peace, and joy.

Help me to regularly seek out the strength that is found in the fellowship of
other believers, that I might freely and openly share with them my burdens and
challenges and so they can encourage me in the way that I should go.

Lead me by Your Holy Spirit into all Truth, so that I might not be deceived
by the enemy into believing the path that I am on is right—only to find
out in the end that the path I have chosen has led me to self-destruction
and death.

In the name of Jesus, Amen.

Know God, Know Love, Love One Another

Dear friends, let us continue to love one another, for love comes from God. Anyone who loves is a child of God and knows God. But anyone who does not love does not know God, for God is love.

—1 JOHN 4:7–8 (NLT)

Heavenly Father,

Grant that as I continue to grow in the knowledge of who You truly are, You would fill me to overflowing with Your perfect love—and grant that that same love with which You have so graciously loved me would pour out from me in love for others.

Show me how all my attempts to love others will be fruitless if I haven't first accepted Your love for me—and that I cannot truly accept Your love for me without first knowing You and experiencing that intimate and personal relationship with You through which You reveal Your great love.

Remind me that I am Your child, made in Your very own image! As such, I was created to be a vehicle of Your love—to share Your love with others—that same love which I have experienced in my own life as a result of knowing You.

Cause the gratitude that I have for Your gracious love for me to move me to see others with Your eyes of understanding, mercy, forgiveness, compassion and grace, and to make intentional choices and take definitive actions to give of myself to others in love—just as Christ did for me.

Grant that as I continue to grow in the knowledge of who You truly are, You would fill me to overflowing with Your perfect love—and grant that that same love with which You have so graciously loved me would pour out from me in love for others.

In the name of Jesus, Amen.

What Love Is, What Love Is Not

Love is patient and kind. Love is not jealous or boastful or proud or rude. It does not demand its own way. It is not irritable, and it keeps no record of being wronged. It does not rejoice about injustice but rejoices whenever the truth wins out. Love never gives up, never loses faith, is always hopeful, and endures through every circumstance.

— 1 Corinthians 13:4–7 (NLT)

Heavenly Father,

Help me to love beyond my mind, will, and emotions—understanding that I only truly love when I am presently, actively engaged in demonstrating the attributes of perfect love toward others.

Work in me that my love might endure long, so that I might be patient and kind at all times, in all situations, and with everyone I encounter—never allowing any hurt, offense, or injustice to cause me to become bitter, resentful, or vengeful.

Keep me from giving into the temptation to become envious of others or to boil over with jealousy. Instead, help me to celebrate the evidence of Your blessing upon their lives—always remaining content and thankful for the blessings You have poured out on my own life.

Keep me from acting prideful, boastful, arrogant, or rude—and may I never think more highly of myself than I ought, but rather with humility acknowledge that anything good in me is only because of You.

Keep me from selfishly demanding my own way. Instead, help me to highly esteem the thoughts and opinions of others, always seeking to understand that I might grow in knowledge and wisdom.

Keep me from being irritable—by helping me to guard the peace You have placed in my heart that comes from knowing You and knowing who I am in Christ.

Help me to freely forgive and release others from any wrongs that they have done to me—so that I have no need to keep a record of those wrongs, making me free to live at peace and in joy *in the here and now*, rather than to be trapped in the past.

Help me to rejoice in truth and justice—as You enable me to discern what is true and just in every situation—and give me the courage and resolve to pursue it.

Show me how to love—so that the love that I offer others will be a love that never gives up, never loses faith, is always hopeful, and endures through every circumstance.

Help me to love beyond my mind, will, and emotions—understanding that I only truly love when I am presently, actively engaged in demonstrating the attributes of perfect love toward others.

In the name of Jesus, Amen.

Like Water Flowing Away

"If only you would prepare your heart
and lift up your hands to him in prayer!
Get rid of your sins,
and leave all iniquity behind you.
Then your face will brighten with innocence.
You will be strong and free of fear.
You will forget your misery;
it will be like water flowing away."

— JOB 11:13–16 (NLT)

Heavenly Father,

Show me the depths of my heart and help me prepare it to come before
You—as I confess and repent of all my sin and iniquity, so I can confi-
dently bring my prayers before You, with my hands lifted up in surrender
and in faith!

Help me to turn forever away from any sin that separates me from You by giving me the strength to confess it and repent of it—to turn my back on it and leave it behind—as I choose to go in a new direction, to follow a better path.

For then You will cause my face to brighten as the darkness of my sin falls away and the innocence of Christ's righteousness shines forth from within me.

You will cause me to become strong with the strength only You can give and I will have no need to fear anything—but can live, by Your grace, with abundant joy and enduring peace.

And I will no longer carry the misery that my sin once poured over me—but will forget it, like water flowing away from me.

Show me the depths of my heart and help me prepare it to come before
You—as I confess and repent of all my sin and iniquity, so I can confi-
dently bring my prayers before You, with my hands lifted up in surrender
and in faith!

In the name of Jesus, Amen.

Not That Important

Share each other's burdens, and in this way obey the law of Christ. If you think you are too important to help someone, you are only fooling yourself. You are not that important.

—GALATIANS 6:2–3 (NLT)

Heavenly Father,

Keep me from getting so caught up in my own self-perceived importance that I fail to be obedient to Your call to share the burdens of those You place in my path.

Give me the heart to do the hard work of sharing the burdens of others—of lightening their load of care and helping them back to the peace and joy that You have called them to in Christ.

In willing obedience, let me submit to the law of Christ—that I would be faithful to love You with all my heart, soul, mind and strength, and allow the love of Christ to reach through me, to love others as I have been so greatly loved.

Save me from the pride and arrogance that tempts me to think more of myself than I ought to think—when I know that any good in me comes from You alone, and can only be seen when I submit myself completely to Your plans and purposes for me.

Keep me from getting so caught up in my own self-perceived importance that I fail to be obedient to Your call to share the burdens of those You place in my path.

In the name of Jesus, Amen.

My Help Comes from the LORD!

I look up to the mountains—
does my help come from there?
My help comes from the LORD,
who made heaven and earth!
He will not let you stumble;
the one who watches over you will not slumber.

— PSALM 121:1–3 (NLT)

Loving LORD,

Help me to remember that all my help comes from You—and then help
me live out my life fully believing that truth!

Don't allow me to dishonor You by putting my hope and trust in lesser things. For You are the One who made the heavens and the earth—and all that is in them—and You alone are the Author and Sustainer of my life.

You are the One who stands forever ready to help me, because of Your infinite and unfailing love for me. So keep me from making an idol of some created thing—thinking it will save me—when my eyes should be looking only to You for my help.

You alone are the all-powerful God who unceasingly watches over me, saving and preserving me in every way—upholding me so I do not stumble along the path of Your will and purpose for my life, for Your glory, honor, and praise.

Help me to remember that all my help comes from You—and then help
me live out my life fully believing that truth!

In the name of Jesus, Amen.

You Offer Forgiveness

LORD, if you kept a record of our sins,
who, O Lord, could ever survive?
But you offer forgiveness,
that we might learn to fear you.

— PSALM 130:3–4 (NLT)

Gracious and Merciful God,

Thank You that for my sin You offer me Your forgiveness—You com-
pletely remove my sin from me and remember it no more—so that there
is nothing left between us to keep me from You.

If You kept a record of my sins, how could I ever survive? For my sin would
be an ever-enlarging, impenetrable wall of judgment that kept me separated
from You—that kept me from the strength of Your presence and left me to face
this world on my own. How could I live without You?

But You, LORD, hold no grudge against me—when I sincerely repent of
my sins—when I turn my back on my sinful behavior, ask for Your forgiveness,
and pursue the ways of truth and life.

You remove my sin—the wall of separation—and You look upon me as if I
had never sinned, so that I can continue in fellowship with You, being strengthened by Your presence, so I can offer You the reverential respect and awe that
is due You.

Help me to use Your model of complete forgiveness when I forgive others—by not keeping a record of wrongs—so that the walls between myself and
others may be torn down and I can live at peace with all men.

Thank You that for my sin You offer me Your forgiveness—You com-
pletely remove my sin from me and remember it no more—so that there
is nothing left between us to keep me from You.

In the name of Jesus, Amen.

To Better Reflect Your Goodness

A good man brings good things out of the good stored up in his heart, and an evil man brings evil things out of the evil stored up in his heart. For the mouth speaks what the heart is full of.

— LUKE 6:45 (NIV)

And now, dear brothers and sisters, one final thing. Fix your thoughts on what is true, and honorable, and right, and pure, and lovely, and admirable. Think about things that are excellent and worthy of praise.

— PHILIPPIANS 4:8 (NLT)

Heavenly Father,

Help me to become a better reflection of Your goodness—one who chooses to fill his heart only with that which is good—so that whatever overflows from my heart and across my lips will always bring You glory!

Let those things I have stored up in my heart be those things that are true, honorable, right, pure, lovely, admirable, excellent, and worthy of praise—so that the life I live will be a pleasing offering to You and be a source of blessing to those around me.

Help me not to allow any evil thoughts, or the lies of the enemy, to have any place in my heart—for if they are allowed to remain, they will corrupt the good treasure of my heart and pollute and poison every part of me.

Through Your Word and by Your Spirit fill my heart with Your Love and Truth—until I overflow with all things good, and become that faithful representative of my Lord, Jesus Christ, that You have called me to be.

Help me to become a better reflection of Your goodness—one who chooses to fill his heart only with that which is good—so that whatever overflows from my heart and across my lips will always bring You glory!

In the name of Jesus, Amen.

To Choose Not to Be Offended

A person's wisdom yields patience;
it is to one's glory to overlook an offense.

— PROVERBS 19:11 (NIV)

Heavenly Father,

Grant me the wisdom that produces patience—rather than anger—and
help me to choose not to be offended by what someone else may say or do.

Help me to be wise enough to watch for Your hand at work in all things that happen to me because of other people's words or actions—that I might control my reactions and remain patient enough to find out what You have to teach me.

Help me not to eagerly embrace every opportunity to be offended by what comes my way, but rather reject the destructive power that an offense can hold over me. Help me let offenses pass me by—as I remain confidently at peace in the truth of who You have shown me I am in Christ.

Help me be slow to become angry but quick to understand, quick to love, quick to show compassion, mercy and grace, and quick to forgive and move forward, unencumbered by the past, in the joy and peace that You call me to walk in—so I can be busy about the good things You have for me to do, for Your glory, honor, and praise.

Grant me the wisdom that produces patience—rather than anger—and
help me to choose not to be offended by what someone else may say or do.

In the name of Jesus, Amen.

The LORD is My Light and My Salvation

The LORD is my light and my salvation—
so why should I be afraid?
The LORD is my fortress, protecting me from danger,
so why should I tremble?

— PSALM 27:1 (NLT)

LORD God Almighty,

You are my light and my salvation! You are the very strength that pro-
tects my life from danger—my fortress and my refuge from harm! So why
should I ever be afraid?

You are the light that shines in me! You are that unfaltering light that dis-
pels all of the darkness—that never-failing light against which evil cannot
stand. So let Your light shine in me and through me, and help me to see it
shining all around me as You keep me in perfect peace and illuminate every
step I take with You.

You are my salvation! You are the One who, through Christ, has saved me
from my sin and blessed me with eternal life in You—the One who has made
me peculiar by calling me to come away from the ways of this world, so I can
live in ongoing fellowship with You—forever.

You are my fortress and my refuge! You are the One, the All-Powerful God
who keeps me safe in every way: my *Defender*—when I am falsely accused;
my *Protector*—from the forces of evil that would seek to destroy me; my
Provider—who gives me all that I need to accomplish Your will for me; and my
Peace—standing firm and unmoved in the midst of every storm.

You are my light and my salvation! You are the very strength that pro-
tects my life from danger—my fortress and my refuge from harm! So why
should I ever be afraid?

In the name of Jesus, Amen.

The Armor and Protection of His Faithful Promises

He will cover you with his feathers.
He will shelter you with his wings.
His faithful promises are your armor and protection.

— PSALM 91:4 (NLT)

Almighty God,

Thank You that out of Your great love for me You cover me—willingly sheltering me under Your wings. Help me to put my hope in the armor and protection of Your faithful promises.

Thank You that You cover me, that You draw me close to You—that You hide me from the attacks of the enemy and shield me from the storms of this life.

Just as a hen gathers her chicks close to herself and covers them with her protective wings, so gather me to Yourself and shelter me there—that my life would be hidden in You.

Thank You that I can know and experience the Truth, that all Your promises are true—and that You are always faithful to Your promises.

For within the Truth of Your faithful promises I find the armor I need to cover me when attacked, and the protection that keeps me from all harm.

Thank You that out of Your great love for me You cover me—willingly sheltering me under Your wings. Help me to put my hope in the armor and protection of Your faithful promises.

In the name of Jesus, Amen.

No Other God

"You shall have no other gods before Me."

— EXODUS 20:3 (NKJV)

*"Get out of here, Satan," Jesus told him. "For the Scriptures say,
'You must worship the Lord your God and serve only him.'"*

— MATTHEW 4:20 (NLT)

Almighty God,

Be for me the only God I serve!

Help me to understand that I am always in danger of allowing the things of this world to take *Your* rightful place in my heart.

Help me to see that I do this when I begin to take my own identity, purpose, and source of security from the things of this world—such as wealth, position, authority, power, fame, and pleasure—instead of from who *You* say that I am in Christ.

Help me to guard against allowing my foolish pride to make a god of *myself*, a desire for wealth or possessions to make *money* a god in my eyes, or a desire to enjoy life to make *pleasure* a god that I would follow.

Help me to remember that Satan would tempt me to make gods of anything in this world that I would value or love, fear or serve, delight in or depend on, more than You.

Help me to come against the temptation to serve any other god with the truth of Your Word—just as Jesus did—and send Satan on his way.

Be for me the only God I serve!

In the name of Jesus, Amen.

Created Anew to Do Good

God saved you by his grace when you believed. And you can't take credit for this; it is a gift from God. Salvation is not a reward for the good things we have done, so none of us can boast about it. For we are God's masterpiece. He has created us anew in Christ Jesus, so we can do the good things he planned for us long ago.

— EPHESIANS 2:8–10 (NLT)

Heavenly Father,

Help me to remember that You created me anew in Christ Jesus to be one of Your masterpieces—that I might do the good things that You planned for me long ago.

Thank you for saving me by Your grace—Your unmerited favor—when I made the choice to believe You.

Always keep me mindful that I didn't earn my salvation, nor do I in any way deserve it because of anything that I did—or might yet do. I simply and freely received salvation when I opened my heart to You and invited You into my life by faith.

When I speak of my salvation, help me give all the glory and praise to You—for Your merciful grace which made it possible—so that I might point others to You that they, too, might be saved.

And when I do any good thing, let me give all the glory and praise to You. For You are the One Who created me to do good—and the power to do good does not come from me but comes from Christ in me.

Don't let me lose sight of the fact that You planned long ago for me to do the good things that I do—that *by my recreation in Christ* You have masterfully and uniquely designed and equipped me to do them according to Your plan—so that my life might glorify You.

Help me to remember that You created me anew in Christ Jesus to be one of Your masterpieces—that I might do the good things that You planned for me long ago.

In the name of Jesus, Amen.

Knowledge Too Wonderful

You have searched me, LORD,
and you know me.
You know when I sit and when I rise;
you perceive my thoughts from afar.
You discern my going out and my lying down;
you are familiar with all my ways.
Before a word is on my tongue
you, LORD, know it completely.
You hem me in behind and before,
and you lay your hand upon me.
Such knowledge is too wonderful for me,
too lofty for me to attain.

— PSALM 139:1–6 (NIV)

Omniscient God,

Help me to see that it is pointless for me to pretend that there is anything
about me that You don't already know altogether—and help me to accept
and trust that You want me to come to You just as I am.

There is nothing about me that ever has been—or ever will be—hidden from You! You have examined my heart and You know everything there is to know about me—for You are my Creator.

You pay careful attention to every detail of everything I do—even if it is just to sit down or to stand up.

You know all of my thoughts even before they are caught by my own mind—and even when I have allowed my heart to stray far from Your heart.

When I travel or when I rest at home, You know everything that I am doing—nothing I do escapes Your notice or Your interest.

You know what I am going to say—even before the words are formed in my mouth—whether they are blessings or curses.

You are the One who goes before me and the One who follows after me, never leaving me, wherever I go—and You are the One who continually blesses me with Your presence and Your unfailing love.

Such knowledge is too wonderful for me to grasp—for You know me in ways that reach far beyond my capacity to understand—yet love me still.

Help me to see that it is pointless for me to pretend that there is anything about me that You don't already know altogether—and help me to accept and trust that You want me to come to You just as I am.

In the name of Jesus, Amen.

My Portion Forever

I was senseless and ignorant;
I was a brute beast before you.
Yet I am always with you;
you hold me by my right hand.
You guide me with your counsel,
and afterward you will take me into glory.
Whom have I in heaven but you?
And earth has nothing I desire besides you.
My flesh and my heart may fail,
but God is the strength of my heart
and my portion forever.

— PSALM 73:22–26 (NIV)

Merciful God,

Whom have I in heaven but You? And what here on earth could I truly
desire besides You?

How foolishly and ignorantly I act at times! How I must seem like a sense-less animal, the way that I carry on in front of You!

Still, all the while You are continually there beside me, claiming me as Your own and holding tightly to my right hand—so that when I stumble I do not fall completely down, so that when I wander I am not lost forever.

By Your counsel, You lovingly guide me along the way I should go—when I make the time to seek Your face and listen—and You will take me home to my glorious destiny, according to the perfect timing of Your plan.

My body may fail me, and my mind, will, and emotions may grow weak, but You will always remain my strength—renewing my spirit forever—for You are mine forever!

Whom have I in heaven but You? And what here on earth could I truly
desire besides You?

In the name of Jesus, Amen.

Truly Free

Jesus replied, "I tell you the truth, everyone who sins is a slave of sin. A slave is not a permanent member of the family, but a son is part of the family forever. So if the Son sets you free, you are truly free."

— JOHN 8:34-36 (NLT)

Heavenly Father,

Help me to fully live out this day in the freedom that was purchased for me on the cross of Christ.

You have called me out of my slavery to sin and have invited me to take my place of freedom as Your very own child—a chosen member of Your own family.

You have made possible my total freedom—so that sin no longer has the power to make me its slave, by controlling me, manipulating me, clouding my mind, will, and emotions, and dictating my every action.

Thank You that through Christ Jesus, Your Son, You have set me free to obey You, as an act of my love for You, and have poured out on me the blessings that flow from that obedience—joy, peace, provision, protection, power, and purpose—as I fulfill Your plan for me by serving You wholeheartedly.

Help me to continue to *choose* to be free—as I seek You out by searching Your Word and placing my confidence in its Truth, and as I listen for Your Voice and respond with loving, obedient submission to You—so that You can continue the work of sanctification in me.

Help me to fully live out this day in the freedom that was purchased for me on the cross of Christ.

In the name of Jesus, Amen.

To Keep Your Commandments, To Reflect Your Decrees

You have charged us
to keep your commandments carefully.
Oh, that my actions would consistently
reflect your decrees!

— Psalm 119:4–5 (NLT)

Heavenly Father,

Help me to carefully keep Your commandments, so that the life I live out
before You would be a consistent reflection my obedience to Your decrees!

LORD, out of Your great love for me You have charged me with this great and awesome responsibility—to keep Your commandments carefully.

In order to do this, I must take the time to discover and seek to understand Your commandments—by reading, studying, and being taught the instructions that are found in Your Word.

This also means I must meditate on Your Word at all times—so the Truth of Your Word will permeate my thoughts and, in turn, will produce in me the godly actions that would bring You glory, honor, and praise.

I must totally surrender control over my heart to Your Spirit—so that You can empower me *not to do* those things I shouldn't do, but also *to do* those things I that I should.

Because of Your great and unending love for me, You have given me Your commandments—so that, *to the extent that I am faithful to follow them,* I can walk in the freedom, peace, protection, provision, and joy that they provide.

Help me to carefully keep Your commandments, so that the life I live out
before You would be a consistent reflection my obedience to Your decrees!

In the name of Jesus, Amen.

To Pay Attention to What God Says

My child, pay attention to what I say.
Listen carefully to my words.
Don't lose sight of them.
Let them penetrate deep into your heart,
for they bring life to those who find them,
and healing to their whole body.

— PROVERBS 4:20–22 (NLT)

Heavenly Father,

Help me to pay attention to what You say—as I listen carefully to Your
words and let them penetrate deep into my heart—so that I can fully
experience the life, health, and wholeness they bring.

With Your Holy Spirit as my teacher, help me fully hear what You would say
to me—when I read and study my Bible, while I listen to teaching and preaching, through my conversations with others, and as I quiet myself before You.

Help me to receive, remember, and treasure every word You would say to
me—allowing the truth of Your words to find a home in the deepest parts of my
heart and abide there forever.

Then help me to apply the truth that I have hidden in my heart to everything I think, say, and do, so that I can truly live for You—walking in health and
wholeness in my body, soul, and spirit, to Your glory, for the rest of my days.

Help me to pay attention to what You say—as I listen carefully to Your
words and let them penetrate deep into my heart—so that I can fully
experience the life, health, and wholeness they bring.

In the name of Jesus, Amen.

The Good Work of Transformation

And I am certain that God, who began the good work within you, will continue his work until it is finally finished on the day when Christ Jesus returns.

— PHILIPPIANS 1:6 (NLT)

Heavenly Father,

Thank You for sending Christ to pay the penalty for the sin of all mankind! Thank You also for the good work of transformation that You began within me on the day I first believed—and for always being faithful to finish what You start!

I know with certainty that it is You who began this work—by the power of Christ in me—and because it is You who began this work, it is a good work, indeed.

I believe that this good work that You began will work within me for the rest of my days—that You will be faithful to attentively continue it throughout my lifetime.

I am completely confident that by Your Spirit, You are enabling me to become more like Christ every day—as I continue to grow and mature in Him according to Your plan and purpose, into the perfected work of Your hand.

I am grateful that You will not leave undone the good work that You have begun in me—but will be faithful to bring this work of love and grace to final completion on that day when I finally see Christ Jesus face to face.

Thank You for sending Christ to pay the penalty for the sin of all mankind! Thank You, also, for the good work of transformation that You began within me on the day I first believed—and for always being faithful to finish what You start!

In the name of Jesus, Amen.

My Hiding Place

You are my hiding place;
you will protect me from trouble
and surround me with songs of deliverance.

— PSALM 32:7 (NIV)

O LORD my God,

Where else, O LORD, can I go to hide? To whom can I turn for protection from my troubles besides You? Who else will surround me with songs of deliverance? My only hope for salvation is found in You!

You alone are my hiding place—my place of safety and comfort, my sanctuary of peace.

In You alone will I find protection from all my troubles.

Only You will surround me with songs of deliverance from all of my enemies.

So help me always run to You.

Where else, O LORD, can I go to hide? To whom can I turn for protection from my troubles besides You? Who else will surround me with songs of deliverance? My only hope for salvation is found in You!

In the name of Jesus, Amen.

Our Hope Is in You Alone!

Let your unfailing love surround us, LORD,
for our hope is in you alone.

— PSALM 33:22 (NLT)

Loving and Merciful LORD,

Let it be that I would place all of my hope in You, LORD—as You faith-
fully surround me with Your unfailing love.

Teach me not to place my hope in my possessions. Help me to understand that what I have is not my own but Yours alone—and remind me that if it were all stripped away from me today, I would have lost nothing because I still have You, the One who is everything to me.

Teach me not to place my hope in other people. Help me to see that other people are human and—just like me—they sometimes disappoint, they sometimes fail, and they sometimes let you down. Remind me that even if everyone else abandoned me, You would still be with me always.

Teach me not to place my hope in my position or in my own strength. Help me to see that any position or strength that I have was given by Your hand—to be used for Your glory and not my own—and that even if I was removed from my position and all strength was drained from me, You would still uphold me in Your everlasting arms.

Let it be that I would place all of my hope in You, LORD—as You faith-
fully surround me with Your unfailing love.

In the name of Jesus, Amen.

Don't Think You Know It All!

Live in harmony with each other. Don't be too proud to enjoy the company of ordinary people. And don't think you know it all!

— ROMANS 12:16 (NLT)

Heavenly Father,

Give me a humble heart and pure motives, so that I might have the privilege of joining in with You—in whatever way You want to use me—to impact the lives of others with Your love.

Help me to live in harmony with those around me—by celebrating the diversity of souls that You have created and making my first consideration my own shortcomings rather than the shortcomings of others.

Keep me from taking a proud and haughty attitude with others—thinking myself better than them—when in truth it is only by Your mercy, grace, and strength that I am able to stand at all.

Teach me to enjoy the company of "ordinary" people—people who are just broken in different ways than I am—and help me to be willing to work alongside them in whatever tasks You have for me to do.

Keep me from thinking that I know it all—so that my thoughts, words, and actions won't be divisive and cause discord between myself and the very ones You have placed before me to love.

Give me a humble heart and pure motives, so that I might have the privilege of joining in with You—in whatever way You want to use me—to impact the lives of others with Your love.

In the name of Jesus, Amen.

To Walk in Wisdom

Those who trust in themselves are fools,
but those who walk in wisdom are kept safe.

— Proverbs 28:26 (NIV)

Heavenly Father,

Save me from the foolishness of trusting in myself and help me to walk as
a wise man—with my eyes fixed on You and with a heart that beats only
after Your own heart!

Don't allow me to start believing that my thoughts are necessarily wise just
because I think them, or that my own strength and power is sufficient to carry
me, or that my own actions could ever be enough to justify me before You.

Keep me ever close to You—and help me to remember that the times that
I am most likely to be deceived by the enemy are those times when I have foolishly wandered from Your Holy Presence.

Make me wise enough to put all my trust in You—in Your power at work in
me, in Your promises given to me, and in Your unfailing love for me—the One
who is faithful to keep safe all those who wisely humble themselves and step
forward in faith to walk with the One who is mighty to save!

Save me from the foolishness of trusting in myself and help me to walk as
a wise man—with my eyes fixed on You and with a heart that beats only
after Your own heart!

In the name of Jesus, Amen.

When You Go Through Deep Waters

When you go through deep waters,
I will be with you.
When you go through rivers of difficulty,
you will not drown.
When you walk through the fire of oppression,
you will not be burned up;
the flames will not consume you.

— Isaiah 43:2 (NLT)

Loving LORD,

You are the One who is always with me—for you have placed Your loving
affection upon me! You take each step of this life with me and are always
faithful—never letting go of my hand—so that I never walk alone!

When I feel as if I am in too deep, like I am no longer able to touch bottom and am drowning in my troubles, You are there to give me my next breath and to help me to regain my footing once again.

When I feel as if I am going to be swept away by the raging currents around me—the tides of evil that come against me—You are there to help me stand firm and to discover that You are my refuge and strength.

When I feel the burning oppression of the enemy seeking to consume my very soul, You are there to shield me in Your loving arms—to remind me of who I am and assure me of Your immeasurable love for me, so that I can continue to walk with You through every attack, in victory.

You are the One who is always with me—for you have placed Your loving
affection upon me! You take each step of this life with me and are always
faithful—never letting go of my hand—so that I never walk alone!

In the name of Jesus, Amen.

To Willingly Submit and Obediently Respond

Cling to your faith in Christ, and keep your conscience clear. For some people have deliberately violated their consciences; as a result, their faith has been shipwrecked.

— 1 TIMOTHY 1:19 (NLT)

Heavenly Father,

Help me always cling to my faith in Christ and keep a clear conscience— as You teach me to willingly submit and obediently respond to every prompting of Your Holy Spirit within me.

Let me truly believe that my faith in Jesus Christ alone is enough to save and deliver me through any circumstance and every situation in which I find myself—and help me listen to Your Spirit speaking through my conscience, as You show me the way that I should go.

Help me be careful not to deliberately violate my conscience—because in doing so I harden my heart to the voice of Your Spirit, weaken my capacity to tell right from wrong, deny my belief in the power of Christ to protect and save me, and ultimately shipwreck my faith.

Help me always cling to my faith in Christ, so that as I submit my will to the tugging of the Holy Spirit at my heart, my conscience will remain clear and my faith will remain strong—and I can better represent my Lord and Savior, Jesus Christ, with my life.

Help me always cling to my faith in Christ and keep a clear conscience— as You teach me to willingly submit and obediently respond to every prompting of Your Holy Spirit within me.

In the name of Jesus, Amen.

A Single Day in Your Presence

A single day in your courts
is better than a thousand anywhere else!
I would rather be a gatekeeper in the house of my God
than live the good life in the homes of the wicked.
For the LORD God is our sun and our shield.
He gives us grace and glory.
The LORD will withhold no good thing
from those who do what is right.

— PSALM 84:10–11 (NLT)

LORD God,

Help me to purpose in my heart to seek out those places where I can
find You and spend time nourishing myself with the abundance of good
things that You have waiting for me there—things which can only be
found when I spend time worshiping in Your Presence.

Let me be content to stand in *whatever* place of service You have for me, in order to serve You where You are at work—rather than to live the so-called "good life" that this world claims to be able to offer me.

For You are my sun and my shield—lighting my way and giving me life, as You guide and direct me through the dangers of this dark and dreary world and shield me from the unrelenting attacks of my enemy.

And You give me grace—which is both that goodwill that You display toward me and the good work that You are doing within me—and glory— which is both the honor that You have given me by adopting me as Your own and the hope that You have given me for that eternity with You which is yet to come.

Thank You for not withholding from me those things which *You have determined* to be for my good, as I seek to walk uprightly before You—doing what is right as my reasonable service to You.

Help me to purpose in my heart to seek out those places where I can
find You and spend time nourishing myself with the abundance of good
things that You have waiting for me there—things which can only be
found when I spend time worshiping in Your Presence.

In the name of Jesus, Amen.

Before The LORD

And each morning and evening they stood before the LORD to sing songs of thanks and praise to him.

— 1 CHRONICLES 23:30 (NLT)

LORD God Almighty,

Fill my heart with unceasing gratitude to You—both for who You are and for all that You have done for me—so that the song of my heart and the melody on my lips will always declare my thanks and praise to You!

In the morning when I rise, let me stand before Your Presence with thankful songs of praise raised to You—for You are good and gracious to me and Your merciful, compassionate, and unfailing love for me endures forever.

Your love for me is so great that You see beyond my own wants and never fail to provide me with what I really need—so that I can walk in peace, joy, hope, and love, through a right relationship of willing obedience to You.

You completely heal my brokenness, perfectly filling every empty longing of my heart—as I accept Your presence with me, and Your power and Your plan for me—so that I am made whole.

So let the meditations of my heart be on who You are—so that my thoughts, words, and actions joyfully celebrate You in praise—and so that the part of this world that I touch might hear of Your wonderful greatness.

For You are worthy of so much more than all the praise, honor, and glory I can give. You are the one and only LORD God Almighty, Creator of everything there is or ever shall be. There is none like You.

And in the evening when I return to rest, let me stand before Your Presence with thankful songs of praise raised to You—for You are good and gracious to me and Your merciful, compassionate, and unfailing love for me endures forever.

Fill my heart with unceasing gratitude to You—both for who You are and for all that You have done for me—so that the song of my heart and the melody on my lips will always declare my thanks and praise to You!

In the name of Jesus, Amen.

You Hear My Voice, I Wait for Yours

In the morning, LORD, you hear my voice;
in the morning I lay my requests before you
and wait expectantly.

— PSALM 5:3 (NIV)

Loving LORD,

Every morning let me call out to You with confidence, humbly placing
my requests before You. Then let me wait expectantly in Your presence,
believing You hear me and will answer the cry of my heart.

Help me come eagerly and boldly before You each morning—with a deep
and abiding reverence for You—knowing my reward will be that I will always
find You lovingly waiting to meet with me.

Help me to approach Your throne with a heart full of gratitude for this
great privilege I have been granted of being welcomed into Your Presence—
and for the interest that You have in every detail of what I have to say to You
about everything I have on my heart.

And when I have shared my heart, help me to remember to be still and
wait, quietly and expectantly in Your presence, for You to speak to me about
Your best plans for me—knowing that You will withhold no good thing from
me, and trusting that You always want what is best for me.

Every morning let me call out to You with confidence, humbly placing
my requests before You. Then let me wait expectantly in Your presence,
believing You hear me and will answer the cry of my heart.

In the name of Jesus, Amen.

Our Father's Hallowed Name

"Pray, then, in this way:
'Our Father who is in heaven,
Hallowed be Your name.'"

— MATTHEW 6:9 (NASB)

Heavenly Father,

Teach me to keep Your Name Holy—set apart as sacred, revered in my heart, and glorified through my life.

Show me how to bring honor to Your Holy Name—in everything I think, say, and do—so others might see in me the mercy, forgiveness, healing, grace, truth, peace, and joy of Your love that is available to all those who call upon Your Name.

Keep me from using Your Holy Name in vain—carelessly throwing it around, shamefully invoking it in unholy ways and bringing dishonor to all the holy perfection that is represented in Your Name.

Fully knowing who I am, as Your dearly loved child, help me to speak and to act boldly—in faith and according to the Truth and Grace that are fully expressed by the perfect Love that is found within Your Holy Name.

Teach me to keep Your Name Holy—set apart as sacred, revered in my heart, and glorified through my life.

In the name of Jesus, Amen.

A Living Sacrifice to You

Therefore, I urge you, brothers and sisters, in view of God's mercy, to offer your bodies as a living sacrifice, holy and pleasing to God—this is your true and proper worship.

— ROMANS 12:1 (NIV)

Merciful and Gracious God,

Help me truly worship You today—in grateful response to Your enduring mercy and abundant grace—by dying to myself and living for You alone.

Because of everything You have done for me, stir within my heart that desire to submit all that I am to You—humbly giving my life completely over to Your plans and purposes for me.

In light of the final atoning sacrifice of Your Son for my sin, help me to make the only sacrifice that is left to make—a living sacrifice of my life—by consciously and continually setting myself apart for Your use.

Help me to offer my true and proper worship to You in every moment of each new day, as You keep me mindful of Your mercy extended toward me—without which I would not have this privilege of life with You, forevermore.

Help me truly worship You today—in grateful response to Your enduring mercy and abundant grace—by dying to myself and living for You alone.

In the name of Jesus, Amen.

The God Who Gives Me the Desires of My Heart

Take delight in the LORD,
and he will give you your heart's desires.
Commit everything you do to the LORD.
Trust him, and he will help you.

— PSALM 37:4–5 (NLT)

Loving LORD,

Let the deepest desires of my heart, my greatest pleasure, and my most complete joy simply be found in experiencing the blessing of Your Presence in my life—as I commit all that I am to You and trust You to help me, no matter what I face.

This day may I truly take delight in You, as I seek to know You in a more intimate and personal way, and as I make this commitment to walk in Your Presence—to walk in a continual consciousness of the truth that You are always right here with me.

As I seek to understand more completely the vastness of Your unfailing love for me, the mystery of the perfection of Your ways, and as I reflect on Your steadfast faithfulness to me, help me learn to trust You even more.

Help me to commit all that I do to You, so my heart's desires will be melded with Your will for my life and so I can walk fearlessly in the plans and purposes that You have for me—as I make the choice to believe that You will always empower and equip me in every way, for the good plans You have for me.

Let the deepest desires of my heart, my greatest pleasure, and my most complete joy simply be found in experiencing the blessing of Your Presence in my life—as I commit all that I am to You and trust You to help me no matter what I face.

In the name of Jesus, Amen.

The Beginning of Knowledge

The fear of the LORD is the beginning of knowledge,
But fools despise wisdom and instruction.

— PROVERBS 1:7 (NKJV)

Loving and Gracious LORD,

Never allow me to take lightly who You are—to fail to acknowledge that
You alone are worthy of all my love, reverence, worship and service, that
You alone are truly awesome in glory, power, and majesty, and that You
alone should I fear.

Help me to hold onto the truth that a proper and worshipful fear and reverent respect for who You are is the very beginning, the ever-firm foundation, the principal part of knowledge—without which I cannot claim to know anything.

For only in fearing You and in serving You obediently—so that each of my thoughts is brought into obedience to Christ—can I profit from the rich blessings that You have promised.

Keep me from the foolishness of despising wisdom and instruction—thinking that I could know anything apart from You—and save me from believing that I don't need Your favor upon my life, or I don't need to fear Your wrath for my disobedience.

Never allow me to take lightly who You are—to fail to acknowledge that
You alone are worthy of all my love, reverence, worship and service, that
You alone are truly awesome in glory, power, and majesty, and that You
alone should I fear.

In the name of Jesus, Amen.

Don't Be Angry! Don't Be Afraid!

Stop being angry!
Turn from your rage!
Do not lose your temper—
it only leads to harm.

— Psalm 37:8 (NLT)

Loving LORD,

Turn me from the destructiveness of feeding my anger until it becomes
rage—whether it be inward rage, outward rage, or both—knowing that
when I lose my temper, it can only lead to harm.

In those moments when I feel my anger rising out of control, help me to remember that the anger I feel comes from a fear that has taken hold of me— then help me question what it is that I am afraid of so that I can return again to that place of peace and joy that I have in You.

Help me to see that these emotions of uncontrolled anger, rage, and losing my temper are symptoms of a bigger issue—a lack of faith on my part—because I am in some way doubting that You are in control, that You love me, and are working in every situation and circumstance for my good.

Help me to continually give my life over to You—that my faith would continue to grow, that I would learn what You want me to teach me, that I would trust You to keep me in every way, and that You would allow me the privilege of being a part of what You are doing in the world around me.

Turn me from the destructiveness of feeding my anger until it becomes
rage—whether it be inward rage, outward rage, or both—knowing that
when I lose my temper, it can only lead to harm.

In the name of Jesus, Amen.

An Example to Follow

I have given you an example to follow. Do as I have done to you.
                                        — JOHN 13:15 (NLT)

Heavenly Father,

Help me to follow the perfect example of Your Son, Jesus Christ. Grant that I would have His heart of love, compassion, and servant leadership toward others.

Thank You for the gift that You so graciously gave to us when You sent Your Son, Jesus Christ, to come and walk upon the earth among us—as an example for us all. Help me to pattern my life after His life of service to all those around Him.

Help me to walk in His humility—having set aside all of my pride—that I might not consider anything You ask me to do to be beneath me, but joyfully and obediently embrace any opportunity You give me to be a part of what You are doing.

Help me to love as He did—as His compassion stirs my heart and I respond with appropriate godly action. Let others experience Christ's love—flowing in me and through me—that You would receive all the glory!

Help me to follow the perfect example of Your Son, Jesus Christ. Grant that I would have His heart of love, compassion, and servant leadership toward others.

In the name of Jesus, Amen.

No Fear of Bad News

Surely the righteous will never be shaken;
they will be remembered forever.
They will have no fear of bad news;
their hearts are steadfast, trusting in the LORD.
Their hearts are secure, they will have no fear;
in the end they will look in triumph on their foes.

— PSALM 112:6–8 (NIV)

Great and Gracious God,

May I live out my life uprightly and in right standing with You, so that my faith is not shaken by the attacks of the enemy, and so my heart remains unafraid and at peace in the face of bad news, because it has found its security in You.

Because of Your unfailing love for me and by the blood of Jesus Christ, You have made me to be righteous—upright and in right standing—before You. Let my life be lived out in that righteousness—as a willing and obedient response to Your love for me—so that the positive impact my life has upon this world might go on forever.

When the world brings me bad news, help me to remain at peace and not be afraid—as I steadfastly trust in You—knowing that my faith is placed in the One Good, Gracious, and Sovereign LORD God who works in all circumstances for my ultimate good.

May my heart remain secure in the knowledge that I can walk in the victory that You have provided for me here, until that day when You take me home to be with You forever, in ultimate and complete victory over every enemy.

May I live out my life uprightly and in right standing with You, so that my faith is not shaken by the attacks of the enemy, and so my heart remains unafraid and at peace in the face of bad news, because it has found its security in You.

In the name of Jesus, Amen.

MARCH 18TH

Thankfulness through Obedience

As I learn your righteous regulations,
I will thank you by living as I should!
I will obey your decrees.
Please don't give up on me!

— PSALM 119:7–8 (NLT)

Merciful and Gracious LORD,

Please don't give up on me! Don't leave me to my own limited understanding and imperfect wisdom—but continue in Your unrelenting, passionate, pursuit of my heart, as You patiently guide me into all Truth.

Let the commandments of Your Word permeate my heart as I listen for Your Spirit to reveal how every commandment plays a part in protecting, providing for, and preserving my life—according to Your perfect plans and purposes.

By that same Spirit within me, strengthen me to live as I should—to fully understand and apply Your righteous regulations to my life—that I might live the abundant life that is available to those who choose to follow after Truth.

And help me to be grateful—not only in my thoughts and words but even more so in the way I live my life—so that my entire life might become a continuous offering of praise to You!

Please don't give up on me! Don't leave me to my own limited understanding and imperfect wisdom—but continue in Your unrelenting, passionate, pursuit of my heart, as You patiently guide me into all Truth.

In the name of Jesus, Amen.

The Choice to Become a Slave

Don't you realize that you become the slave of whatever you choose to obey? You can be a slave to sin, which leads to death, or you can choose to obey God, which leads to righteous living.

— ROMANS 6:16 (NLT)

Heavenly Father,

Help me to remember that I become the slave of whatever I choose to obey—and help me always choose to fix my heart on obedience to Christ and His calling upon my life.

Help me to be careful in every choice I make today, to choose that which honors You—so that in my choosing I don't enslave myself once again to sin.

Let my choice always be obedience to You in all things—as I look to the Truth of Your Word to be my guide to life and as I choose to make myself a slave to righteous living through the power of Christ at work in me.

And in my obedience, take me down that path of right standing with You, toward holiness—so that I can stand in that place of intimate and personal relationship with You, where I find the abundant life You have hidden there for me in Christ.

Help me to remember that I become the slave of whatever I choose to obey—and help me always choose to fix my heart on obedience to Christ and His calling upon my life.

In the name of Jesus, Amen.

LORD Be My Rock Fortress, My Home High in the Mountains

You have been deceived by your own pride
because you live in a rock fortress
and make your home high in the mountains.
'Who can ever reach us way up here?'
you ask boastfully.

— OBADIAH 1:3 (NLT)

Dear LORD God,

Be for me my rock fortress, my home high in the mountains, as I walk
humbly before You.

Don't ever allow me to be deceived, by my own foolish pride, into believing that I am somehow protected by the work of my own hands—as if I could build a place of safety apart from You.

Let my only boast be in You—the One who made me, the One who loves me and cares for me, the One who keeps me safe in every way and unfolds the story of my life before me, according to His plans and purposes—as I walk humbly before You.

Let me make my home in You—in the refuge of those high places of intimate relationship with the author of my life, the redeemer and sustainer of my soul, and my LORD, forevermore!

Be for me my rock fortress, my home in the high mountains, as I walk
humbly before You.

In the name of Jesus, Amen.

Trusting the One Who Is Able to Save

The idols of the nations are merely things of silver and gold,
shaped by human hands.
They have mouths but cannot speak,
and eyes but cannot see.
They have ears but cannot hear,
and noses but cannot smell.
And those who make idols are just like them,
as are all who trust in them.

— PSALM 135:15–18 (NLT)

Heavenly Father,

Save me from worshiping anything—or anyone—but You.

Keep me from counting on anything made with human hands—as if those things could save me.

Let me instead count on You—the One who created all there is by the power of Your Word.

Keep me from worshiping anything that cannot speak to me—that cannot reveal the Truth.

Let me instead worship only You—and listen to hear You speaking to me through Your Word and Your Spirit, in every moment of every day.

Keep me from looking to anything that cannot see and understand what I am going through.

Let me instead look to You—the One who is personally and intimately acquainted with every trial I face.

Keep me from crying out to something that cannot hear or help.

Let me instead cry out to You—the One who patiently and compassionately waits to hear my cry for help and is ready and able to supply all my needs.

Keep me from trusting in anything that cannot sniff out trouble coming my way.

Let me instead trust You—to smell the stench of evil coming and warn me by Your Spirit, so I can avoid the disaster of succumbing to its temptations.

Keep me from becoming like those things I am tempted to put in front of You—powerless and unable to speak, see and hear the truth, and unable to smell trouble coming and avoid it.

Let me instead be empowered by You—to become more like Your Son, Jesus.

Keep me from merely making You first among the many objects of my worship.

Let me instead worship You—and You alone.

Save me from worshiping anything—or anyone—but You.

In the name of Jesus, Amen.

Comforted, So That
I Can Comfort Others

All praise to God, the Father of our Lord Jesus Christ. God is our merciful Father and the source of all comfort. He comforts us in all our troubles so that we can comfort others. When they are troubled, we will be able to give them the same comfort God has given us.

— 2 Corinthians 1:3–4 (NLT)

Merciful and Comforting Father God,

Teach me to show others the same mercy and extend to them the same loving comfort that You pour out on me when I am weighed down with troubles.

Help me be careful to give You all the praise—as the Father of My Lord and Savior, Jesus Christ, and the source of all comfort—for Your continuing faithfulness to bring good out of all my troubles.

Don't let me forget that You allow hardships, so that I can experience Your faithfulness in my hardships—whether You choose to deliver me from them altogether or walk with me through them to ultimate victory in Christ.

Remind me that as I find comfort and help from You in my troubles, You are equipping me then to be able to offer that same comfort to others who are troubled—and to point them to the only true source of help and hope.

Teach me to show others the same mercy and extend to them the same loving comfort that You pour out on me when I am weighed down with troubles.

In the name of Jesus, Amen.

Giving Every Burden to the LORD

Give your burdens to the LORD,
and he will take care of you.
He will not permit the godly to slip and fall.

— PSALM 55:22 (NLT)

Loving LORD,

Keep me from dishonoring You by trying to carry my own burdens—
when You are right here with me waiting to carry them for me, wanting
to take care of my every need and well able to keep me, in every possible
way, from slipping and falling.

Help me truly turn over every care and concern that burdens my heart to
You—not merely saying that I trust You, when it is evident by the lack of peace
in my heart that I have not.

Help me to continue in trusting You—so that when I give You my burdens,
I don't turn around and try to take them back from You!

Help me to believe that just as You are faithful to sustain me each and every
day—giving me exactly what I need to accomplish Your will and purpose for
me—You are also well able to carry my heaviest burden, so that I do not have
to slip and fall trying to do it on my own.

Keep me from dishonoring You by trying to carry my own burdens—
when You are right here with me waiting to carry them for me, wanting
to take care of my every need and well able to keep me, in every possible
way, from slipping and falling.

In the name of Jesus, Amen.

Show Me My Heart

All the ways of a man are clean and innocent in his own eyes [and he may see nothing wrong with his actions],
But the LORD weighs and examines the motives and intents [of the heart and knows the truth].

— PROVERBS 16:2 (AMP)

All-Knowing LORD,

You alone know the truth about the motives and intents of my heart—so I ask You to show me my heart. And then help me to surrender all of my ways to You—so that You can make my heart Your home.

Don't allow me to deceive myself into believing that all my ways are clean and innocent—but help me to find the truth behind the reasons for what I do, so that I can more perfectly submit my thoughts, words, plans, and actions to Your will for me.

Help me to live every moment of my life in willing obedience to the instruction of Your Word and according to the promptings of Your Holy Spirit—so that I can live an emotionally, mentally, physically, and spiritually healthy life of Truth.

Help me never to try to hide my impurity from You, but openly come before You to confess and repent of my sin and ask You to change me by Your mercy, forgiveness, and grace—fully aware that You already know every imperfection in me but love me anyway.

You alone know the truth about the motives and intents of my heart—so I ask You to show me my heart. And then help me to surrender all of my ways to You—so that You can make my heart Your home.

In the name of Jesus, Amen.

Bringing No Sorrow
by the Way That I Live

And do not bring sorrow to God's Holy Spirit by the way you live. Remember, he has identified you as his own, guaranteeing that you will be saved on the day of redemption.

— EPHESIANS 4:30 (NLT)

Heavenly Father,

Help me not to bring sorrow to Your Holy Spirit within me by the way that I live.

I don't want to be that guy who takes for granted Your presence and power within me—living my life in careless offense to Your Spirit by refusing to submit to Your power to change me.

Help me to realize that the degree to which I am conscious of Your presence working within me, and through me, is an indication of the genuineness of my faith in You—and the closeness of my walk with You is a sign of my submission to Your Spirit.

Help me to remember that Your presence within me is the confirmation that I am a child of God, the assurance that You have secured eternal life for me, and evidence of Your power at work in me to transform me in the here and now, until that time when my transformation is made complete in eternity with You.

Help me not to bring sorrow to Your Holy Spirit within me by the way that I live.

In the name of Jesus, Amen.

Words and Thoughts
That Please You, LORD

May the words of my mouth
and the meditation of my heart
be pleasing to you,
O LORD, my rock and my redeemer.

— PSALM 19:14 (NLT)

Father God,

May this simple prayer—and the high and holy standard it sets forth—be
true in my life today: let every word that I say and every thought I ponder
be pleasing to You.

Let my heart be so filled with gratitude and love for You, that I would
always allow Your love—*for me and for others*—to form every word that I say
and permeate my every thought!

Let every word that escapes from my lips go forth with Your blessing—and
be released to Your delight, for Your glory, honor, and praise!

Let every thought that I invite to dance within my head and dwell within
my heart carry Your approval—and bring You great pleasure!

Help me live in the truth that my life is not my own to live, but is to be lived
for the One who is my Rock and my Redeemer, who redeemed me from the
consequence of my sin—which was certain death—and gave me a new life with
You, forever!

May this simple prayer—and the high and holy standard it sets forth—be
true in my life today: let every word that I say and every thought I ponder
be pleasing to You.

In the name of Jesus, Amen.

The Blessing of Protection, Provision, Pardon, and Peace

The LORD bless you and keep you;
the LORD make his face to shine upon you and be gracious to you;
the LORD lift up his countenance upon you and give you peace.

— NUMBERS 6:24–26 (NKJV)

Loving and Gracious LORD,

Let me fully walk in the favor of Your blessings of protection, provision,
pardon, and peace each and every day!

Thank You for making Your blessing available to any person who opens his or her heart to receive it—so that we can all live in contentment and joy, as we are kept safe in every way within that blessing.

Thank You for the way You make Your face to shine upon us, to smile on us, to enlighten us and give us comfort and life—just as the sun that You hung in space shines upon the earth and warms it to bring it life.

Thank You for lifting up Your countenance upon us in loving adoration—like a gentle and caring father who gazes upon his children with such amazing love that they are always at peace, assured of the special favor and unreserved acceptance that is theirs in him.

Thank You that within Your blessing I am protected and provided for—by the power of the Creator of all things; I am pardoned for all of my sin—by the gracious sacrifice of my Lord Jesus; and I have peace—because my Comforter, the Spirit of peace, lives within me.

Let me fully walk in the favor of Your blessings of protection, provision,
pardon, and peace each and every day!

In the name of Jesus, Amen.

The Truth that Is Found in Christ

Don't let anyone capture you with empty philosophies and high-sounding nonsense that come from human thinking and from the spiritual powers of this world, rather than from Christ.

— COLOSSIANS 2:8 (NLT)

Heavenly Father,

May my heart never be taken captive by any of the empty philosophies and high-sounding nonsense that come from human thinking and the spiritual powers of this world. Let me only live in the Truth—Truth which comes from Your Word, Jesus Christ!

In my search to know the Truth, let me not be satisfied to accept those philosophies that are merely built on human thinking—but always look to Your Word to reveal Your Truth to me.

Don't let me be misled by man's deceitful words—which, despite the fact that they may sound right, are only counterfeits of the Truth, twisted by the enemy to entrap my heart in lies, in order to lead me to destruction.

Keep me from *blindly* assuming that the traditions of man are Truth—those practiced ideas that have been widely accepted as Truth but are not confirmed by Your Word—since I know that the spiritual powers of this world are lying in wait to capture me and keep me from the freedom that I find in Christ alone.

May my heart never be taken captive by any of the empty philosophies and high-sounding nonsense that come from human thinking and the spiritual powers of this world. Let me only live in the Truth—Truth which comes from Your Word, Jesus Christ!

In the name of Jesus, Amen.

As Long as I Live, To My Last Breath

I will sing to the LORD as long as I live.
I will praise my God to my last breath!
May all my thoughts be pleasing to him,
for I rejoice in the LORD.

— PSALM 104:33–34 (NLT)

Heavenly Father,

Oh that all my thoughts would be pleasing to You—that You would be
the source of all my joy and the object of all my praise for as long as I live!

Give me a voice to sing Your praises—and I will sing praises to You, my God, because of who You are and for all that You have done, until my final breath!

Remind me to praise You, LORD—for the precious gift of life You have given me, for the love that You have freely showered on me, and for the opportunity that You have opened before me to experience personally Your amazing grace!

Let my heart rejoice with gratitude for everything You have done, everything that You are doing, and everything that You have yet to do—so that my thoughts would always be pleasing to You!

Oh that all my thoughts would be pleasing to You—that You would be
the source of all my joy and the object of all my praise for as long as I live!

In the name of Jesus, Amen.

Show Me, Lead Me, Teach Me, Save Me

Show me the right path, O LORD;
point out the road for me to follow.
Lead me by your truth and teach me,
for you are the God who saves me.
All day long I put my hope in you.

— PSALM 25:4–5 (NLT)

LORD my GOD,

Show me the right path—the road that I should follow, the way that I
should go. Lead me by Your Truth, teach me by Your Spirit, and save me
in every way—as I put all my hope in You through every moment of each
new day.

Help me to find the path that is right and good—the road where I find
myself walking in intimate, personal relationship with You—where I choose
to humbly serve You and obediently submit to Your will for me in all things.

By the power of Your Holy Spirit at work within me, open up my heart to
receive the Truth You have waiting for me in Your Word—as You teach me to
apply that Truth to every situation and circumstance, so I might always journey
forward, moving ever closer to You.

Help me never forget that You are the God who saves me in every way—
emotionally, mentally, physically, and spiritually—so that I put all of my hope
in You no matter what I face.

Show me the right path—the road that I should follow, the way that I
should go. Lead me by Your Truth, teach me by Your Spirit, and save me
in every way—as I put all my hope in You through every moment of each
new day.

In the name of Jesus, Amen.

Called, Equipped, and Empowered to be Holy

For God did not call us to be impure, but to live a holy life. Therefore, anyone who rejects this instruction does not reject a human being but God, the very God who gives you his Holy Spirit.

— 1 THESSALONIANS 4:7–8 (NIV)

Heavenly Father,

I am grateful that You not only call me to live a holy life, but You also have equipped me to live that life by giving me the Holy Spirit, who empowers me for this journey toward holiness.

Help me never forget that the instruction to live a holy life does not come from a man but from You—and is given to me out of Your unsurpassed wisdom for my own benefit, because of Your great and unfailing love for me.

Let me always remember that when I reject this instruction—instead of allowing it the opportunity to work in me the protections and blessings it brings—I am not rejecting a man but I am rejecting You, the LORD GOD, my Creator and Protector.

Help me see that in doing so, I have grieved Your Holy Spirit within me—and have separated myself from the very One who You have given to me to make it possible for me to turn from impurity and choose to live a holy life.

Help me to understand fully that when I choose impurity over Your call to holiness, I don't have my own best interests at heart—because I have rejected You and Your very best for me.

I am grateful that You not only call me to live a holy life, but You also have equipped me to live that life by giving me the Holy Spirit, who empowers me for this journey toward holiness.

In the name of Jesus, Amen.

Hearing, Trusting, Walking—Giving Myself to You

Let me hear of your unfailing love each morning,
for I am trusting you.
Show me where to walk,
for I give myself to you.

— PSALM 143:8 (NLT)

O LORD of Love That Never Fails,

With each new morning, help me to listen and hear how You love me, and respond to Your love—by offering my love in return, by giving myself to You.

Too often I have rushed into a new day—self-centeredly pursuing my own plans and ideas—without first spending time to listen for what You would say to me, to hear of Your unfailing love for me.

Help me not to forget how critical it is that I open the Bible—*Your love story written to me*—and allow You to speak to me, by Your Holy Spirit, as I read—*and as You reveal*—the Truth that is waiting there for me.

As I study Your Word each morning, help me to hear the message of Your unfailing loving kindness for me and teach me of the goodness of Your ways—so that I will be drawn into an ever-closer relationship with You and my faith will be made increasingly stronger.

As I come before You in prayer, help me submit my will to Yours alone and allow You to show me the ways that I should go.

Help me to follow the best path for me—where I can experience Your strength, Your plan, Your provision, Your protection, Your peace, Your joy, but most of all Your unfailing love for me.

With each new morning, help me to listen and hear how You love me and respond to Your love—by offering my love in return, by giving myself to You.

In the name of Jesus, Amen.

He Who Heals My Broken Heart

He heals the brokenhearted
and bandages their wounds.
He counts the stars
and calls them all by name.
How great is our Lord! His power is absolute!
His understanding is beyond comprehension!

— PSALM 147:3–5 (NLT)

Gracious God,

You alone know and understand the brokenness in the depths of my
heart—so to whom can I bring my broken heart for healing but to You?

By Your absolute power and understanding, You count the stars of Your
own creation and call each one by name—yet You choose to set Your compassionate love and affection on us.

You are intimately familiar with every wound I carry—every hurt, every
pain, every injustice, every disappointment and worldly betrayal—and You
know how the enemy has tried to scar my heart permanently with each one.

Only You are infinite in Your understanding and hold the mighty power
to heal my heart—to bind up every wound left by the evil of this fallen world.

Even when I cannot understand myself—when I am at a loss to explain
my own thoughts, words, or actions—You understand me altogether perfectly
and love me completely, in spite of my sin—and You desire to bring me back to
wholeness again.

How I need for You to remove from me any self-serving thoughts or
motives, so You can become the center of all my desires—and so I might then
begin to comprehend better who You are—and who You have made me to be
in Christ.

You alone know and understand the brokenness in the depths of my
heart—so to whom can I bring my broken heart for healing but to You?

In the name of Jesus, Amen.

The One Who Goes with You

"Be strong and of good courage, do not fear nor be afraid of them; for the LORD your God, He is the One who goes with you. He will not leave you nor forsake you."

— DEUTERONOMY 31:6 (NKJV)

O LORD, My God,

No matter what opposition or challenges that the forces of evil may put before me today, grant that I would be strong and courageous—confidently trusting in the Truth that You are the One who goes with me, who never leaves me nor forsakes me.

Let my strength be found in the Truth of Your immeasurable strength within me.

Let my courage be demonstrated by my faith in Your ever-abiding Presence.

Let fear be far from me because I have been filled to overflowing with the knowledge and experience of Your unfailing love for me.

Let my testimony be that my God goes with me wherever I go—has never left my side and has never let me down—so I have no reason to fear!

No matter what opposition or challenges that the forces of evil may put before me today, grant that I would be strong and courageous—confidently trusting in the Truth that You are the One who goes with me, who never leaves me nor forsakes me.

In the name of Jesus, Amen.

Identifying the Enemy

For we are not fighting against flesh-and-blood enemies, but against evil rulers and authorities of the unseen world, against mighty powers in this dark world, and against evil spirits in the heavenly places.

— EPHESIANS 6:12 (NLT)

Almighty God,

Help me not to lose sight of the fact that my enemies are not people—nor is my enemy even myself—but rather, my enemies are the spiritual forces of evil at work in this dark world.

Help me to remain at peace with all people—knowing that You have made mankind Your most prized creation and that You sent Your Son, Jesus, as a sacrifice for the redemption of *every* one of us.

Help me to realize that the real battle is a battle to deceive me—to turn me from the truth of Your Word to empty lies which bring destruction and death.

Help me to recognize the spiritual weapons that the devil and his demons use against me, as by Your Holy Spirit You reveal the truth of Your Word to my heart—so I can come against them with the authority of Christ Himself.

Help me not to lose sight of the fact that my enemies are not people—nor is my enemy even myself—but rather, my enemies are the spiritual forces of evil at work in this dark world.

In the name of Jesus, Amen.

Defense Against Those More Opportune Times

When the devil had finished every temptation, he [temporarily] left Him until a more opportune time.

— LUKE 4:13 (AMP)

Almighty God,

Help me remember that the devil never stops lying, that he never stops trying to deceive me—that even when it looks as if he has given up on coming against me, he is only waiting for a better opportunity to tempt me into sin.

Thank You that because of Your Son, Jesus, I can have victory over the temptations that come my way—I am no longer a slave to my sin.

Thank You that I can resist the attacks of the enemy—that I resist him by *knowing* and *speaking* Your Word, just as Christ did.

But don't let me forget that walking in a season where the temptations are not as frequent or as strong doesn't mean that the enemy is finished trying.

Keep me mindful that I must always stand guard over my heart, because the enemy will always be looking for another opportunity to attack when I least expect it.

Thank You for showing me that my best defense against the devil is to stay in close fellowship with You—filling my heart with the truth of Your Word and allowing Your Spirit to fill it with Your presence and power—so that my weapon arsenal will be well stocked against his next attack.

Help me remember that the devil never stops lying, that he never stops trying to deceive me—that even when it looks as if he has given up on coming against me, he is only waiting for a better opportunity to tempt me into sin.

In the name of Jesus, Amen.

God Listens, When My Heart Is Right

Come and listen, all you who fear God,
and I will tell you what he did for me.
For I cried out to him for help,
praising him as I spoke.
If I had not confessed the sin in my heart,
the LORD would not have listened.
But God did listen!
He paid attention to my prayer.
Praise God, who did not ignore my prayer
or withdraw his unfailing love from me.

— PSALM 66:16–20 (NLT)

Heavenly Father,

I praise You, God, for You do not ignore my prayers—but You listen and lavish Your unfailing love on me!

Let me boldly declare to anyone who will listen, but especially to those who fear You, the marvelous things You have done for me—not in a prideful way but only to give honor and praise to You and as an encouragement to others to put their hope in You.

For You are my hope and it is to You alone that I cry out for help, praising Your greatness all the while—for I know the power of the One from whom my help comes.

Keep me mindful, though, of the futility of coming before You, harboring any sin in my heart—treating it as if it were my friend—rather than confessing and repenting of it, in order that my prayers would continue to be heard and answered according to Your great love for me.

And though I am still a sinful man, when You look upon my heart, may You find within me not a heart after sin but a heart after Your own heart.

I praise You, God, for You do not ignore my prayers—but You listen and lavish Your unfailing love on me!

In the name of Jesus, Amen.

The Perfect Peace of All Who Trust in You

You will keep in perfect peace
all who trust in you,
all whose thoughts are fixed on you!
Trust in the LORD always,
for the LORD GOD is the eternal Rock.

— ISAIAH 26:3–4 (NLT)

LORD GOD of Peace,

Help me to abide—to truly live—in that perfect and constant peace that can only be found in trusting You.

You have promised perfect peace to all who trust in You—to all whose thoughts are fixed on You.

So help me to place all of my trust in You—no matter what hardship or pain, no matter what circumstances or situations I may face—knowing that You will deliver me out of, or carry me safely through, every attempt of the enemy to steal my peace.

And help me to fix my thoughts on You rather than trying to find my own way out of my troubles—because it is only in You will I find the answers that I am looking for.

Grant that I would live in the kind of peace that not only remains in me, but radiates outwardly from deep within me—to a world that needs Your peace so desperately.

Establish within my heart this unchanging truth: that You are, and forever will be, my strength and the firm, unchanging and never-failing Rock upon which all of my faith and hope stands.

Help me to abide—to truly live—in that perfect and constant peace that can only be found in trusting You.

In the name of Jesus, Amen.

Transform Me, Change the Way I Think!

Don't copy the behavior and customs of this world, but let God transform you into a new person by changing the way you think. Then you will learn to know God's will for you, which is good and pleasing and perfect.

— ROMANS 12:2 (NLT)

Heavenly Father,

Transform me into a new person by changing the way I think—so I can learn to know Your good and pleasing and perfect will for me.

Grant me the wisdom not to copy any of those behaviors, customs, and values of this world, which are birthed out of selfish pride and nurtured with corruption—those things that this world so quickly and casually accepts.

Do the work of transformation in me—by the power of Your Holy Spirit—so that my thoughts will be like Your thoughts and Your ways will become the only ways that I choose to follow.

Help me to learn to know Your will for me—and to trust that Your will is good, pleasing, and perfect—so that I can walk down every path You place before me in willing obedience, confident that it will lead to Your very best for me.

Transform me into a new person by changing the way I think—so I can learn to know Your good and pleasing and perfect will for me.

In the name of Jesus, Amen.

You Are God!

Before the mountains were born
Or You gave birth to the earth and the world,
Even from everlasting to everlasting, You are God.

— PSALM 90:2 (NASB)

Everlasting God,

I worship You for who You are—the God who always was, always is, and
always shall be the only One worthy of my worship!

I worship You for only You are timeless! Only You existed before time began—before You created everything that now exists, put it all in order, and set in motion, thus creating time itself.

I worship You, for among the so-called gods and other worshiped things of this world, only You are the Living God—the One who gives life to all things! Yes, You are alive and choose to live here—both with me and within me—so that I can know You through Your Word, as revealed by Your Spirit, and so I can personally experience Your great affection for me as Your dearly loved child.

I worship You, for out of all of that which begs my worship, only You will remain steadfast and unchanging for all eternity—only You will always love me with an unfailing love that passionately and unrelentingly pursues me. And only You will remain worthy of my love and worship and devotion forevermore.

I worship You for who You are—the God who always was, always is, and
always shall be the only One worthy of my worship!

In the name of Jesus, Amen.

Mark Out a Straight Path

Mark out a straight path for your feet;
stay on the safe path.
Don't get sidetracked;
keep your feet from following evil.

— PROVERBS 4:26–27 (NLT)

Heavenly Father,

With each new day, help me to mark out the straight path for my feet—
the path which leads to a more abundant life!

Keep me on the safe path of willing obedience to Your will and Your decrees—as You prove Your loving faithfulness to me by keeping me in every way each step along the way.

And don't allow me to get sidetracked by the distractions of this world—but let me stay focused on the next best step that You have planned for me.

Then my feet will not follow after evil—and I won't find myself lost along the way home to You.

With each new day, help me to mark out the straight path for my feet—
the path which leads to a more abundant life!

In the name of Jesus, Amen.

APRIL 11TH

Help Me to Watch and Pray

"Watch and pray, lest you enter into temptation. The spirit indeed is willing, but the flesh is weak."

— MATTHEW 26:41 (NKJV)

Heavenly Father,

Help me to watch and pray.

Help me keep watch against all the schemes of the enemy by living each moment of my life in prayerful fellowship with You—so that my spirit will remain sensitive to every prompting of Your Holy Spirit within me, and my life can be lived in the peace You offer to those who will trust and obey.

By Your Holy Spirit, make me wise and help me to be discerning—so I can expose every evil lie sent against me that might cause me to fall to temptation. Help me to stand against those lies with the truth of Your Word—so I might live in the freedom that can only be found in Truth.

I know that though my spirit is willing, my flesh remains weak. Help me to depend on Your Spirit to strengthen me and enable me to resist every temptation I face—so that my life will be filled with only Your very best for me.

Help me to watch and pray.

In the name of Jesus, Amen.

All of Us, Just Like Sheep

All of us, like sheep, have strayed away.
We have left God's paths to follow our own.
Yet the LORD laid on him
the sins of us all.

— ISAIAH 53:6 (NLT)

Loving LORD,

Like a shepherd lead me along Your path today,
and teach me by Your Spirit's voice never to stray away.

I need You to lead me today. Because just like a sheep, if left on my own, I will wander from the path of Your will for me—and follow a path marked by my own self-centered desires.

Sometimes I do it somehow blindly unaware of my wandering—as if I were sleepwalking—failing to wake up to the error of my way, until I am lost and a long way from home.

Sometimes I fall back into my old ways of stubborn and willful rebellion—fully aware but wanting what I want, more than wanting what You want for me.

And yet always, even in my sin, You call me to return to You—having laid all of my sin upon Jesus, so that I might stand in the peace and protection of Your Presence once again.

So help me to keep my eyes fixed on You—and to value Your Presence with me as I should—so I can hear Your instruction then choose to follow after You in obedience—as You lead me to every good thing that You have prepared for me.

Like a shepherd lead me along Your path today,
and teach me by Your Spirit's voice never to stray away.

In the name of Jesus, Amen.

This Gracious Invitation into Your Glorious Presence

Hear me as I pray, O LORD.
Be merciful and answer me!
My heart has heard you say, "Come and talk with me."
And my heart responds, "LORD, I am coming."

— PSALM 27:7–8 (NLT)

Gracious and Loving LORD,

When within my heart I hear You calling, "Come and talk with me," let
my response always be an eager, "LORD, I am coming!"

Grant me the kind of faith that fully believes that You hear me when I pray—and that You answer me in Your perfect timing and according to Your sovereign purpose and plan for my life, always with my best interest at heart.

Let me experience the wonders of the depths of Your merciful love and goodness—as You faithfully answer me and draw me into the unfathomable peace of Your abiding presence once again.

Give me the strength to push aside every distraction and accept this gracious invitation into Your glorious presence, knowing that it is in Your presence—within that place of intimate fellowship with You—that everything I need to accomplish Your will for my life is supplied.

When within my heart I hear You calling, "Come and talk with me," let
my response always be an eager, "LORD, I am coming!"

In the name of Jesus, Amen.

The One Who Leads into All Truth

"If you love me, obey my commandments. And I will ask the Father, and he will give you another Advocate, who will never leave you. He is the Holy Spirit, who leads into all truth."

— JOHN 14:15–17A (NLT)

Lord of my life,

Let me never fail to demonstrate my love for You through my willing obedience to Your commandments, as I look to the Holy Spirit within me to guide me into all Truth.

May my love for You be so much more than just words that I push carelessly across my lips without thinking. Rather, let my words be a reflection of my love for You—a love which permeates everything that I think, say, and do.

Help me to look to the Advocate—the Holy Spirit of God—to be my Comforter when I am hurting, my Encourager when I am discouraged, my Counselor when I need guidance, my Helper when the work gets hard, my Strengthener when I need to take a stand, my Friend when I need to know I am never alone, and my Teacher when I need to hear and know the Truth.

Keep me sensitive to Your Spirit alive within me at all times, so that I might not miss anything good thing that You have for me along my journey to know You more and to make Your great name known here upon earth.

Let me never fail to demonstrate my love for You through my willing obedience to Your commandments, as I look to the Holy Spirit within me to guide me into all Truth.

In Your most Precious and Holy Name, Lord Jesus.

In the Everlasting Grip of Your Unfailing Love

The LORD directs the steps of the godly.
He delights in every detail of their lives.
Though they stumble, they will never fall,
for the LORD holds them by the hand.

— PSALM 37:23–24 (NLT)

Heavenly Father,

Thank You for delighting in every detail of my life—for holding my hand and directing my steps—so that even if I stumble I will never fall, because I am held firmly in the everlasting grip of Your unfailing love!

What an amazing thought, that You would take pleasure and joy in every detail of my life—that You would want to be intimately involved with me!

You make every moment that I live an opportunity for me to see Your faithfulness and love extended toward me!

You direct me into each "next step" along the path of my life, and take every single step with me, never leaving my side—never giving me reason to fear!

You take me by the hand to guide me in paths of safety and even when I falter You do not allow me to fall completely down, because Your grip on me never fails!

You keep me from being destroyed by the harm that my own inexperience or inattentiveness might cause me and rescue me according to Your mighty power, mercy, forgiveness, grace, and love!

Thank You for delighting in every detail of my life—for holding my hand and directing my steps—so that even if I stumble I will never fall, because I am held firmly in the everlasting grip of Your unfailing love!

In the name of Jesus, Amen.

I Know My Redeemer Lives

I know that my redeemer lives,
and that in the end he will stand on the earth.
And after my skin has been destroyed,
yet in my flesh I will see God;
I myself will see him
with my own eyes—I, and not another.
How my heart yearns within me!

— JOB 19:25–27 (NIV)

Living God, My Redeemer,

I know that my Redeemer lives—and that it is You who redeems me to
the uttermost!

Thank You for giving me the faith to believe that You will one day return and stand upon the earth again to vindicate the sufferings of this life and set all things right—as my personal and risen Redeemer.

Though my body is assaulted and failing, I believe I will yet see You for myself—though death may bring my body to decay in the grave, I will yet see Your redemption come, in my own body, with my own eyes.

How overwhelming is the comfort of this knowledge! How steadfast is my hope as I remain in this Truth!

I know that my Redeemer lives—and that it is You who redeems me to
the uttermost!

In the name of Jesus, Amen.

Overwhelming Victory
Is Ours through Christ

Can anything ever separate us from Christ's love? Does it mean he no longer loves us if we have trouble or calamity, or are persecuted, or hungry, or destitute, or in danger, or threatened with death?

No, despite all these things, overwhelming victory is ours through Christ, who loved us.

— ROMANS 8:35, 37 (NLT)

Loving Heavenly Father,

May I always rejoice in the knowledge that there is nothing that can ever separate me from the constant and continuous love of Christ—which never wavers, never diminishes, never fails, and never ends.

In the tough and troubled times of my life, help me to cling to this Truth: You will use everything that I may suffer to help me to identify more closely with Christ's sufferings on my behalf, so I can more fully realized the depth of His love for me and be drawn into ever closer fellowship with You.

Use those times of my life to help me to understand how totally dependent I am on You to provide everything I need, not only survive but also to thrive along this journey here—as I watch You prove Your faithfulness to me every step along the way.

Let me never forget that no matter what may come I have no need to fear, for overwhelming victory is mine through Christ—who, *because of His great love for me*, heals my brokenness with Truth; who, *through His mercy*, forgives my sin and makes me completely whole; and who, *out of His amazing grace*, grants me abundant and eternal life with Him.

May I always rejoice in the knowledge that there is nothing that can ever separate me from the constant and continuous love of Christ—which never wavers, never diminishes, never fails, and never ends.

In the name of Jesus, Amen.

Walking in Paths of Joy

Joyful are people of integrity,
who follow the instructions of the LORD.
Joyful are those who obey his laws
and search for him with all their hearts.
They do not compromise with evil,
and they walk only in his paths.

— PSALM 119:1–3 (NLT)

Heavenly Father,

Thank You for giving me a path to follow that strengthens me with last-ing joy!

Your Word tells me that if I will trust You enough to walk uprightly and follow Your ways, that as I search for You with all my heart, I will find joy—complete and blessed happiness—in You.

Help me to remember that Your instructions are for my benefit, to keep me safe or out of trouble—not to imprison me but to set me free to walk in all the blessings that obedience brings—for my own good.

Help me to remember that in order to know You and follow Your will, I must search for You—resolve to persistently and purposefully look for You for myself, to seek carefully and thoroughly for You with expectation, confident that I *can* know You personally and intimately.

Your Word further reminds me that in order to stay in this joy, I cannot compromise with evil by walking in any path that is not Your own. So I ask You to help me stay on the path You have instructed me to walk down and remain in Your joy.

Thank You for giving me a path to follow that strengthens me with last-ing joy!

In the name of Jesus, Amen.

Expectantly Waiting for the Lord

I wait for the Lord, I expectantly wait, and in His word do I hope. I am looking and waiting for the Lord more than watchmen for the morning, I say, more than watchmen for the morning.

— PSALM 130:5–6 (AMPC)

Heavenly Father,

I wait for You and confidently place my trust in this hope—that the fulfillment of all of the promises of Your Word is more certain than the rising of the sun each morning.

I wait for You—with even greater expectation than I have for the morning itself to come—confident that You will come to me with relief and comfort by the power of Your mercy, grace, and love, as I place all of my hope in You.

I wait for You—looking for You to reveal Yourself more fully to me—believing that as I am careful to look, I will see Your hand at work in every moment of my day.

I wait for You—knowing Your plans and purposes for me are good—knowing You will direct my every step as I submit my will to You.

I wait for You—asking that I might wait with patient expectation, as I long to see that what You have promised—looking to no one else but making You my only hope.

I wait for You and confidently place my trust in this hope—that the fulfillment of all of the promises of Your Word is more certain than the rising of the sun each morning.

In the name of Jesus, Amen.

Good News Worth Sharing

And this same God who takes care of me will supply all your needs from his glorious riches, which have been given to us in Christ Jesus.

— PHILIPPIANS 4:19 (NLT)

Provider God,

I praise You for You are always faithful to take care of me—to supply all my need according to Your glorious riches in Christ Jesus!

Because of who You are and out of Your unfailing love for me, I have always had everything that I needed to be able to carry out Your plans and purposes for me—each and every day that I have lived.

Thank You for continuing in Your faithfulness to me, providing every resource that I need to carry me through whatever opportunities or challenges, trials, or troubles that may come my way—as I remain in Christ Jesus and seek after You with all my heart.

Never let me forget that the supplying of my needs is not according to any of the limited resources that I can see here in the natural, but rather according to the supernatural and inexhaustible supply of Your glorious riches—prepared for us who have found our life in Christ Jesus.

Help me to be faithful to carry this message of hope to others—that this same abundant and glorious supply is available to all who believe have and received the redemptive gift of Your Son, Jesus Christ.

I praise You for You are always faithful to take care of me—to supply all my need according to Your glorious riches in Christ Jesus!

In the name of Jesus, Amen.

In This Time of Our Deep Need

I have heard all about you, LORD.
I am filled with awe by your amazing works.
In this time of our deep need,
help us again as you did in years gone by.
And in your anger,
remember your mercy.

— HABAKKUK 3:2 (NLT)

Merciful LORD,

In this time of our deep need, please help us once again! Though we deserve Your anger, even still have mercy upon us according to Your loving kindness!

As I search the words of Your Holy Scriptures, fill me with awe and wonder—with reverential fear and respect—because of Your amazing works and the demonstrations of Your unlimited power and unfailing love for Your people.

Remind me of all the times that You have tempered Your anger toward the unfaithfulness of Your people with Your mercy—so that they were not completely destroyed and the glory of Your Name could continue to be proclaimed throughout the world by the remnants of the faithful.

And grant us again today Your mercy—that Your glory might yet shine from within us, that we would return to You in repentance, and find You waiting there to help us just as You did in years gone by.

In this time of our deep need, please help us once again! Though we deserve Your anger, even still have mercy upon us according to Your loving kindness!

In the name of Jesus, Amen.

The Plans You Have for Me

For I know the plans I have for you," says the LORD. "They are plans for good and not for disaster, to give you a future and a hope.
— JEREMIAH 29:11 (NLT)

Dear LORD,

Thank You that I can trust You with my life—because there is no uncertainty within You. I trust that Your plans for me are for my good and extend throughout eternity, as evidence of Your love for me. I live at peace in this hope.

Interwoven among all the things that have ever happened, the things that are happening now, and anything that has yet to happen is that marvelous plan for my individual life that was authored by You.

Limited by my humanness, I do not fully understand where I have been, where I am now, or where I am going. I do not even fully know my own heart and I am uncertain of my own mind at times.

But there is no uncertainty within You. You know everything—past, present, and future—and have designed a plan to bring me good and not disaster, to give me a future with You and with that great hope as I put my trust in You.

Thank You that I have no reason to fear anything that may have happened in the past, nor the things that are happening around me now, nor anything that may happen to me next—because the plan You have for me is a plan to use it all to greatly benefit me and not to cause me harm.

And though trouble may come to me—because I live in a fallen world full of evil—You will always be working in the midst of every circumstance I find myself in, to carry me through it in peace and bring good out of it for me.

Thank You that I can trust You with my life—because there is no uncertainty within You. I trust that Your plans for me are for my good and extend throughout eternity, as evidence of Your love for me. I live at peace in this hope.

In the name of Jesus, Amen.

Joy, Peace, and Confident Hope - Because We Trust God

I pray that God, the source of hope, will fill you completely with joy and peace because you trust in him. Then you will overflow with confident hope through the power of the Holy Spirit.

— ROMANS 15:13 (NLT)

Gracious and Loving God,

Be for me my source of hope—and fill me completely with the joy and peace that comes when I put all of my trust in You. By Your Holy Spirit, cause that confident hope to overflow from deep within me—for Your glory, honor, and praise.

Forever remain the very source of hope within me. Let my continuing experience of Your patient goodness, loving kindness, and enduring faithfulness to me give me cause to trust in You more and more—with every moment that passes.

And as I learn to trust You more and more, giving every hurt and worry to You, fill me completely with Your joy and peace—so I am no longer disheartened or dismayed no matter what circumstances I may face.

By the power of Your Holy Spirit at work within me, cause that confident hope that is mine to overflow out of me to all those around me—as a testimony to Your great mercy, grace, and love for us all.

Be for me my source of hope—and fill me completely with the joy and peace that comes when I put all of my trust in You. By Your Holy Spirit, cause that confident hope to overflow from deep within me—for Your glory, honor, and praise.

In the name of Jesus, Amen.

The Comfort That Gives Me
Renewed Hope and Cheer

I cried out, "I am slipping!"
but your unfailing love, O LORD, supported me.
When doubts filled my mind,
your comfort gave me renewed hope and cheer.

— Psalm 94:18–19 (NLT)

Loving LORD,

When I feel myself slipping in any way, help me to cry out to You in
faith—knowing that You will hear my cry and You will support me in
Your unfailing love.

Help me to fix my eyes upon You at all times, so that I won't slip or fall but rather will allow Your unfailing love to sustain me in every way—physically, emotionally, mentally, and spiritually.

But in those times when I find myself under attack from the deceiver—the one who floods my mind with doubts and lies, and tempts me to question all that I know in my heart is true—help me to cry out to You.

For You, O LORD, are the only One who can save me, comfort me, and bring me renewed hope and cheer.

When I feel myself slipping in any way, help me to cry out to You in
faith—knowing that You will hear my cry and You will support me in
Your unfailing love.

In the name of Jesus, Amen.

No One Like You

"How great you are, O Sovereign LORD! There is no one like you. We have never even heard of another God like you!"

— 2 SAMUEL 7:22 (NLT)

O Sovereign LORD,

Let all that I am boldly and freely declare—to anyone who will hear—how uniquely great and marvelously wonderful You are!

There is no god that surpasses Your greatness, for it is from You alone that greatness flows! Anything or anyone that is made great is made so by Your divine design, according to Your divine purposes, and ultimately for Your highest glory, honor, and praise!

There is no other god that is Sovereign but You! For it is You who created all things and holds all power and authority in Your hand—assigning that power and authority to those You choose!

There is no other god that is like You—alive and living within those who believe! For You didn't wait for me to love You and desire a relationship with You, but rather You loved me first—when I was bound in filthy sin—and called me to Yourself and made my heart Your home, forever!

Why would I follow after some other god—when I have never even heard of another God like You? None better, none greater, none higher, none like You!

Let all that I am boldly and freely declare—to anyone who will hear—how uniquely great and marvelously wonderful You are!

In the name of Jesus, Amen.

A Spirit of Power, of Love, and of a Sound Mind

For God has not given us a spirit of fear, but of power and of love and of a sound mind.

— 2 TIMOTHY 1:7 (NKJV)

Heavenly Father,

Thank You for showing me that I don't have to be afraid—for reminding me that You didn't create me to be timid or to act cowardly or fearfully—but that the spirit You have given me is a spirit of power, of love, and of a sound mind.

You have given me a spirit of power to resolutely face any trouble, opposition, or obstacle with courage—since You have delivered me from any cowardice or timidity by the strength of the Greater One who lives in me.

You have given me a spirit of love, *both for You*—which gives me the faith and the freedom to rise above any fear of man or circumstance—*and for the souls of others*—which gives me the desire and the power to compassionately reach out to my neighbor with truth and grace.

You have given me a spirit of a calm and well-balanced and sound mind, so that with that quietness of mind, I can remain peacefully disciplined—as I surrender control to Your Spirit and entertain only thoughts that are true and life-giving.

Thank You for showing me that I don't have to be afraid—for reminding me that You didn't create me to be timid or to act cowardly or fearfully—but that the spirit You have given me is a spirit of power, of love, and of a sound mind.

In the name of Jesus, Amen.

A Harvest of Joy and Blessing

Those who plant in tears
will harvest with shouts of joy.
They weep as they go to plant their seed,
but they sing as they return with the harvest.

— PSALM 126:5–6 (NLT)

Gracious God,

How miraculously You restore my life and renew my joy from the depths
of my pain and brokenness!

Thank You that You feel my sadness and see my tears and are preparing a harvest of great joy and blessing for me—because You are ever working for my good.

Even in my sadness help me consistently plant my seeds of faith in You and seek to do what is right in Your sight—knowing that Your ability to bring good out of my pain is far beyond my ability to understand it.

Help me to wait patiently for Your faithful hand to work for my good—knowing that You work in ways I cannot know.

How miraculously You restore my life and renew my joy from the depths
of my pain and brokenness!

In the name of Jesus, Amen.

Dwelling in the Secret Place
of the Most High

He who dwells in the secret place of the Most High
Shall abide under the shadow of the Almighty.

— PSALM 91:1 (NKJV)

Almighty and Most High God,

Let me live in Your secret, sheltering place—that place where I find seren-
ity, security, and safety. Let me abide forever in that place where You
have called me to remain—within Your Holy Presence!

Help me remember that I am drawn into that secret place when I live in constant, prayerful communion with You; as I allow the Truth of Your Word as revealed by Your Spirit to fill me; and as I make that choice to believe Your promises to me.

Help me to find my place of rest in Your shadow—in closest proximity to You, under Your covering, firmly held in Your everlasting arms of love.

Help me not to wander in and out of that secret place, but rather make it my place of permanent residence—so I can remain under Your protection, provision, and peace—where You are my rescue, refuge and rest, and my only hope forevermore.

Let me live in Your secret, sheltering place—that place where I find seren-
ity, security, and safety. Let me abide forever in that place where You
have called me to remain—within Your Holy Presence!

In the name of Jesus, Amen.

To Live My Life in Christ,
His Words Made Alive in Me

*If you abide in Me, and My words abide in you, ask whatever you wish,
and it will be done for you.*

— JOHN 15:7 (NASB)

Lord Jesus,

*Let me never walk away from Your Presence within me, and help me to
keep every word that You have spoken alive in my heart and proven by
my life, so that my deepest desire—the thing I wish for the most—would
always be the very best that You have for me.*

May I always live my life in You—being vitally and necessarily joined with
You and making You the center of everything I think, say, and do—always conscious that apart from You, I am nothing.

Cause Your words to remain in my heart—so I can remember to rely on
them, continually contemplate them, use them as my strict standard for that
which I do, graciously grow by them, carefully cling to them for my hope, and
evermore establish them as the Truth in my life.

For I know that in as much as I am truly able to do this, not only will my
thoughts, words, and actions be in harmony with Your plans and purposes for
my life, but every desire of my heart will be conformed to Your will.

*Let me never walk away from Your Presence within me, and help me to
keep every word that You have spoken alive in my heart and proven by
my life, so that my deepest desire—the thing I wish for the most—would
always be the very best that You have for me.*

This I pray in Your Holy Name, Lord Jesus, Amen.

No Escaping Your Presence

Where can I go from your Spirit?
Where can I flee from your presence?
If I go up to the heavens, you are there;
if I make my bed in the depths, you are there.
If I rise on the wings of the dawn,
if I settle on the far side of the sea,
even there your hand will guide me,
your right hand will hold me fast.

— PSALM 139:7–10 (NIV)

Omnipresent LORD,

Thank You that no matter where I wander, You are already there waiting
for me—just as You have always been—holding within Yourself every-
thing that I will ever need and making it freely available to me, if I will
only turn and seek You with my whole heart.

Never let me forget that though I cannot see You—and though I may not
always sense Your Spirit with me—You *never* leave me, but rather are constantly and compassionately watching over me according to Your unfailing love
for me.

When in my foolishness I have gone my own way and feel like I am far
from where You are, help me to remember that I only need to look for You and
that in calling out for You, I will find that You are right there with me—having
never left my side, having never let go of my hand—ready to forgive me and
restore me to fellowship with You once again.

May the knowledge of Your constant presence with me create within me
the courage to faithfully follow wherever Your Spirit might take me—trusting
that Your hand will guide me and Your strength will support me no matter
where Your perfect path for me may lead.

Thank You that no matter where I wander, You are already there waiting
for me—just as You have always been—holding within Yourself every-
thing that I will ever need and making it freely available to me, if I will
only turn and seek You with my whole heart.

In the name of Jesus, Amen.

This Amazing Book of Instruction

"Study this Book of Instruction continually. Meditate on it day and night so you will be sure to obey everything written in it. Only then will you prosper and succeed in all you do. This is my command—be strong and courageous! Do not be afraid or discouraged. For the LORD your God is with you wherever you go."

— Joshua 1:8–9 (NLT)

O LORD My God,

Thank You for giving us Your Word—this amazing Book of Instruction—which tells us everything we need to know in order to navigate the challenges of life here on earth and fulfill our purpose as Your chosen people.

Help me to study Your Word continually and meditate on its Truth day and night—so that I will not only be careful to fully understand Your instruction, but also be able to apply its Truth to my life in willing obedience to Your instruction.

For I know that it is Your will that I prosper and succeed in all that I do—when I am obedient to Your instruction and call—and that in Your blessing upon my life, others will see You at work and be drawn into relationship with You.

Keep me far from fear and discouragement—comforted by knowing that though Your way for me may not always seem easy, it will always be right.

Help me to remain strong and courageous at all times—in every circumstance and situation I face—because I know that You are always with me wherever I go.

Thank You for giving us Your Word—this amazing Book of Instruction—which tells us everything we need to know in order to navigate the challenges of life here on earth and fulfill our purpose as Your chosen people.

In the name of Jesus, Amen.

United with Christ Jesus

God has united you with Christ Jesus. For our benefit God made him to be wisdom itself. Christ made us right with God; he made us pure and holy, and he freed us from sin. Therefore, as the Scriptures say, "If you want to boast, boast only about the Lord."

— 1 CORINTHIANS 1:30–31 (NLT)

Merciful and Gracious God,

Let me never boast about anything except Jesus, my Lord!

Thank You for uniting me with Christ Jesus, Your Son, so that I can walk in the blessing of being joined with wisdom itself.

Thank You that because I believe and have confessed that Christ died and rose again for me—because I have received Him into my heart and life by faith as my Lord—I am made right with You.

Thank You that by Christ's transforming power, I am made pure and holy— and by His death and resurrection, the power that sin once had over me has been broken, and I am free to choose good over evil.

Help me always remember that anything good in me has come through Christ who is Worthy of all of the Honor, Glory, and Power forevermore!

Let me never boast about anything except Jesus, my Lord!

In the name of Jesus, Amen.

Sustained with Joy, Filled with Life

If your instructions hadn't sustained me with joy,
I would have died in my misery.
I will never forget your commandments,
for by them you give me life.

— PSALM 119:92–93 (NLT)

Father God,

Thank You for the sustaining joy and the abundant life that You give
to those who listen to Your instructions—to those who are careful to
remember and to obey Your commandments!

Too much of my life I wandered from Your instructions—reaping the
consequences of my disobedience—until finally I learned that each of Your
instructions are meant to benefit me, not to harm me or hold me back from
life in any way.

When I learned to follow Your instructions and ordered my steps by Your
commandments, trouble still came my way—but misery could not take away
my life, for You sustained me with joy!

Let me never forget Your commands, for by them You give me abundant
life—life that is rich, deep, and full and overflowing, so that I can be a blessing
to those around me.

Thank You for the sustaining joy and the abundant life that You give
to those who listen to Your instructions—to those who are careful to
remember and to obey Your commandments!

In the name of Jesus, Amen.

The LORD Who Rescues Me

The LORD says, "I will rescue those who love me.
I will protect those who trust in my name.
When they call on me, I will answer;
I will be with them in trouble.
I will rescue and honor them.
I will reward them with a long life
and give them my salvation."

— PSALM 91:14–16 (NLT)

O LORD my GOD,

Thank You for all the promises that I find in Your Word—and help me to
do my part to secure those promises in my life.

Your Word promises me that You will rescue me—*if I love You.*

Your Word promises me that You will protect me—*when I put my trust in*
Your name.

Your Word promises me that You will answer me—*every time I call to You.*

Your Word promises me that You will be with me—*even when I find myself*
in trouble.

Your Word promises me that You will honor me—*as I humbly depend on*
You alone.

Your Word promises me that You will reward me with long life—*long*
enough for me to accomplish Your purposes for me here and to make me ready to
meet You there.

Your Word promises me that You will give me Your salvation—*as I reach*
out and take it by faith.

Thank You for all the promises that I find in Your Word—and help me to
do my part to secure those promises in my life.

In the name of Jesus, Amen.

To Let the Holy Spirit Guide My Life

So I say, let the Holy Spirit guide your lives. Then you won't be doing what your sinful nature craves.

— GALATIANS 5:16 (NLT)

Heavenly Father,

Grant me the wisdom to allow Your Holy Spirit to guide all of my life—so I won't find myself doing what my sinful nature desires to do.

Let my actions reflect my character—and let my character be an overflow of the love, joy, peace, patience, kindness, goodness, faithfulness, gentleness, and self-control that I find in Christ.

Help me to be able to discern the difference between my own subjective feelings and the leading of Your Holy Spirit—as I commit to listen for, hear, and willingly obey all of the instructions You give me through Your Word and Your Spirit.

Strengthen me to continue to live every moment of my life under the guidance and control of Your Spirit—allowing the words of Christ to fill my thoughts, to determine my actions, and to be the power within me that keeps control of my selfish and sinful desires.

Grant me the wisdom to allow Your Holy Spirit to guide all of my life—so I won't find myself doing what my sinful nature desires to do.

In the name of Jesus, Amen.

Whatever Seems Right to Me...
Or According to Your Truth?

In those days Israel had no king; all the people did whatever seemed right in their own eyes.

— JUDGES 21:25 (NLT)

My LORD and My King,

Let me forever look to You as my LORD and King, so that the way I conduct my life will be according to Your Truth and not according to my own opinion.

Help me to submit my will to Your will, my plans to Your plans, my desires to Your desires, and my motives to Your motives, so that my heart beats only after Your own heart—and my actions only reflect the revelation of Your Truth to my spirit.

Keep me from the chaos that comes from deciding for myself what is right and what is wrong—based on my own limited and flawed intellect and perspective—and give me the faith to trust You for the best answers, knowing Your intellect is infinitely beyond my own and Your perfect perspective is limitless.

As I commit to obediently follow Your instructions—as revealed to my spirit by the Holy Spirit through Your Word—let my actions reflect Your standards for morality, mercy, forgiveness, grace, justice, truth, and above all, love.

Let me forever look to You as my LORD and King, so that the way I conduct my life will be according to Your Truth and not according to my own opinion.

In the name of Jesus, Amen.

Leading Me with Unfailing Love and Faithfulness

The LORD is good and does what is right;
he shows the proper path to those who go astray.
He leads the humble in doing right,
teaching them his way.
The LORD leads with unfailing love and faithfulness
all who keep his covenant and obey his demands.

— PSALM 25:8–10 (NLT)

Good and Righteous LORD,

Thank You for continuing to show me the proper path and for teaching me to humbly follow Your way—as You lead me with unfailing love and faithfulness.

Since You are always good and always do what is right, help me look to You forever—as the only standard for my life here and now and my only hope for the life which is to come.

When I foolishly leave the path You put me on and go my own way, lovingly guide me back to the proper path—that path that leads to life and peace.

Help me always to walk humbly before You and empty me of any pride, haughtiness, or arrogance that would cause me to think more highly of myself than I ought—so my heart will remain teachable and I can learn to do right.

Lead me with unfailing love and faithfulness. Help me to see my value as measured through You alone—as I surrender myself to live in covenant relationship with You and choose to be obedient to You in all my ways.

Thank You for continuing to show me the proper path and for teaching me to humbly follow Your way—as You lead me with unfailing love and faithfulness.

In the name of Jesus, Amen.

The Course of My Life

Guard your heart above all else,
for it determines the course of your life.

— PROVERBS 4:23 (NLT)

Heavenly Father,

Help me to guard my heart above all else—understanding that what I
allow to fill my heart will determine the course of my life.

Help me to see that the battle for my heart is a battle that is waged against
the enemy, in my mind, for the rights to occupy that sacred space, which is
my heart—it is a battle over what thoughts (good or bad) and beliefs (right or
wrong) that I will allow to fill my heart, and thus determine my life's course.

Help me remember that You are always with me in this battle and that I am
armed with the Truth of Your Word, the Bible—so that I have the strength that
I need to stand against the enemy and the weapons I need to defeat him and
defend the holy ground of my heart.

Help me to make my heart a space that only You can fill—with Your
Presence and Power—as I wage every battle of my mind by holding every
thought captive until it lines up with the Truth of the Word as revealed to my
heart by the Holy Spirit.

Help me to guard my heart above all else—understanding that what I
allow to fill my heart will determine the course of my life.

In the name of Jesus, Amen.

Loving God, Myself, and Others

Jesus replied: "'Love the Lord your God with all your heart and with all your soul and with all your mind.' This is the first and greatest commandment. And the second is like it: 'Love your neighbor as yourself.' All the Law and the Prophets hang on these two commandments."

— MATTHEW 22:37–40 (NIV)

Heavenly Father,

Grant that I might truly love You—with everything within me—so that I can love myself and others as I should and obey Your commandments, as a demonstration of my love for You.

Help me to reap the benefits of having a personal and intimate relationship with You—the kind of relationship that comes from spending time to get to know and understand You—so that I might have right relationships with others as well.

In loving You, help me to focus on the things I *should* do to show my love for You and others, rather than things that I *should not* do—so much so that I come to a point where I have left no room to even consider that which I *should not* do.

Help me learn to love myself by understanding how much You love me—despite the way that I sometimes behave. And help me to understand that same love that You have for me is extended to every single person on earth—no matter how *they* behave.

Give me the desire and the ability to love them as You have loved me, by helping me to see *them* with the same love with which You have looked upon *me*.

Grant that I might truly love You—with everything within me—so that I can love myself and others as I should and obey Your commandments, as a demonstration of my love for You.

In the name of Jesus, Amen.

To Really Love Others

Don't just pretend to love others. Really love them. Hate what is wrong. Hold tightly to what is good.

— ROMANS 12:9 (NLT)

Lord of Love,

With Christ as my example, teach me to love others in Spirit and in Truth—hating what is wrong and holding tightly to what is good.

Keep me from the hypocrisy of only pretending to love others—from "loving" others out of impure motives that falsely promise to serve me well, but in the end leave me empty and far from You.

Out of a grateful heart for Your love for me, help me to love others as You do—with complete selflessness—putting the needs of others before my own selfish wants and desires, so that they might see Your love for them through me.

Like Christ, help me to fight passionately against all wrong—wherever it may raise its ugly head—by always speaking truth, always giving grace, and always walking in His perfect love.

And help me to hold tightly to what is good—help me to cling to You—knowing You are the source of all things good.

With Christ as my example, teach me to love others in Spirit and in Truth—hating what is wrong and holding tightly to what is good.

In the name of Jesus, Amen.

Search Me, Know Me, Lead Me

Search me, O God, and know my heart;
test me and know my anxious thoughts.
Point out anything in me that offends you,
and lead me along the path of everlasting life.

— PSALM 139:23–24 (NLT)

Holy God,

Search me and know my heart—and by the continuing work of the power
of Christ in me, point out and remove anything that is offensive to You, so
I can walk more perfectly with You the path that leads to everlasting life.

As You test the integrity of the motives of my heart and as You reveal my secret fears, grant me the strength to endure Your testing and the faith to overcome my fears—so I might learn to let all my trust and hope remain in You.

Grant me the courage to allow You to shine the light of Your love on the hidden places of my heart to dispel the darkness—indeed the evil—of anything in me that offends You, as I repent and run to You.

Grant me the peace and the joy that comes when I invite You to lead me down the path of everlasting life—to that place where nothing remains that would keep me from that close, personal, intimate relationship that You desire to have with me, and which I so desperately need to have with You.

Search me and know my heart—and by the continuing work of the power
of Christ in me, point out and remove anything that is offensive to You, so
I can walk more perfectly with You the path that leads to everlasting life.

In the name of Jesus, Amen.

To the LORD Who Saves

Let the whole earth sing to the LORD!
Each day proclaim the good news that he saves.

— 1 CHRONICLES 16:23 (NLT)

LORD Who Saves,

Let the whole earth be filled with singing—proclaiming the Good News that You save!

With each new day You give, fill my heart with gratitude, LORD—for Your life-giving power which saves.

Then let that uncontainable fullness of my heart spill over my lips in expressions of thanksgiving to You, LORD—in unending life-songs of praise to You for Your unfailing love for us all.

And quicken my spirit within me so that I would know that You are present with me—in each moment that I live. Let me feel You power at work in me, through me and all around me, as You change me and use me in Your plan and for Your purposes!

Each day, let my life proclaim the Good News—through my thoughts, words, and actions—as a testimony to how Your love continually saves me in every way, as I put all of my trust in You!

Let the whole earth be filled with singing—proclaiming the Good News that You save!

In the name of Jesus, Amen.

Guide Me, Advise Me, Watch Over Me

The LORD says, "I will guide you along the best pathway for your life.
I will advise you and watch over you.
Do not be like a senseless horse or mule
that needs a bit and bridle to keep it under control."

— PSALM 32:8–9 (NLT)

Loving LORD,

Guide me along the best pathway for my life—advise me and watch over
me always. Let my heart be fully submitted to Your will, Your plan, and
Your purpose for me.

I don't want to find myself fighting against You—like a senseless or stubborn horse or mule—only to end up having to endure the discipline and deal with the consequences of my foolish disobedience.

Help me to remember that the path You lead me down is the best way for me to go—the way that will keep me safe and the direction in which I will find my every need met according to Your plan and Your perfect timing.

Help me to seek out Your counsel, listen for Your advice, willingly obey Your instruction—and then, by faith, rest in Your provision, protection, peace, and joy.

Guide me along the best pathway for my life—advise me and watch over
me always. Let my heart be fully submitted to Your will, Your plan, and
Your purpose for me.

In the name of Jesus, Amen.

The Overcoming Power of Compassion

Jesus wept.

— JOHN 11:35 (NASB)

Compassionate Lord Jesus,

Thank You for the deep, deep love of humanity that You expressed to us in the tears that You shed.

Thank You for loving me enough to come to earth and take on the *flesh and blood* and the *mind and emotions* of a man, to experience all of the tests and trials and grief and pain that I face—*and so much more*—so I would know that *You know* how I feel.

Thank You that there is healing from my hurts and pains in the tears that You designed for me to shed—that it's okay to cry—and that in crying I should cry out to You, the only One who can help me live an *overcoming* life of peace and victory.

Thank You for Your example of loving compassion and how it reminds me of my obligation to open my heart that I might be overcome by Your Spirit with compassion for all those around me—for life in this world is not easy, especially for those who do not know You.

Thank You for the deep, deep love of humanity that You expressed to us in the tears that You shed.

In Your Matchless Name I pray, Jesus, Amen.

Your Amazing Grace

The LORD is compassionate and merciful,
slow to get angry and filled with unfailing love.
He will not constantly accuse us,
nor remain angry forever.
He does not punish us for all our sins;
he does not deal harshly with us, as we deserve.
For his unfailing love toward those who fear him
is as great as the height of the heavens above the earth.
He has removed our sins as far from us
as the east is from the west.

— PSALM 103:8–12 (NLT)

Heavenly Father,

Thank You for Your undeserved favor—that merciful compassion, perfect
patience, complete forgiveness, and unfailing love that You demonstrate
toward me every day.

Though I seem to manage to disappoint You in some way every day, You are slow to get angry with me—because of Your unfailing love.

You don't constantly chide me about what I've done wrong or hold a grudge against me—but rather, You give me the opportunity to recognize my sins and turn my back on them, in order that I might return to You.

Though there are consequences that inevitably follow after my sin and disobedience, You do not punish me for all my sin, nor do You punish me as harshly as I deserve.

Your unfailing love for me is as great as the immeasurable distance of the heavens above the earth—because I choose to reverently fear You.

Though the enemy constantly accuses me of my past, You remind me who I am in Christ—and that You see me spotlessly sin-free—so I don't have to let my past keep me from the good plans You have for me today or in the days to come.

For by the sacrifice of Your Son, You have removed all of my sin from me— past, present, and future—as far as the east is from the west, so that I and my sin need never meet again.

Thank You for Your undeserved favor—that merciful compassion, perfect
patience, complete forgiveness, and unfailing love that You demonstrate
toward me every day.

In the name of Jesus, Amen.

Return to Me, for I Have Redeemed You

I have swept away your offenses like a cloud,
your sins like the morning mist.
Return to me,
for I have redeemed you.

— ISAIAH 44:22 (NIV)

O LORD, My God and My Redeemer,

Let me forever live in the truth of the work of redemption Your performed,
when You removed all my offenses and sins so that I could return to You!

You have swept away my offenses like a cloud that the wind carries away—
so that Your light can shine on me, in me, and through me.

My sins are gone—like the morning mist that evaporates in the warmth of
the rising sun. You have done this for me—out of Your immeasurable love for
me—to make a way for me to return to You!

So when I sin, make my heart eager to repent and return to You, my feet
ready to run to You—for my salvation is found in You alone!

Let me forever live in the truth of the work of redemption Your performed
when You removed all my offenses and sins, so that I could return to You!

In the name of Jesus, Amen.

Live Like Those Who Are Wise

So be careful how you live. Don't live like fools, but like those who are wise. Make the most of every opportunity in these evil days. Don't act thoughtlessly, but understand what the Lord wants you to do.

— EPHESIANS 5:15–17 (NLT)

Heavenly Father,

Help me to live like one who is wise—like one who makes the most of every opportunity You give—as I take the time to consider, understand, and submit to Your will, Your plan, and Your purpose for me.

Help me to be careful how I live. Help me not to live foolishly, but help me carefully consider and seek to understand what You would have me do—as I pour out my heart to You in prayer, search Your Word for truth, and as I listen for and trust the promptings of Your Spirit to guide me.

Reveal Your will for me, and help me to be willing to eagerly and obediently walk with You wherever You lead—knowing that Your plan is the very best path for me to walk, and will always bring You glory, honor, and praise.

And keep me always ready to accept Your invitation to join You in the opportunities You put before me to advance Your Kingdom here on earth—as I choose to live every day of my life with the intention and purpose of taking on more and more of the character of Jesus Christ.

Help me to live like one who is wise—like one who makes the most of every opportunity You give—as I take the time to consider, understand, and submit to Your will, Your plan, and Your purpose for me.

In the name of Jesus, Amen.

Resolve to Not Hide These Truths

We will not hide these truths from our children;
we will tell the next generation
about the glorious deeds of the LORD,
about his power and his mighty wonders.
So each generation should set its hope anew on God,
not forgetting his glorious miracles
and obeying his commands.

— PSALM 78:4, 7 (NLT)

LORD God,

Help me resolve to leave a legacy of Truth to my children and to the next
generation—to commit to tell them of Your glorious deeds, Your unlim-
ited power, and Your mighty wonders—that they would set their hope
anew on You, would remember Your glorious miracles, and would obey
all Your commands.

Help me to remember that the Truth is never something that should be hidden away, but rather boldly and fearlessly shared with anyone who will listen—especially with my own children and with all of those of the next generation.

Help me to share freely what Your Word says about You, but also how You have proven Your Word to be Truth in every situation or circumstance that I have ever faced—as You have demonstrated Your compassion, mercy, forgiveness, and grace in every moment of the story that You have written of the pages of my life.

Let it be that those who follow after me would set their hope anew on You—because they heard, believed, remembered, and obeyed the Truth of Your Word—and may they, too, leave that same legacy to those who follow after them.

Help me resolve to leave a legacy of Truth to my children and to the next
generation—to commit to tell them of Your glorious deeds, Your unlim-
ited power, and Your mighty wonders—that they would set their hope
anew on You, would remember Your glorious miracles, and would obey
all Your commands.

In the name of Jesus, Amen.

Never Changing That We Might Thrive

"But you are always the same;
you will live forever.
The children of your people
will live in security.
Their children's children
will thrive in your presence."

— PSALM 102:27–28 (NLT)

Ever Constant God,

Though all creation continually changes around me, You are always the
same forevermore and it is Your desire that I would continually thrive in
Your presence—that it may be well with me, my children, and my chil-
dren's children, forever.

Thank You for being the God who never changes—the God I can believe
and in whom I can place all of my hope and confidence.

As You teach me how to simply *be* in Your presence—as I submit my will
to Yours and look for only Your will in each moment—You are faithful to cause
me not to merely *survive* the challenges, tests, and trials that come my way, but
to actually *thrive* in the midst of them.

In You I find the fullness I need to thrive—joy, peace, provision, protection,
mercy, grace, forgiveness, and salvation in every way through Your unfailing love.

Your desire for me to thrive is not only for my benefit, but also so that in
my thriving I might pass down these principles of fullness of life in You to the
generations to come.

Though all creation continually changes around me, You are always the
same forevermore and it is Your desire that I would continually thrive in
Your presence—that it may be well with me, my children, and my chil-
dren's children, forever.

In the name of Jesus, Amen.

To Have the Light That Leads to Life

Jesus spoke to the people once more and said, "I am the light of the world. If you follow me, you won't have to walk in darkness, because you will have the light that leads to life."

— JOHN 8:12 (NLT)

Gracious Heavenly Father,

Thank You for sending Your Son, Jesus, to be the Light of the World—so that we wouldn't have to walk in darkness!

Thank You that the darkness of evil doesn't have the power—nor will it ever have the power—to overcome that Light we find in the Creator of life itself, Jesus Christ, whose life brings light to all humankind.

Thank You that though I once was a prisoner to the evil at work in me—an evil which held me captive in sin—I am now free from its bondage, because of the Light that exposed the works of darkness and showed me my desperate need for a Savior.

Thank You that as I follow after Jesus, I don't have to walk in darkness—blindly stumbling through life, driven by evil to fall into sin—but I can choose to walk in the Light of Your Truth, which leads me to life, because of the power of Christ within me!

Thank You that in Jesus, I experience Your presence with me, Your love for me, Your protection over me, Your provision for all my needs, and Your guidance as You reveal Your plan for me to truly live in the freedom of Your marvelous Light!

Thank You for sending Your Son, Jesus, to be the Light of the World—so that we wouldn't have to walk in darkness!

In the name of Jesus, Amen.

To Return, Rest Quietly, and Wait for His Help

This is what the Sovereign LORD,
the Holy One of Israel, says:
"Only in returning to me
and resting in me will you be saved.
In quietness and confidence is your strength.
But you would have none of it."
So the LORD must wait for you to come to him
so he can show you his love and compassion.
For the LORD is a faithful God.
Blessed are those who wait for his help.

— ISAIAH 30:15, 18 (NLT)

Sovereign LORD,

Grant that I would always come to You and find my strength renewed as
I rest quietly and confidently in You—held by the assurance of Your love
and compassion, and the truth of Your faithfulness to me.

Thank You that no matter how hard the circumstances that I face may be, I find my salvation in You—if I choose to come to You and wait for Your help.

So may I always be quick to turn to You—to come into Your presence, allow You to quiet my soul, and confidently rest in Your promises—so that my strength is renewed and You can show me Your love and compassion.

And may I always choose to remain in that strength and safety that I find in Your presence and never fall to the temptation to put my hope in anyone or anything other than the mighty power of my Creator and Redeemer.

Grant that I would always come to You and find my strength renewed as
I rest quietly and confidently in You—held by the assurance of Your love
and compassion, and the truth of Your faithfulness to me.

In the name of Jesus, Amen.

Teach Me That I May Live

Teach me your ways, O LORD,
that I may live according to your truth!
Grant me purity of heart,
so that I may honor you.

— PSALM 86:11 (NLT)

LORD my God,

Teach me Your ways that I may live according to Your Truth—honoring
You with a pure and undivided heart.

Help me to live my life according to the Truth of Your Word—and not be satisfied to settle with living according to anything less.

Grant me great discernment so that I never fall for the lies of the world in which I live—lies that are put forth as truth but fall far short of conforming to fact or reality.

Help me never to believe the lies that the enemy speaks to me—lies put forth to tempt me to question what I know to be true—but hold up every idea that comes into my mind to see if it agrees with the Truth of Your Word.

And show me my own heart, so that any sin that I harbor there may not stand against the light of Truth—and so my heart may be united in Christ with Your own heart.

Then help me to guard my heart with Your Truth, that it may be pure and solely given to Truth—making me free to serve and honor You with all that I am.

Teach me Your ways that I may live according to Your Truth—honoring
You with a pure and undivided heart.

In the name of Jesus, Amen.

To Worship the Creator,
Not the Creation

They traded the truth about God for a lie. So they worshiped and served the things God created instead of the Creator himself, who is worthy of eternal praise! Amen.

— ROMANS 1:25 (NLT)

Creator God,

Keep me from ever trading the truth about You for a lie—and may I never fail to worship only You, as the Creator of all that there is and all that there will ever be!

Help me to hold onto the Truth of who You are and stand against the assault of lies that this world would have me believe—as I fill my mind, my heart, and my mouth with the truth of Your Word and act out of that truth alone.

Help me quickly to repent any time that I allow myself to make an idol—an object of worship—out of something that You have created and intended for my good, but not for my worship.

Strengthen my resolve to follow after Truth by giving me great wisdom and discernment—so that I allow nothing to take Your rightful place of worship in my heart and so my eternal praise is offered to You alone.

Keep me from ever trading the truth about You for a lie—and may I never fail to worship only You as the Creator of all that there is and all that there will ever be!

In the name of Jesus, Amen.

Your Unfailing Love,
Better Than Life Itself

Because your love is better than life,
my lips will glorify you.
I will praise you as long as I live,
and in your name I will lift up my hands.
I will be fully satisfied as with the richest of foods;
with singing lips my mouth will praise you.

— PSALM 63:3–5 (NIV)

Loving and Faithful LORD,

For as long as I live let me praise You! Let me lift my hands to You in
prayer! Let me praise you forever with songs of joy!

Let me praise You! Your unfailing love is better than life itself—for there is
no life outside of Your love!

Let me praise You! With my hands lifted up and my palms open wide in
prayer to You, let me offer all that I am to You! And make me ready, open, and
willing to receive from You all that You have for me today!

Let me joyfully sing praise songs to You! Grant that I would find my contentment in Your Presence here with me! And let my soul be satisfied in my
experience of the rich feast of Your loving faithfulness, which You set before me
daily—knowing that my every need is met in You!

For as long as I live let me praise You! Let me lift my hands to You in
prayer! Let me praise you forever with songs of joy!

In the name of Jesus, Amen.

Never Too Short To Save

Surely the arm of the LORD is not too short to save,
nor his ear too dull to hear.
But your iniquities have separated
you from your God;
your sins have hidden his face from you,
so that he will not hear.

— ISAIAH 59:1–2 (NIV)

Dear LORD God,

Help me to listen to Your Word, follow Your commands, and turn and
run away from sin, so that I can fully experience the joy and peace that
comes from being in Your presence, and I can be confident that You will
hear me and answer when I pray.

Thank You that no matter how far I stray from You, Your arm is never too short to reach me where I am and draw me back to the safety of fellowship with You.

Thank You that no matter where I find myself, you will hear me—if I turn my back on my sin and call to You in true repentance. And You are ever faithful to forgive me of my sin and restore to me the joy of my salvation.

Help me not to forget that it is *my* iniquities—*my* sins—that have separated me from You—that *I* am the one who has walked away from You.

And how foolish I am to expect that You would hear my prayers and answer me if I don't first listen to You and respond to the love that You first showed me—with obedience!

So give me a listening ear and an obedient heart, so I might never leave the safety of Your powerful presence or the joy and peace that come from having intimate fellowship with You—my LORD God, the Creator and the Sustainer of my life.

Help me to listen to Your Word, follow Your commands, and turn and
run away from sin, so that I can fully experience the joy and peace that
comes from being in Your presence, and I can be confident that You will
hear me and answer when I pray.

In the name of Jesus, Amen.

Throwing Out the Garbage
in Order to Gain Christ

Yes, everything else is worthless when compared with the infinite value of knowing Christ Jesus my Lord. For his sake I have discarded everything else, counting it all as garbage, so that I could gain Christ and become one with him. I no longer count on my own righteousness through obeying the law; rather, I become righteous through faith in Christ. For God's way of making us right with himself depends on faith.

— PHILIPPIANS 3:8–9 (NLT)

God of Mercy and Grace,

Help me to discard—as I would garbage—anything and everything in my life that is a barrier which prevents me from fully embracing Christ Jesus as my Lord, becoming one with Him and being made right with You through my faith in Him.

Remind me that for me, there should be no greater pursuit than the pursuit of my faith in Christ—that I might know Him and experience His power at work in me to make me more like Him.

Help me to hold very lightly to those things with which I have been blessed, so that if they were taken away from me today, I would still find everything that I need in Christ—in whom my joy remains complete.

Forgive me for those times when my focus turns away from You and onto things I *think* I need—and help me remember that You will supply everything that I truly need when I first seek Christ in my life.

Let my total dependence be on Christ, since I know that in all my striving I can never be made right with You in my own strength—for it is only found in Your grace extended to me through Christ, as I simply receive it by faith.

Help me to discard—as I would garbage—anything and everything in my life that is a barrier which prevents me from fully embracing Christ Jesus as my Lord, becoming one with Him and being made right with You through my faith in Him.

In the name of Jesus, Amen.

I Will Put My Hope in God!

Why am I discouraged?
Why is my heart so sad?
I will put my hope in God!
I will praise him again—
my Savior and my God!

— PSALM 42:11 (NLT)

Heavenly Father,

In those times when I am tempted to become discouraged, help me to
reason with my heart—and remind myself that You alone are worthy to
receive all of my hope and praise.

Help me to see that when I become discouraged, I have "miss-placed" my
hope—that I have placed my hope in something or someone other than the
One in whom all my hope is found.

Help me to see that when my heart is saddened, I need only raise my voice
to You, the One to whom all praise is due—and You will lift me up once again
into your Presence, where I find joy in my salvation and in the abundant life
that You offer me.

You are my Savior and my God—the One who drives away all doubt and
fear by Your love and renews my courage, hope, and joy—so I will sing praises
to You yet again!

In those times when I am tempted to become discouraged, help me to
reason with my heart—and remind myself that You alone are worthy to
receive all of my hope and praise.

In the name of Jesus, Amen.

Salvation from the LORD

The LORD is good to those who depend on him,
to those who search for him.
So it is good to wait quietly
for salvation from the LORD.

— LAMENTATIONS 3:25–26 (NLT)

Good and Loving LORD,

Thank You for being so faithful to show me Your goodness in those times that I have depended on You the most—and help me today to trust You completely, to seek after You continuously, and to quietly wait for Your salvation.

Help me remember all the ways that have You poured out Your goodness on me in the past—and how, because of Your goodness, You have either delivered me *out of* each distressing circumstance in which I found myself, or sustained me *in the midst of it*, in order to deliver me *through* it.

Help me to make more room for You in my life as I simply talk with You throughout this day—through my heartfelt prayers and my loving worship of You—and as, within the peace of my stillness, I listen for the quiet whisper of Your Voice.

Help me not to be anxious about those things that I don't have—and may never have—all figured out. Remind me to keep my peace by remembering that You are my hope and You will provide for me, protect me, and save me—because You are my LORD.

Thank You for being so faithful to show me Your goodness in those times that I have depended on You the most—and help me today to trust You completely, to seek after You continuously, and to quietly wait for Your salvation.

In the name of Jesus, Amen.

Peace, Be Still

Then He arose and rebuked the wind, and said to the sea, "Peace, be still!" And the wind ceased and there was a great calm. But He said to them, "Why are you so fearful? How is it that you have no faith?"

— MARK 4:39–40 (NKJV)

Heavenly Father,

Increase in me my faith, so that when the storms of life are raging against me, I will rebuke the wind and confidently speak to the waves, in Your Name, "Peace, be still!" and watch as You still the winds and bring great calm to my soul.

Help me to not be fearful—when I am tormented, battered, and tossed about in the midst of the circumstances in which I find myself—but help me to act in faith.

Help great faith to rise up within me that I would command peace to my circumstances—in Your all-powerful Name—and wait in total trust that You will calm the storm.

And help me to receive Your peace—the calm You offer for my heart, that peace which far surpasses my ability to comprehend—until the storms have passed.

Increase in me my faith, so that when the storms of life are raging against me, I will rebuke the wind and confidently speak to the waves, in Your Name, "Peace, be still!" and watch as You still the winds and bring great calm to my soul.

In the name of Jesus, Amen.

As for Me

As for me, I look to the LORD for help.
I wait confidently for God to save me,
and my God will certainly hear me.

— MICAH 7:7 (NLT)

God of My Salvation,

Help me to remember that You are my source of help—that all my help
surely comes from You!

Help me to look to You and wait—in quietness of spirit and in confidence of heart—for You to save me from whatever circumstance or situation in which I find myself.

And help me to see Your hand at work on my behalf, through every place and person that I come upon along the path that You lead me down—as You teach me more about Your ways and show me Your plan and purpose for me.

Let me freely cry out to You—knowing that You will always hear me— because You know my thoughts even before I put them into words and are ever eager to answer the cries of my heart.

Help me to remember that You are my source of help—that all my help
surely comes from You!

In the name of Jesus, Amen.

Like a Father to His Children

The LORD is like a father to his children,
tender and compassionate to those who fear him.
For he knows how weak we are;
he remembers we are only dust.

— PSALM 103:13–14 (NLT)

Heavenly Father,

Thank You that You know my every weakness and deal with me with
tenderness and compassion as my loving Heavenly Father.

You know me better than I know myself, for You are the one who knit me together in my mother's womb—I am *Your* creation.

Out of Your tender compassion for me You show me Your patience when I am impatient, You comfort me when I am sick, You pick me up when I fall, You forgive me when I repent of my sin, and You bring understanding to me of things I do not understand.

You show me that when I walk with You—submitting my will to Yours— You will set right every injustice done to me—in Your perfect timing—and give me everything I need to live my life for You.

Because You know the frailty of my flesh (this body in which I live) and the weakness of my soul (my mind, will, and emotions), You demonstrate Your tender compassion to me by not allowing me to suffer more than I can handle, as I confidently place my trust in You.

Thank You that You know my every weakness and deal with me with
tenderness and compassion as my loving Heavenly Father.

In the name of Jesus, Amen.

For Everyone Who Believes

We are made right with God by placing our faith in Jesus Christ. And this is true for everyone who believes, no matter who we are. For everyone has sinned; we all fall short of God's glorious standard. Yet God freely and graciously declares that we are righteous. He did this through Christ Jesus when he freed us from the penalty for our sins.

— ROMANS 3:2224 (NLT)

Heavenly Father,

Help me not to think of myself as better than anyone else—for all of us have sinned and fall short of Your glorious standard.

Help me to remember that my right standing with You—along with all the blessings that flow from that relationship—came by the grace that You showed me, in light of my faith in Jesus Christ, and is available to anyone who believes.

Help me to show others how You freely and graciously declare that *all who believe*—no matter who they are—are righteous through their faith in Jesus Christ.

And help me to live in the freedom that You granted me from the penalty that my sin demanded—by humbly and obediently living my life for Your glory, honor, and praise.

Help me not to think of myself as better than anyone else—for all of us have sinned and fall short of Your glorious standard.

In the name of Jesus, Amen.

Your Word Hidden in My Heart

Your word I have hidden in my heart,
That I might not sin against You.

— PSALM 119:11 (NKJV)

Heavenly Father,

Help me to store up more and more of Your Word in my heart, so it can
cleanse me and keep me from sinning against You—as it continuously
washes over my soul.

Thank You that Your Word answers everything that I encounter on my
earthly journey—so that I never have to feel lost—and takes me down the path
of abundant and everlasting life in Christ, both now and forevermore.

Help me truly know Your Word. Let it be so much more than simply lines
that I recall having read. Help me to grasp the depth of meaning contained in
every verse—so that, with Your Spirit as my teacher, I can receive all the life-
giving Truth that each word offers me.

Don't let my hunger for Your Word ever wane, but let me always seek to
hide it—so as not to lose the great treasure that it is—within the deepest parts
of my heart. And strengthen me as I commit to meditate daily on Your Word
and apply each truth that I find there to my life—in obedience to all Your
instruction.

Help me to store up more and more of Your Word in my heart, so it can
cleanse me and keep me from sinning against You—as it continuously
washes over my soul.

In the name of Jesus, Amen.

Your Will, Not Mine

He went on a little farther and bowed with his face to the ground, pray-ing, "My Father! If it is possible, let this cup of suffering be taken away from me. Yet I want your will to be done, not mine."

— MATTHEW 26:39 (NLT)

Heavenly Father,

Help me to embrace the example of Jesus—who, when faced with the hardest of decisions, found peace in asking that Your will would be done over His own.

In all of my praying to You—in all of my asking—let my requests always hinge on Your will being done rather than my own. But also, let my heart become so in union with Your heart that I would no longer ask for anything that was not within Your will.

And keep me ever mindful that Your will is not only *best* but that Your will is always *the best for me*—that Your will encompasses an *infinite perception* of all that has ever been, that is now, and that will ever be while my will is clouded by my *limited, finite perception.*

Grant me the peace that comes from knowing that You use everything I experience to draw me closer to You—as the source of my peace, provision, and protection—and move me forward with You—in Your *good* plan to break my will, to mold me, and to make me more like Jesus.

Help me to embrace the example of Jesus—who, when faced with the hardest of decisions, found peace in asking that Your will would be done over His own.

In the name of Jesus, Amen.

The Perfect Instructions of the LORD

The instructions of the LORD are perfect,
reviving the soul.
The decrees of the LORD are trustworthy,
making wise the simple.

— Psalm 19:7 (NLT)

Dear LORD,

Thank You for giving me Your Word—the perfect instruction manual for
my life! For Your Word brings new life to my soul and shows me how even
a simple man like me can become wise.

Thank You that Your instructions are perfect and pure—not corrupted in any way—full of only that which is good for me, and designed to equip me in every way to every good work that You have planned for me.

Thank You that Your instructions revive and refresh my mind, will, and emotions, with new strength—strength to obey Your Word—so that I can walk in that close, personal relationship with You which brings me life.

Thank You that Your decrees are trustworthy—that Your words represent Your holy will and go forth in Your power. They endure throughout all the generations of man and beyond, and they fulfill their purpose as I honor them with my life.

Thank You that as simple-minded as I am, through Your words You cause me to grow in understanding and judgment, give me insight into Your ways, and even grant me revelation of things that are yet to come. Your words make me wise.

Thank You for giving me Your Word—the perfect instruction manual for
my life! For Your Word brings new life to my soul and shows me how even
a simple man like me can become wise.

In the name of Jesus, Amen.

The Wisdom of Living in the Truth

Don't be impressed with your own wisdom.
Instead, fear the LORD and turn away from evil.

— PROVERBS 3:7 (NLT)

All-Wise Father,

Keep me from being impressed with my own wisdom—as though any
wisdom that comes through me could have originated with me! For You
are the Holy God, only All-Wise Father, and Originator of all things—
and my pride is that evil which separates me from You.

Don't allow me to think that my own intellect or reasoning will produce
any wisdom outside of You—but let me pray to You to make me wise as You
reveal Your Truth to me by Your Spirit and through Your Word.

Help me humbly and reverently fear and worship You alone and turn my
back on all that is evil—repenting of all my sin and determining to find Your
best for me—by submitting myself to Your will, plans, and purposes for my life.

Grant me the wisdom always to seek You first, in all things, so that my
life would be lived out in Truth—both in private moments and in public
moments—as a testimony to others, all for Your glory, honor, and praise.

Keep me from being impressed with my own wisdom—as though any
wisdom that comes through me could have originated with me! For You
are the Holy God, only All-Wise Father, and Originator of all things—
and my pride is that evil which separates me from You.

In the name of Jesus, Amen.

To Be Strong and Fearlessly Walk the Path

Say to those with fearful hearts,
"Be strong, and do not fear,
for your God is coming to destroy your enemies.
He is coming to save you."

— ISAIAH 35:4 (NLT)

Just and Merciful God,

In these disquieting times, quiet my fearful heart so that I can be strong and fearlessly walk the path that You have placed before me—fully believing that soon You will come to destroy my enemies and save me completely from this evil world in which I now live.

Help me to see that Your perfect morality is evident in Your complete hatred of immorality—*which is sin*—and it leads to Your perfect execution of judgment on all who have sinned.

But help me to be assured that Your perfect morality is also revealed in Your absolute and unfailing love for all of humanity—which leads to Your perfect exercise of mercy for those of us who, though we have sinned, have sincerely loved Your Son, Jesus, and placed all our hope in Him.

With confidence help me to rest in the knowledge that You are coming soon to destroy all that is evil and set *all things* right—every hurt, every offense, every injustice—according to Your perfect judgment and mercy, in order to restore us completely to Yourself.

In these disquieting times, quiet my fearful heart so that I can be strong and fearlessly walk the path that You have placed before me—fully believing that soon You will come to destroy my enemies and save me completely from this evil world in which I now live.

In the name of Jesus, Amen.

Gifted for a Purpose

In his grace, God has given us different gifts for doing certain things well. So if God has given you the ability to prophesy, speak out with as much faith as God has given you. If your gift is serving others, serve them well. If you are a teacher, teach well. If your gift is to encourage others, be encouraging. If it is giving, give generously. If God has given you leadership ability, take the responsibility seriously. And if you have a gift for showing kindness to others, do it gladly.

— ROMANS 12:6–8 (NLT)

Heavenly Father,

Thank You for the gifts that You have given me for doing certain things well.

Help me to be aware of the things that I do well, so that I can focus my energy there.

Help me to understand that there are things that You have gifted me for—and there are things that You have chosen not to gift me for—according to Your design, so that I might share my gifts with others and allow them to share their gifts with me.

Help me to understand that because You gift each of us uniquely, I don't have to become overwhelmed by trying to do everything, but I can concentrate my efforts on those things that You have put on the inside of me that I am good at doing.

Help me to remember that the gifts that You placed in me were placed there with a purpose—and that purpose was so that I would use those gifts not for selfish personal gain, but rather so that I could use them in service to You by helping others.

Help me be aware of the opportunities that You put before me to serve others and be willingly use what You have given me, not holding anything back.

Thank You for the gifts that You have given me for doing certain things well.

In the name of Jesus, Amen.

The Joy of the LORD is My Strength

They read from the Book of the Law of God, making it clear and giving the meaning so that the people understood what was being read.

Then Nehemiah the governor, Ezra the priest and teacher of the Law, and the Levites who were instructing the people said to them all, "This day is holy to the LORD your God. Do not mourn or weep." For all the people had been weeping as they listened to the words of the Law.

Nehemiah said, "Go and enjoy choice food and sweet drinks, and send some to those who have nothing prepared. This day is holy to our Lord. Do not grieve, for the joy of the LORD is your strength."

The Levites calmed all the people, saying, "Be still, for this is a holy day. Do not grieve."

Then all the people went away to eat and drink, to send portions of food and to celebrate with great joy, because they now understood the words that had been made known to them.

— NEHEMIAH 8:8–12 (NIV)

Heavenly Father,

Let my joy never waver, my strength never wane as You help me to understand the truth of the good plans You have laid out clearly before me in the pages of Your Word.

As I come to understand Your Word more and more—and in that understanding, my sins are brought to light before me—help me not only to mourn my sin and repent, but help me even more to rejoice in the power of Your love to remove my sin from me, so my joy in You might not waver and cause me to lose strength.

Help me to live in the understanding that my joy in You will strengthen me to be obedient to the things that You have placed before me to do and cause me to be able to resist any temptations from the enemy to do the wrong thing.

Help me to spread the joy that acceptance of Your salvation and obedience to Your Word brings by sharing with others the abundant blessings You have placed on my life—materially, physically, and spiritually.

Let my joy never waver, my strength never wane as You help me to understand the truth of the good plans You have laid out clearly before me in the pages of Your Word.

In the name of Jesus, Amen.

The Work of Telling Others

But my life is worth nothing to me unless I use it for finishing the work assigned me by the Lord Jesus—the work of telling others the Good News about the wonderful grace of God.

— ACTS 20:24 (NLT)

Heavenly Father,

My life is worth nothing to me if I live it outside of Your will for me—so help me to submit my will to Yours at all times and willingly and obediently do the work that You have placed before me.

My heart's desire is that I might finish strong in the days I have left here on earth—by completing the work that You have assigned me through Jesus Christ.

Help me to remember that You have uniquely gifted each one of us—placed within us certain talents and strengths—and called us to use those gifts for Your plans and purposes, to Your honor and glory.

And while my life may not look anything like the person next to me, and the way that we approach the work that You have given us to do may be completely different, the assignment is always the same.

So let my heart overflow with love for You and for others—so that every thought that comes through my mind is permeated with compassion and an unquenchable desire to share the Good News about Your wonderful grace with others.

May my words always be carefully crafted by Your Spirit—to consistently bring Your message of hope and healing to the lost, hurting, and dying.

And may my every action demonstrate and stand as evidence of the truth of this amazing grace that is mine through Your Son, Jesus Christ—so that others might be drawn to You.

My life is worth nothing to me if I live it outside of Your will for me—so help me to submit my will to Yours at all times and willingly and obediently do the work that You have placed before me.

In the name of Jesus, Amen.

You Must be Holy, Because I Am Holy

For I, the LORD, am the one who brought you up from the land of Egypt,
that I might be your God. Therefore, you must be holy because I am holy.

— LEVITICUS 11:45 (NLT)

Holy LORD,

Thank You for being the One who called me and brought me out of my
slavery to sin, in order that You might be my God—for being the One
who makes me holy in Christ Jesus.

I praise You for You are holy! Just as You brought Your people, Israel, up
out of their slavery in Egypt, so have You brought me up out of my slavery to
sin through the redeeming sacrifice of Your Son, Jesus.

I exalt You for You are holy! Just as You called Your people, Israel, to be
holy—set apart and uniquely different from the world around them—so have
You called me to be set apart and uniquely different from the world around me.

I worship You for You are holy! Just as You desired to be the only God of
Your people, Israel, so You have called me into relationship with You through
Christ—that I would reflect the love and holiness of Christ to this world—so
my life would be a living testimony of my worship of the One True Living God!

Thank You for being the One who called me and brought me out of my
slavery to sin, in order that You might be my God—for being the One
who makes me holy in Christ Jesus.

In the Name of Jesus, Amen.

The LORD's Command to Call and His Promise to Answer

"This is what the LORD says, he who made the earth, the LORD who formed it and established it—the LORD is his name: 'Call to me and I will answer you and tell you great and unsearchable things you do not know.'"

— JEREMIAH 33:2–3 (NIV)

O LORD of All Creation,

How wonderfully amazing it is that You—the One who made the earth and everything in it, who formed it and established it by Your Word— would not only invite me to call to You, but would also promise to answer me and tell me great and unsearchable things that I do not know!

May I forever remain in reverent fear and awe of Your power and majesty— as You continue to surround me with the glories of Your creation and reveal to me the intricacies of the order by which You alone have established all things.

Through Your unfailing love for me, teach me to know more perfectly Your will and Your ways—so that my will would be conformed to Yours, and so my prayers would be offered up in harmony with Your will, Your plans, and Your purposes for me.

Grant me the courage to call out boldly to you with my prayers of faith. And help me to believe that You always hear and will answer my call—and that You will reveal to me great things that I cannot discover within my own intellect or power.

How wonderfully amazing it is that You—the One who made the earth and everything in it, who formed it and established it by Your Word— would not only invite me to call to You, but would also promise to answer me and tell me great and unsearchable things that I do not know!

In the name of Jesus, Amen.

JUNE 12TH

Strong Nails and a Heavy Hammer

Those who belong to Christ Jesus have nailed the passions and desires of their sinful nature to his cross and crucified them there.

— GALATIANS 5:24 (NLT)

Heavenly Father,

Help me once again today as I choose to nail the passions and desires of my sinful nature to the cross of Christ and crucify them there.

Thank you that because of the sacrifice of Your Son, Jesus, on the cross and my acceptance of His gift of salvation, I have been set free from sin's power over me—so that now, I can choose not to give in to sin.

Show me that even though the Holy Spirit is alive and living in me, my flesh still remains—along with all of its self-serving inclinations. It is at war with my recreated heart—and must be nailed to the cross and made to die there, so that Christ may be seen in me.

So help me as I commit to surrender my sinful nature to Your control and draw on the power of Your Spirit—in every moment of my day—to give me the strength to overcome. Give me strong nails and a heavy hammer, so that what I take to the cross stays on the cross and is left there to die.

Help me once again today as I choose to nail the passions and desires of my sinful nature to the cross of Christ and crucify them there.

In the name of Jesus, Amen.

My Greatest Joy

I take joy in doing your will, my God,
for your instructions are written on my heart.

— Psalm 40:8 (NLT)

Father God,

Let my greatest joy be found in doing Your will!

Help me to remain passionate about discovering Your will for me—as I take the time to quiet my mind, to search the scriptures, and to allow Your Spirit to reveal to me the Truth that is waiting there for me in Your Word—so that Your instructions would be established within my heart and that I might faithfully apply them to my life.

Let my *earnest seeking after Your will* result in Your instructions being written so deeply within my heart that *that which is my duty to do*—as a follower of Christ—*will truly become my joy and delight and privilege to do!*

Then help me to live out the rest of my life in Your Truth—and experience the joy and the peace that come when I put all my trust in You and follow Your instructions in willing and heartfelt obedience to Your will for me.

Let my greatest joy be found in doing Your will!

In the name of Jesus, Amen.

Hidden Safely in Your Hand

My name is the LORD of Heaven's Armies.
And I have put my words in your mouth
and hidden you safely in my hand.

— Isaiah 51:15b–16a (NLT)

O LORD of Heaven's Armies,

Thank You for being the self-existent One, the redemptive God—for all
who choose to believe, receive, and respond to Your passionate, unrelent-
ing, and pursuing love. You are the God of all the armies of Heaven—and
the One who holds me safely hidden in the palm of Your hand!

It is You who has put Your words in my mouth—that I might boldly proclaim the Truth of all that You are and of all that You have done—so that You
would receive all the glory and honor and praise that You are due.

You have chosen me as an ambassador of the Good News—placing Your
hand of blessing upon me, so that my entire life would be a testimony to everyone that You place in my path of the power and glory of the God that I worship.

And it is You who holds me safely hidden in Your hand and shielded from
my enemies—that is, kept perfectly at peace against any storm of evil that
would try to come against me physically, spiritually, emotionally or mentally.

Thank You for being the self-existent One, the redemptive God—for all
who choose to believe, receive, and respond to Your passionate, unrelent-
ing, and pursuing love. You are the God of all the armies of Heaven—and
the One who holds me safely hidden in the palm of Your hand!

In the name of Jesus, Amen.

Safely Kept In Christ

Those who love their life in this world will lose it. Those who care nothing for their life in this world will keep it for eternity.

— JOHN 12:25 (NLT)

Heavenly Father,

Thank You for showing me that the very best life that this world has to offer me is nothing when compared to the unending and unfailing life that You have promised me—a life that is safely kept in Christ, both now and for eternity.

Help me to hold every blessing of my life in an open hand, lifted up to You—as I freely allow You to take and give to me the things that make up my life here on earth—so that a lust for "things" won't cause me to miss out on one moment of the incomparable joy of living my life in Your presence.

Save me from my own selfish ways that tempt me to buy into the lies that positions will give me power, material things will bring me security, and pleasures will make me satisfied—so I can clearly see that only in You can I ever hope to experience true power, real security, and lasting satisfaction for my soul.

Help me to totally surrender my life here into Your care and control—to live for Christ and allow Christ to live in me—so my life would in some way serve Your purposes and bring glory to Your name.

Thank You for showing me that the very best life that this world has to offer me is nothing when compared to the unending and unfailing life that You have promised me—a life that is safely kept in Christ, both now and for eternity.

In the name of Jesus, Amen.

Let Your Soul Delight
Itself in Abundance

Why do you spend money for what is not bread,
And your wages for what does not satisfy?
Listen carefully to Me, and eat what is good,
And let your soul delight itself in abundance.

— ISAIAH 55:2 (NKJV)

Heavenly Father,

Help me not to spend my money and my time chasing after that which
does not satisfy the hunger of my soul—when You have invited me to let
my soul freely delight in the abundance that You have prepared for me.

Help me to listen carefully and expectantly to You—as You speak to me
through Your Word and by Your Spirit—that I would not only hear what You
would say but also apply Your Truth to my life by faith.

For only then can I both receive the promise of everlasting life and fully live
now in the abundance of peace and joy, provision and strength, and protection
and safety that You provide in this life for those who follow You.

Make my life so much more than what I consume with my physical body—
and help me to feed my spirit on Your Truth and Grace—for only then will the
deepest longings of my soul be satisfied in abundance.

Help me not to spend my money and my time chasing after that which
does not satisfy the hunger of my soul—when You have invited me to let
my soul freely delight in the abundance that You have prepared for me.

In the name of Jesus, Amen.

To Choose to Rejoice Always

We can rejoice, too, when we run into problems and trials, for we know that they help us develop endurance. And endurance develops strength of character, and character strengthens our confident hope of salvation. And this hope will not lead to disappointment. For we know how dearly God loves us, because he has given us the Holy Spirit to fill our hearts with his love.

— ROMANS 5:3–5 (NLT)

Heavenly Father,

Help me to choose to rejoice always even in the face of any problems and trials I may face. Let me look beyond them to see the working of Your plan—a plan to help me to endure all things as I grow in strength of character, in hope of Your salvation and in knowledge of Your love for me.

Help me to endure every hardship I face with complete faith and trust in You—knowing that You use life's difficulties and even the enemy's attacks against me to strengthen my character.

Then use my strengthened character to build my confident hope that You will always be faithful to save me in, through, or out of every situation or circumstance that I may face—even death itself.

Remind me that as long as my hope is in You alone I will never be disappointed, and help me to truly embrace how much You dearly love me—as Your Holy Spirit fills my heart with Your love.

Help me to choose to rejoice always even in the face of any problems and trials I may face. Let me look beyond them to see the working of Your plan—a plan to help me to endure all things as I grow in strength of character, in hope of Your salvation and in knowledge of Your love for me.

In the name of Jesus, Amen.

You Lift Me Up from the Depths of the Earth

You have allowed me to suffer much hardship,
but you will restore me to life again
and lift me up from the depths of the earth.
You will restore me to even greater honor
and comfort me once again.

— PSALM 71:20–21 (NLT)

Loving and Gracious LORD,

In Your sovereign and infinite wisdom You have allowed me to suffer much hardship over the course of my life—but the story You are writing with my life is not finished yet!

In every trouble I have faced, I have always seen Your hand at work to take each hardship that I am going through and turn it to something good—something that brings me closer to the abundant life that I find only in You.

So I pray that You would help me to continue look for You in every difficulty that You allow me to suffer and that I would see Your faithfulness again as You lift me up from the depths of this earth—as You pull me from the heartache, pain, and evil of this fallen world and restore me to life again in You.

Let me find my only comfort in this world in You, as You graciously honor me by taking me to those higher and deeper places I have yet to discover in Christ—as by Your grace you help me surrender all of my life to His Lordship.

Keep me and sustain me in every way, and may my life here bring You glory, honor, and praise, until such time as You choose to rescue me completely out of this world—and take me to my forever home with You.

In Your sovereign and infinite wisdom You have allowed me to suffer much hardship over the course of my life—but the story You are writing with my life is not finished yet!

In the name of Jesus, Amen.

The Kind of Sorrow that God Wants Us to Experience

For the kind of sorrow God wants us to experience leads us away from sin and results in salvation. There's no regret for that kind of sorrow. But worldly sorrow, which lacks repentance, results in spiritual death.

— 2 CORINTHIANS 7:10 (NLT)

Heavenly Father,

When I sin, let me experience the kind of sorrow that leads me away from sin and ends with no regret—because of the salvation that You bring to anyone who truly repents.

Lead me by Your Spirit—in my sorrow over my sins—so that I would be carried far away from continuing in the sin and fully experience the joy of my salvation.

Steer me clear of any pretense of repentance over my sin and help me recognize any world-like sorrow in myself—any tendency to only be sorry that my sin was found out and exposed, rather than to be willing to immediately stop, turn away, and flee from my sin.

Help me to see my heart clearly—and help me to purge from within me any tendency to hide the evil that remains there, so I can run into Your rescuing arms and find the abundant life You have for me in Christ.

When I sin, let me experience the kind of sorrow that leads me away from sin and ends with no regret—because of the salvation that You bring to anyone who truly repents.

In the name of Jesus, Amen.

This is the Way You Should Go

Your own ears will hear him.
Right behind you a voice will say,
"This is the way you should go,"
whether to the right or to the left.

— ISAIAH 30:21 (NLT)

Heavenly Father,

Your Word assures me that if I will listen, I will hear Your Voice telling
me, "This is the way you should go," so I can stay on the right path—that
path that leads to life—as I obediently place my life in Your Hands.

Help me always look forward—with great excitement and expectation—to
the honor of hearing Your Voice guiding me in each new moment of the day, as
You unfold Your wondrous plan before me.

Help me remain willing to move obediently forward with energy and
enthusiasm—eager to participate in the things that You have planned for me to
learn and experience—knowing You work in all things for my good.

Help me to trust the Truth that there is nothing hidden from You and that,
because of Your Unfailing Love for me, You will never leave me and will keep
me in every way as I remain in You—as I listen for Your Voice and obey.

Your Word assures me that if I will listen, I will hear Your Voice telling
me, "This is the way you should go," so I can stay on the right path—that
path that leads to life—as I obediently place my life in Your Hands.

In the name of Jesus, Amen.

Abstain, Withdraw, and Keep Away

Abstain from every form of evil [withdraw and keep away from it].
— 1 THESSALONIANS 5:22 (AMP)

Heavenly Father,

Help me deliberately choose not to have anything to do with evil—to withdraw from any temptation to join in with it and keep away from it!

Because Christ has broken sin's power over me—by the sacrifice of His life on the cross for my sin—I have been given the freedom to choose not to sin.

So grant me the strength to walk with You in integrity and with purity of heart—always conscious that I am called to represent Christ to this dark and evil world—in my thoughts, with my words, and by my actions.

And when I feel this world of evil crowding in on me, when I feel my peace being stolen from me, or when I am tempted to buy into the lies of darkness and join in its evilness, be for me a refuge from the storm, a strong tower—where I can run and where I am kept safe in every way.

Keep me from the temptation to try to see how close I can come to evil and yet still not sin. And let me also abstain from even the *appearance of evil*—from anything that might even look like it could be sin.

Help me consistently choose to move away from darkness and toward the Light of true holiness that can only be found in You.

Help me deliberately choose not to have anything to do with evil—to withdraw from any temptation to join in with it and keep away from it!

In the name of Jesus, Amen.

Never be Fuel for the Fire

Fire goes out without wood, and quarrels disappear when gossip stops.

— PROVERBS 26:20 (NLT)

Heavenly Father,

Help me never allow myself—in any way—to be the wood that fuels fires of contention and strife by joining in with others in gossip.

Let the thoughts, motives, and intents of my heart be right, pure, and holy, so that those things which fill my heart—and flow from my mouth—will produce the good fruit of one who loves by only speaking words of truth and grace.

Help me remember that it is not enough to refuse to start or repeat gossip—I must also refuse to listen to gossip—refuse to allow my ears to receive and my heart to be polluted by that which is garbage to my soul.

So help me to be bold and loving enough to challenge anyone who chooses to gossip, to stop—in the hope that they might repent and that we all would benefit from the peace and unity that comes when gossip stops.

Help me never allow myself—in any way—to be the wood that fuels fires of contention and strife by joining in with others in gossip.

In the name of Jesus, Amen.

The Indescribable Joy of Dwelling in Your Presence

One thing I ask from the LORD,
this only do I seek:
that I may dwell in the house of the LORD
all the days of my life,
to gaze on the beauty of the LORD
and to seek him in his temple.

— PSALM 27:4 (NIV)

O LORD my God,

May the only thing I seek be the indescribable joy of dwelling in Your Presence—of gazing on Your beauty in an abiding, unbroken, intimate relationship with You!

David wrote of his desire to make Your house his home—knowing that Your house was where Your presence could be found, and that in Your presence he would find everything that He needed.

And so it is true for me that in Your Presence I can experience provision for all my needs, protection from all my enemies, comfort for all my sorrows, wisdom to discern the truth of Your Word, a knowledge beyond my intellect, the power, strength, and courage to do Your will, and a peace that surpasses my own understanding.

Help me to be cognizant of Your abiding Presence with me at all times, so that I can personally experience all the grace and truth of the abundant life that You so freely offer me through Your Son, Jesus.

May the only thing I seek be the indescribable joy of dwelling in Your Presence—of gazing on Your beauty in an abiding, unbroken, intimate relationship with You!

In the name of Jesus, Amen.

JUNE 24TH

The Wealth of True
Godliness with Contentment

Yet true godliness with contentment is itself great wealth. After all, we brought nothing with us when we came into the world, and we can't take anything with us when we leave it. So if we have enough food and clothing, let us be content.

— 1 TIMOTHY 6:6–8 (NLT)

Generous God,

Let my aim in life never be to accumulate as many things as I can from that which this world has to offer, but rather to find true godliness with contentment—so that I might experience the depths of great gain that a godly walk and a contented relationship with You provide.

Grant me the peace I find within an ever deepening relationship with Your Son, Jesus—so that I am able to remain content with those things that You have entrusted into my hands and experience the pure wealth that comes when I use them for Your glory.

Help me remember that I brought nothing into this world and that every good thing in my life has surely come from You—that there is nothing that I own for it all belongs to You. And keep me mindful that I can take nothing of this earth with me when I leave to come to home to You—for there is no eternal value in earthly things.

Help me to trust You to see to it that I will have every good thing that I truly need—like food and clothing—and within that trusting, help me find my contentment made complete in You.

Let my aim in life never be to accumulate as many things as I can from that which this world has to offer, but rather to find true godliness with contentment—so that I might experience the depths of great gain that a godly walk and a contented relationship with You provide.

In the name of Jesus, Amen.

Pure Wisdom from Above

But the wisdom from above is first of all pure. It is also peace loving, gentle at all times, and willing to yield to others. It is full of mercy and good deeds. It shows no favoritism and is always sincere. And those who are peacemakers will plant seeds of peace and reap a harvest of righteousness.
— JAMES 3:17–18 (NLT)

Heavenly Father,

Help me to allow that pure wisdom—which only You can give—guide me through every new day. And let me enjoy the harvest of right standing with You that comes when I plant seeds of peace wherever I go.

Grant that every choice I make today would flow from a pure heart—a heart that is after Your own heart.

Show me how to be peace loving—to seek out the paths of peace rather than follow the ways of contention and division.

Let me handle others with gentle care and have a willingness not to insist on my own way but yield to others—as long as it does not compromise my heart being yielded to You.

Help me extend mercy to others—just as I have been shown mercy—and do good things for the benefit of those around me, in order to bring You glory and to lead others to Christ.

May I sincerely treat all people with the same respect and honor that is due every one of Your unique creations—out of the knowledge that You love each one of us both greatly and equally.

Show me how to be a wise peacemaker, not just a peace keeper, by making me willing to plant the seeds of the Truth and Grace from Your Word in others—and to water them generously with love.

Help me to allow that pure wisdom—which only You can give—guide me through every new day. And let me enjoy the harvest of right standing with You that comes when I plant seeds of peace wherever I go.

In the name of Jesus, Amen.

A Shelter for the Oppressed, A Refuge in Times of Trouble

The LORD is a shelter for the oppressed,
a refuge in times of trouble.
Those who know your name trust in you,
for you, O LORD, do not abandon those who search for you.

— PSALM 9:9–10 (NLT)

Loving LORD,

Thank You that You never turn away from those who search for You but rather, You allow Yourself to be found so that we can know Your Name and place all our trust in You—and in You find shelter from oppression and refuge from all our troubles.

Thank You that the more I seek You, the more I can come to know the power and perfection of Your Holy Name—and the character of the One whose Name is above all names—as I become personally and intimately acquainted with You.

Thank You that when I put my trust in You, You become my place of refuge—a high and strong tower of safety and peace for my soul—even in the midst of the oppressive storms of trouble that may surround me on every side.

And though in this world I cannot escape the trouble and suffering that comes to us all, by Your grace and mercy You are always here with me to carry me safely through it all in perfect peace—using it all together for my ultimate good.

Thank You that You never turn away from those who search for You but rather, You allow Yourself to be found so that we can know Your Name and place all our trust in You—and in You find shelter from oppression and refuge from all our troubles.

In the name of Jesus, Amen.

Led by the Spirit, Children of God

Therefore, dear brothers and sisters, you have no obligation to do what your sinful nature urges you to do. For if you live by its dictates, you will die. But if through the power of the Spirit you put to death the deeds of your sinful nature, you will live. For all who are led by the Spirit of God are children of God.

— ROMANS 8:12–14 (NLT)

Heavenly Father,

Thank You that I don't have to do what my sinful nature urges me to do—that through the power of the Spirit, I can put to death those evil deeds and find life everlasting.

Your Word tells me that if I live according to the dictates of my sinful nature—giving into the wants and desires of my self-centered and self-motivated flesh—my sin will lead me to death.

But praise be to You, my God, not only for showing me the way I should go but also for supplying—through the Holy Spirit—the power I need to put to death the deeds of my sinful nature and live!

And thank You for the privilege of being called Your child—as I listen and obey the leading of Your Spirit and as You walk me through this fallen world to bring me safely home with You.

Thank You that I don't have to do what my sinful nature urges me to do—that through the power of the Spirit, I can put to death those evil deeds and find life everlasting.

In the name of Jesus, Amen.

As the Day Approaches

Let us hold tightly without wavering to the hope we affirm, for God can be trusted to keep his promise. Let us think of ways to motivate one another to acts of love and good works. And let us not neglect our meeting together, as some people do, but encourage one another, especially now that the day of his return is drawing near.

— HEBREWS 10:23–25 (NLT)

Heavenly Father,

Help me to demonstrate an unwavering trust in You by living out my testimony of Your love and kindness for me, through acts of love and good works, as I motivate and encourage others, and as I purpose to seek out the strength I find in fellowship with other believers.

With unwavering faith, may I hold tightly to the hope that I have in You and boldly and publicly declare it to be true—knowing You are forever faithful to do everything that You have promised to do.

Show me ways to motivate others—both by my words and by my actions—to do acts of love and good works that I, too, may be motivated to do the same and that You might be glorified in all of our lives.

Help me not to miss opportunities to grow in faith and strength by meeting with other Christians often—both to give and receive encouragement, help and strength, in the face of the many spiritual struggles that will come as the day of Christ's return approaches.

Help me to demonstrate an unwavering trust in You by living out my testimony of Your love and kindness for me, through acts of love and good works, as I motivate and encourage others, and as I purpose to seek out the strength I find in fellowship with other believers.

In the name of Jesus, Amen.

The Path That Leads
to Your Very Best for Me

*Then if my people who are called by my name will humble themselves
and pray and seek my face and turn from their wicked ways, I will hear
from heaven and will forgive their sins and restore their land.*

— 2 CHRONICLES 7:14 (NLT)

Loving LORD,

*Thank You for giving me the opportunity make a choice with every new
moment of each new day that comes. Help me to choose wisely—to humble myself, seek Your face, turn away from my wicked ways, and take the
path that leads to Your very best for me.*

As one of Your very own people—as Your dearly loved child who is called
by Your Name—teach me what it is to humbly walk in true repentance from
my sin.

Show me Your faithfulness as you hear my prayers, forgive me of my sin,
and restore me again to a right relationship with You.

Move by Your Spirit on all of Your people, so that we all would humble ourselves and pray, seek Your face, and turn from our wicked ways—for then You
will hear from heaven, You will forgive our sins, and You will restore our land.

*Thank You for giving me the opportunity make a choice with every new
moment of each new day that comes. Help me to choose wisely—to humble myself, seek Your face, turn away from my wicked ways, and take the
path that leads to Your very best for me.*

In the name of Jesus, Amen.

My Deepest Longing,
My Most Essential Need

"Seek the LORD [search diligently for Him and long for Him as your most essential need] so that you may live...."

— Amos 5:6a (AMP)

LORD of Life,

Let me forever keep my relationship with You in its rightful place as the most important thing in my life—so that I can truly live.

Give me a heart to seek after You—to search for You diligently—that I would know and better understand Your character and Your attributes as You reveal them to me in Your Word and by Your Spirit.

Within my understanding of who You are, help me also to discover who I am to You—along with Your expectations for how I should relate to You.

Be my deepest longing and help me to realize that You alone are my most essential need. For in You I find everything I need for life here on earth and for the life that is yet to come, with You there.

Let me forever keep my relationship with You in its rightful place as the most important thing in my life—so that I can truly live.

In the name of Jesus, Amen.

By the Way That I Live

"Prove by the way you live that you have repented of your sins and turned to God."

— MATTHEW 3:8 (NLT)

Father God,

May the way that I live be evidence of my repentance for my sins—my decision to leave my old ways behind and to turn and run to You.

Save me from the hypocrisy of claiming that I have repented of my sins when there is no visible proof of my claim to be found in the way that I live my life.

Instead, help me show others—by the way I live my life—that I have been changed, been set apart to do Your will, and that I am submitted to Your plan and purpose for my life.

Let the best evidence of this change in me be seen in the way that I love others—with all of the compassion, kindness, patience, mercy, forgiveness, and grace that only Christ can give.

May the way that I live be evidence of my repentance for my sins—my decision to leave my old ways behind and to turn and run to You.

In the name of Jesus, Amen.

This Kind of Fruit in Our Lives

But the Holy Spirit produces this kind of fruit in our lives: love, joy, peace, patience, kindness, goodness, faithfulness, gentleness, and self-control. There is no law against these things!

— GALATIANS 5:22–23 (NLT)

Heavenly Father,

Let my life continually abound with the good fruit that is produced by Your Spirit—as I submit to Your will for me and embrace Your power at work within me to change me.

Teach me to be a person who loves You and loves others—with the deep, God-kind of love that can only come from You.

Teach me to be a person who overflows with unrelenting joy—because of the strength you give me for today and the hope for tomorrow that is mine in Christ.

Teach me to walk in that peace that only You can give, which passes understanding—and in as much as is my part, to live at peace with everyone.

Teach me to patiently bear with others with kindness and gentleness—just as You have always been patient, kind, and gentle with me.

Teach me to remain faithful to You—at all times and in every situation—just as You have always proven Yourself faithful to me.

Teach me to have a gentleness of spirit and exercise self-control at all times—as I humble myself and surrender my control to Your Spirit for Your glory and honor.

Teach me to reflect the character of my Lord and Savior, Jesus Christ, always.

Let my life continually abound with the good fruit that is produced by Your Spirit—as I submit to Your will for me and embrace Your power at work within me to change me.

In the name of Jesus, Amen.

When I Am Afraid

But when I am afraid,
I will put my trust in you.
I praise God for what he has promised.
I trust in God, so why should I be afraid?
What can mere mortals do to me?

— PSALM 56:3–4 (NLT)

Heavenly Father,

Overwhelm me by an ever-deepening revelation of Your amazing love
for me—so that I will place all of my trust in You and see all my fears
brought down to nothing!

Help me resist the times when my mind tries to take me to those dark places that open an entrance for fear to come rushing into my heart. And let the light of Your promises fill me up inside—flooding me with truth and driving the darkness of fear away—as I make the choice to believe You.

Let me ever praise You—out of a heart that is overwhelmed by the love You have for me—as Your Spirit brings back to my remembrance every promise that You have given me in Your Word.

Help me to see the folly of fearing what mortal man can do to me when it is You, the Ever-living LORD of all Creation, in whom I have placed my trust—that it is You who holds my life firmly and forever in His grip!

Overwhelm me by an ever-deepening revelation of Your amazing love
for me—so that I will place all of my trust in You and see all my fears
brought down to nothing!

In the name of Jesus, Amen.

Doing My Part to Live at Peace with Everyone

Never repay anyone evil for evil. Take thought for what is right and gracious and proper in the sight of everyone. If possible, as far as it depends on you, live at peace with everyone.

— ROMANS 12:17–18 (AMP)

Prince of Peace,

Let Your peace remain in me by helping me to be a person who resists the impulse of my flesh to repay evil with evil and chooses the better way—the way that is right, gracious, and proper—so that my actions don't diminish the possibility of me living at peace with everyone.

Help me to remember that any evil that I do to others in response to evil they have done to me will only breed more evil—and that if I choose this destructive course, evil will always have me in its ever-tightening grip.

Let me instead enjoy the freedom that comes from being one who walks uprightly before others—being careful to love others in the same way You have loved me—so that I might represent You well and sow seeds of peace wherever I go.

And while I know that it will not always be possible for me to live at peace with everyone, remind me that I must always do *my part* to be a peacemaker—by speaking only the truth, granting an abundance of grace to all, letting Your love guide my thoughts, and making that same love be the sole motive behind everything I say and do.

Let Your peace remain in me by helping me to be a person who resists the impulse of my flesh to repay evil with evil and chooses the better way—the way that is right, gracious, and proper—so that my actions don't diminish the possibility of me living at peace with everyone.

For the glory of Your Name, Jesus, Amen.

To Have Life, and Have It More Abundantly

The thief does not come except to steal, and to kill, and to destroy. I have come that they may have life, and that they may have it more abundantly.

— John 10:10 (NKJV)

Heavenly Father,

Grant me the wisdom and discernment that I need this day to make right choices—choices that will lead me back to that abundantly rich and fully satisfying life with You, which You always intended for me to have from the beginning.

Help me not to buy into the hidden lies of the enemy whose only purpose is to keep me from having that which is rightfully mine—to keep me from returning to the fullness of life that was bought back for me through the death and resurrection of Jesus Christ, my Savior.

Give me the strength of mind to boldly expose the lies that the enemy would speak into my head in an attempt to steal truth from me, kill my hope, and destroy my calling.

And help me just as boldly to replace his lies with Truth—the Truth that You have revealed to me in Your Word and by Your Spirit—that I would live in that Truth all the rest of my days.

Thank You that I don't have to live in an empty and unsatisfying "less-than" life—because I can choose to truly live an abundant life overflowing with joy, peace, purpose, meaning, and love.

Grant me the wisdom and discernment that I need this day to make right choices—choices that will lead me back to that abundantly rich and fully satisfying life with You, which You always intended for me to have from the beginning.

In the name of Jesus, Amen.

The Depths of Each Heart Around Me

Each heart knows its own bitterness,
and no one else can fully share its joy.

— PROVERBS 14:10 (NLT)

Heavenly Father,

Help me to remember that only You can fully know the depths of the
hearts of the those around me—and help me to carefully consider that
truth in all my dealings with them.

Teach me to look through eyes of compassion at each person I encounter,
realizing that I do not fully know the particular experiences that have helped
to shape them into the persons that they now are—whether for the good or for
the bad.

Don't let me forget that each person's heart carries its own bitterness and
pain—each heart its own hurts, wounds, and brokenness—which cry out,
searching for healing wherever it might be found.

Use me to help point the brokenhearted to Your Son and our Savior, Jesus—
the only One who can bring true healing to the broken—as I speak truth and
grace, motivated by love, into their lives.

And help me also to rejoice with those whose hearts are rejoicing—though
I can never fully share the joy that is uniquely theirs—in order that my own joy
would be awakened within me and I would give you glory.

Help me to remember that only You can fully know the depths of the
hearts of the those around me—and help me to carefully consider that
truth in all my dealings with them.

In the name of Jesus, Amen.

Looking Out for Others

Do nothing out of selfish ambition or vain conceit. Rather, in humility value others above yourselves, not looking to your own interests but each of you to the interests of the others.

— PHILIPPIANS 2:3–4 (NIV)

Heavenly Father,

Save me from my own self-centeredness and any impure, attention-seeking motive in me—so that I might walk in true humility thinking of others as more important than myself. Help me not to look out only for my own interests but take an interest in others, too.

Help me not to be selfish—always looking at everything to see what's in it for me rather than how it might be an opportunity for me to be a part of what You are doing to benefit others.

Help me not to try vainly to impress others but simply just do all I can to please You—as by faith I follow Your will, plan, and purpose for me in each and every moment You give me.

Keep me humble before You and before others—and help me to value them above myself, so that I am never found to be arrogant, irritable, or unapproachable.

Help me not to look out for my own interests alone—but make my first effort to look out for the interests of others with the love of Christ.

Save me from my own self-centeredness and any impure, attention-seeking motive in me—so that I might walk in true humility, thinking of others as more important than myself. Help me not to look out only for my own interests but take an interest in others, too.

In the name of Jesus, Amen.

Loving Instruction

*Those who love your instructions have great peace
and do not stumble.*

— Psalm 119:165 (NLT)

Heavenly Father,

May I always love the instruction I find as I search the truth of Your Word.

Thank You for showing me the way to find great peace—that peace of mind and heart that the world so longs for but so often fails to find.

Help me to share what I have found so that others might come to know that peace for themselves—which comes through following the instruction of Your Word.

Thank You that as I apply Your instruction, You keep me from stumbling—that You keep my steps sure and guide my way in safety.

Help me to show others that they don't have to get tripped up by the temptations of this world—if they will only learn and apply the instruction of Your Word.

May I always love the instruction I find as I search the truth of Your Word.

In the name of Jesus, Amen.

As I Wait for His Return

Be on guard. Stand firm in the faith. Be courageous. Be strong. And do everything with love.

— 1 CORINTHIANS 16:13–14 (NLT)

Heavenly Father,

In these difficult and uncertain times as I wait for the return of Your Son, Jesus, help me always to be on guard, to stand firm in my faith, to be courageous and strong—and to do everything You have called me to do with love.

Help me to stay alert, aware, and ready to respond to any attack from the enemy—whether it is an obvious threat to my physical safety or a subtle attempt to deceive me and entice me down a path of destruction.

Help me to hold fast to the revelation of Truth that I have found in Your Word and refuse to exchange it for the so-called "wisdom" of this world—remembering, at all times, that it is by this faith alone that I am able to stand against temptation and, in Christ, overcome the world.

Make me fearlessly courageous and forever strong by never letting me forget who I am in Christ and by keeping me sensitive to Your Spirit—ready to obediently take action as You speak to my spirit and as I acknowledge that I am completely dependent on You and Your Almighty Power and Presence at work in me.

As I move forward boldly and courageously in Your strength, cause grace and truth to coexist within my heart—in the purest form of love—and let my thoughts, my words, and my actions be a God-honoring reflection of the love of Jesus Christ.

In these difficult and uncertain times as I wait for the return of Your Son, Jesus, help me always to be on guard, to stand firm in my faith, to be courageous and strong—and to do everything You have called me to do with love.

In the name of Jesus, Amen.

To Listen Closely, To Understand More

Then he added, "Pay close attention to what you hear. The closer you listen, the more understanding you will be given—and you will receive even more. To those who listen to my teaching, more understanding will be given. But for those who are not listening, even what little understanding they have will be taken away from them."

— MARK 4:24–25 (NLT)

Heavenly Father,

I want to be "all in" so that I may continue to grow in understanding— and not lose the little understanding that I have gained up until now.

Help me to pay close attention to what I hear from You—to listen for Your voice as You speak to me by the Holy Spirit—both through Your Word and in the words of others who would speak Truth to my heart.

Help me to understand that the closer I listen the more I will understand— and the more Your Truth will be revealed to me.

Help me to apply the Truth that You speak to both my heart and my actions, so that I may continue to grow in understanding as I live out Your Truth.

I don't want to be a casual Christian who carries the name of Christ but not His heart—and so miss out on the promises You bring to a life lived in Him.

I want to be "all in," so that I may continue to grow in understanding— and not lose the little understanding that I have gained up until now.

In the name of Jesus, Amen.

As I Enter God's House

As you enter the house of God, keep your ears open and your mouth shut. It is evil to make mindless offerings to God. Don't make rash promises, and don't be hasty in bringing matters before God. After all, God is in heaven, and you are here on earth. So let your words be few.

— ECCLESIASTES 5:1–2 (NLT)

Almighty God,

Help me carefully guard my steps as I enter Your house—as I come into Your Presence—that I might not foolishly dishonor You.

Let me never come before You unless my ears are ready to hear, my heart is ready to receive, and my flesh is ready to be obey all that You would ask of me.

Help me to thoughtfully consider every offering that I bring to You—that I might offer it with the humble acknowledgment that You alone are the One who takes each thing that I have to offer and makes it worthy to be received.

Keep me from making rash promises to You and to others—but help me consider my weaknesses and my propensity to fail to deliver on my promises apart from Your power at work in me enabling me to do so.

Never allow me to come before You carelessly, abruptly, irreverently, or arrogantly—as if I deserved Your attention or could dictate to You what You should do to accommodate my wishes.

For You are the LORD of Heaven and Earth, God Almighty, the Creator and Sustainer of all there is and all that there will ever be. So let my words be few.

Help me carefully guard my steps as I enter Your house—as I come into Your Presence—that I might not foolishly dishonor You.

In the name of Jesus, Amen.

To You Who Are Willing to Listen

"But to you who are willing to listen, I say, love your enemies! Do good to those who hate you. Bless those who curse you. Pray for those who hurt you."

"Do to others as you would like them to do to you."

— LUKE 6:27–28, 31 (NLT)

Heavenly Father,

Help me be willing to listen to and to follow Your instructions. Help me to love and do good to everyone—even those who hate and curse me. Help me to do to others just as I would want others to do to me.

Help me not to allow how others treat me or mistreat me to determine the path that I walk down—but rather make my path straight and my way sure as I listen and follow the example that was set before me in Christ.

But also show me how truly loving another person does not mean enabling them to continue to sin—for in doing so, I become an active participant in the sin. Instead, help me always to stand for both Truth and Grace—as expressed through Christ's perfect love—as equally necessary parts of any good relationship I might have.

Let my actions reflect my love for You and let my love for others be an outflow of that love for You—as I surrender the desires of my mind, will, and emotions to the control of Your Holy Spirit, so I can walk in the freedom and the joy You have reserved for those who choose to follow Christ obediently.

Help me do good to those who hate me, bless those who curse me, and always pray for those who hurt me—so that they might be rescued by Your love from the sin that enslaves them, and so I won't destroy my own life by harboring an unforgiving heart.

Help me be willing to listen to and to follow Your instructions. Help me to love and do good to everyone—even those who hate and curse me. Help me to do to others just as I would want others to do to me.

In the name of Jesus, Amen.

Obedience, Without Delay

I pondered the direction of my life,
and I turned to follow your laws.
I will hurry, without delay,
to obey your commands.

— PSALM 119:59–60 (NLT)

Heavenly Father,

Let this be my story that I continue to tell for the rest of my life—that I pondered the direction of my life and I turned to follow Your laws; that I hurried, without delay, to obey Your commands.

To that end, remind me to make time to frequently stop and ponder the direction of my life—and to consider the extent to which I am hurrying, without delay, to obey Your commands.

Show me the state of my heart—and how my obedience (or my disobedience) to You is continually determining the course of my life—and help me to travel down those paths of surrender toward perfect submission to You.

Help me to be quick to follow Your commands—fully trusting that my obedience will always bring Your best for me and the upmost glory to You.

Let this be my story that I continue to tell for the rest of my life—that I pondered the direction of my life and I turned to follow Your laws; that I hurried, without delay, to obey Your commands.

In the name of Jesus, Amen.

When You Search for Me
with All Your Heart

Then you will call upon Me and come and pray to Me, and I will listen to you. You will seek Me and find Me when you search for Me with all your heart.

— JEREMIAH 29:12–13 (NASB)

Loving LORD,

Help me to call upon You, to come to You, to pray to You—with the steadfast confidence that You listen to my every prayer. Help me to seek You with my whole heart, fully believing that You are the God who can be found—the God who desires to be found—by all of His children.

Thank You that You are not a god who is unconcerned about those things that concern me—but rather the God who is intimately acquainted with my every need and with every desire of my heart.

Thank You that when I come to You in prayer, You are eager to put into action Your already existing plan to provide for my every need—in accord with what is the very best for me—because You always have my best interests at heart.

So help me to seek You with all my heart—holding nothing back—knowing that as I seek You, You will reveal Yourself to me and draw me into that close, intimate, and personal relationship that You desire to have with me.

Help me to call upon You, to come to You, to pray to You—with the steadfast confidence that You listen to my every prayer. Help me to seek You with my whole heart, fully believing that You are the God who can be found—the God who desires to be found—by all of His children.

In the name of Jesus, Amen.

Faith Walking

For we walk by faith, not by sight.

— 2 CORINTHIANS 5:7 (NKJV)

Heavenly Father,

Help me remember that as long as I am here on earth, I am to walk by faith and not by sight—that faith is given to me for this world and that true sight is yet awaiting me in the world to come.

Help me not to be fooled into believing a lie—deceived by my own natural eyes—when that which I *cannot* see—that is, the realm of the Spirit—is truer and more real than anything I can now see.

Help me to understand that faith is mine to help me get through *this* life until that day when I join You there and will know all things as they are—when faith will no longer be needed.

Remind me that my part is just to *believe* that You are who You are and that what You have told me is true and then wait—as according to Your perfect will, plan, and purpose, You choose to reveal to me how those things that I have believed are true.

Help me remember that as long as I am here on earth, I am to walk by faith and not by sight—that faith is given to me for this world and that true sight is yet awaiting me in the world to come.

In the name of Jesus, Amen.

Even Before God Made the World

Even before he made the world, God loved us and chose us in Christ to be holy and without fault in his eyes. God decided in advance to adopt us into his own family by bringing us to himself through Jesus Christ. This is what he wanted to do, and it gave him great pleasure.

— EPHESIANS 1:4–5 (NLT)

Loving and Gracious Father God,

Thank You for Your wondrous plan to make me holy and without fault in Your own eyes through Christ—so that You could bring me to Yourself and adopt me as Your very own.

Thank You that before the beginning—before You created the heavens and the earth, before You put it all in order, and before You created time by setting it all into motion—You decided that mankind would be the focus of Your love.

Thank You that even before You created me, You so greatly desired to be able to have a loving relationship with me, that You made a way for me to come to You—a way for my sin debt to be paid—through the sacrifice of Your Son, Jesus Christ.

Thank You that You wanted me so very much that You chose me—even though I did not deserve it and did nothing to earn it—and that I get to choose You back and be adopted into Your family as Your dearly loved child!

Thank You for the overwhelming love that I feel, in knowing that You not only wanted to do this but got great pleasure in doing it for me—and for all those You call to accept the free gift of salvation.

Thank You for Your wondrous plan to make me holy and without fault in Your own eyes through Christ—so that You could bring me to Yourself and adopt me as Your very own.

In the name of Jesus, Amen.

If We Ever Forget the LORD Our God

"But I assure you of this: If you ever forget the LORD your God and fol-low other gods, worshiping and bowing down to them, you will certainly be destroyed. Just as the LORD has destroyed other nations in your path, you also will be destroyed if you refuse to obey the LORD your God."

— DEUTERONOMY 8:19–20 (NLT)

O LORD My God,

Help us, Your people, to never forget You—by turning our backs on all You have done and worshiping and bowing down to the gods of this world— thereby assuring our own destruction because of our disobedience.

Help us—as individuals, as Your Church, and as a nation—to remember Your many blessings to us and Your provision for every need that we have had, and turn our hearts back to You.

Help us to arise from our sleep, repent of our sin, return to our God, and worship You alone—that revival might sweep across our land for Your glory, honor, and praise.

Remove not Your hand of mercy and grace from us, but cleanse us from our unrighteousness that You may once again use us for Your glory to change our world for good.

Help us, Your people, to never forget You—by turning our backs on all You have done and worshiping and bowing down to the gods of this world— thereby assuring our own destruction because of our disobedience.

In the name of Jesus, Amen.

Freedom through Truth

Jesus said to the people who believed in him, "You are truly my disciples if you remain faithful to my teachings. And you will know the truth, and the truth will set you free."

— JOHN 8:31–32 (NLT)

Heavenly Father,

Thank You that if I remain faithful to the Truth—the Truth that You teach me by Your Spirit and through Your Word—I can walk in that freedom which only comes in my obedience.

Help me to understand that to truly be Your disciple, I must be a student of Your Word, so You can reveal the Truth of Your Word to me—through Your Holy Spirit. And I must purpose to be obedient to all Your teachings as I allow Your revealed Truth to guide me in all my affairs.

Don't allow me to forget that Jesus is that Truth and help me to steadfastly cling to Him. For He is the One who sets me free from my slavery to sin—from my tendency to do the wrong thing, my inclination to deceive myself, and my propensity to believe the lies of the enemy.

Let me always remember that the freedom You give is freedom to walk out my life in obedience to Christ—the one true example of everything that is right and just—and that as I am obedient to Him, He makes it possible for me to become everything You intended for me to be and experience the peace, protection, provision, sustaining strength, and abounding joy that only You can give.

Thank You that if I remain faithful to the Truth—the Truth that You teach me by Your Spirit and through Your Word—I can walk in that freedom which only comes in my obedience.

In the name of Jesus, Amen.

Nothing Can Ever Separate Us

*And I am convinced that nothing can ever separate us from God's love.
Neither death nor life, neither angels nor demons, neither our fears for
today nor our worries about tomorrow—not even the powers of hell can
separate us from God's love. No power in the sky above or in the earth
below—indeed, nothing in all creation will ever be able to separate us
from the love of God that is revealed in Christ Jesus our Lord.*

— ROMANS 8:38–39 (NLT)

Ever Faithful God,

*Thank you for the way that You daily demonstrate just how great Your
love is for me—as evidenced by Your unrelenting, passionate, pursuit of
my heart.*

I know that I can be sure of this: there is nothing that will in any way stop,
alter, or diminish the love You have for me—as revealed to me in Christ Jesus
my Lord.

Your love is passionately unrelenting and unconditional—always seeking
to fill every corner of my heart and drive out any shadow of darkness in me.

There is *nothing* in all creation that can remove me from Your love. Your
love knows no time or distance. It cannot be cut off and it never fades in the
least.

I cannot escape Your love. I cannot hide from Your love. I cannot change
Your love by anything I say or do now or in the future. Your love abides with
me forever.

Your love never fails to reach me. No matter where I am, no matter the
circumstances I face, no matter what my fears and faith failures may be—You
still lavish Your love on me in order to draw me back into fellowship with You.

*Thank you for the way that You daily demonstrate just how great Your
love is for me—as evidenced by Your unrelenting, passionate, pursuit of
my heart.*

In the name of Jesus, Amen.

To Seek You Now

Seek the LORD while you can find him.
Call on him now while he is near.
Let the wicked change their ways
and banish the very thought of doing wrong.
Let them turn to the LORD that he may have mercy on them.
Yes, turn to our God, for he will forgive generously.

— ISAIAH 55:6–7 (NLT)

O LORD, my God,

Grant me the wisdom to seek You now—to call on You while You are near—knowing that in my repenting I will see Your mercy and forgiveness and find myself made complete in You.

Let me seek You with my whole heart—along the way that has been made for me through Your Son, Jesus, as Your Holy Spirit guides me, and in obedience to the instruction of Your Word, so that You would be glorified in my life.

Help me to repent of my sin—to turn from any wickedness that remains in me and run to You—and help me banish the very thought of doing wrong from my heart, so that nothing separates me from You.

Pour out Your mercy and forgiveness generously on all of us who choose to turn to You in faith and obedience—as You show Yourself faithful to everything that You have promised to do to redeem us to Yourself.

Grant me the wisdom to seek You now—to call on You while You are near—knowing that in my repenting I will see Your mercy and forgiveness and find myself made complete in You.

In the name of Jesus, Amen.

Rest for My Soul

"Come to me, all you who are weary and burdened, and I will give you rest. Take my yoke upon you and learn from me, for I am gentle and humble in heart, and you will find rest for your souls. For my yoke is easy and my burden is light."

— MATTHEW 11:28–30 (NIV)

Dear Lord Jesus,

Thank You for not only inviting me but urging me to come to You—so that You can teach me how to enter into the rest You give, both here and forever, to all who will come.

In my weariness and brokenness, help me to continue to come to You and lay down those heavy burdens of the world—which, in my own willfulness, I have piled high upon myself—so that I might find peace and quiet for my soul in Your gentle presence.

Help me to balance and carry out the responsibilities of those things that You have called me to do with the inner strength that only You can give—strength I can only find in Your presence.

Help me remember that Your yoke is easy to bear when contrasted with going life on my own, and that the burden You give me is light—because You are always there with me to do the heavy lifting—when I remain in Your presence.

Thank You for not only inviting me but urging me to come to You—so that You can teach me how to enter into the rest You give, both here and forever, to all who will come.

This I pray in Your Glorious Name, Amen.

Properly Clothed as God's Chosen

Therefore, as God's chosen people, holy and dearly loved, clothe your-selves with compassion, kindness, humility, gentleness and patience. Bear with each other and forgive one another if any of you has a grievance against someone. Forgive as the Lord forgave you. And over all these vir-tues put on love, which binds them all together in perfect unity.

— COLOSSIANS 3:12–14 (NIV)

Gracious God,

In response to Your immeasurable love for me, I want to go forth into this new day clothed in Your holiness.

Help me to wear the tender mercies of Your compassion for each person you place in my path today.

Help me to clothe myself in kindness to all, considering others before I consider myself.

Help me to put on the garment of quiet and gently disciplined strength.

Let the clothing of patience which is tireless be mine to wear as I bear with those around me, forgiving them freely, quickly, and completely—just as You through Your Son, Jesus, have forgiven me.

And over all these, help me to wear Your love which holds every virtue in perfect unity, so that Christ may be seen in me.

In response to Your immeasurable love for me, I want to go forth into this new day clothed in Your holiness.

In the name of Jesus, Amen.

Maker and Giver of Life

"The Spirit of God has made me,
And the breath of the Almighty gives me life."

— JOB 33:4 (NKJV)

Almighty God,

Let me never take for granted that it is Your Spirit that has made me and
Your breath that gives me life.

Your Spirit has made me according to Your image—and I bear the imprint of my Father God upon my spirit.

You, O LORD—the same God who breathed out the stars and galaxies—are the life-breathing God that spoke life into me and sustains my life in every moment by Your Word and for Your good purposes.

To You alone do I owe my everything—everything I have and everything I am—for every good thing found in me comes from You.

Let me never take for granted that it is Your Spirit that has made me and
Your breath that gives me life.

In the name of Jesus, Amen.

To Please God

*For we speak as messengers approved by God to be entrusted with the
Good News. Our purpose is to please God, not people. He alone examines
the motives of our hearts.*

— 1 THESSALONIANS 2:4 (NLT)

Heavenly Father,

*Let my highest goal—my all-consuming, life-long mission—be to please
You in everything that I do!*

Thank You for approving me to be entrusted with the Good News—the
Gospel of Jesus Christ—and for sending me out to be one of Your messengers
of truth, grace, and love, because of this hope which is mine as a follower of
Christ.

Keep me mindful that in order to please You, I must live by faith, out of a
clean and obedient heart that is dedicated and submitted to You alone—so that
everything I think, say, and do will honor You regardless of what others might
think of me.

You alone know the motives of my heart, so I ask You to convict me, by
Your Holy Spirit, me when my motives are not pure—when I've allowed my
mind, will, and emotions to stray from the truth and to taint my heart—and
give me the strength to repent, so I can live more completely in Christ.

*Let my highest goal—my all-consuming, life-long mission—be to please
You in everything that I do!*

In the name of Jesus, Amen.

To Experience Firsthand the Practical Demonstration of Truth

But don't just listen to God's word. You must do what it says. Otherwise, you are only fooling yourselves. For if you listen to the word and don't obey, it is like glancing at your face in a mirror. You see yourself, walk away, and forget what you look like. But if you look carefully into the perfect law that sets you free, and if you do what it says and don't forget what you heard, then God will bless you for doing it.

— JAMES 1:22–25 (NLT)

Heavenly Father,

Help me not only to listen to Your Word but also to seek to experience firsthand the Truth of Your Word practically demonstrated in my life—as I receive that Truth deep in my heart and apply that Truth to every aspect of my life in careful, willing, and even eager obedience to Your every instruction.

Save me from the self-deception that I am accomplishing something good when I merely listen to Your Word but then simply walk away—failing to embrace and apply the instructions that You have placed there for my benefit.

Help me always to approach Your Word carefully and with proper reverence for the power of the Truth that it holds—Truth that invites me to live in the abundant blessings of liberty.

Help me to invest the time to look carefully into the perfect law that sets me free that I might understand and do what it says—being careful to remember what I have heard—so I can walk in the freedom of those blessings that you have waiting for those who obey.

Help me not only to listen to Your Word but also to seek to experience firsthand the Truth of Your Word practically demonstrated in my life—as I receive that Truth deep in my heart and apply that Truth to every aspect of my life in careful, willing, and even eager obedience to Your every instruction.

In the name of Jesus, Amen.

Our Refuge and Strength, Always Ready to Help

God is our refuge and strength,
always ready to help in times of trouble.

— PSALM 46:1 (NLT)

LORD God Almighty,

Thank You for being my place of shelter and protection, my source of strength for every moment I face in life—and for always being ready to help me in my times of trouble!

Thank You that this is not only something that I believe, but it is something that I have seen proven again and again in my relationship with You—throughout my entire lifetime.

It is Your presence with me and Your magnificent power—alive within me, flowing through me, and at work all around me—which has delivered me through, or out of, every trouble that I have ever faced.

Help me always remember Your faithfulness to me, so that—in response to Your demonstrated love for me—I might become ever more faithful in my relationship with You.

Thank You for being my place of shelter and protection, my source of strength for every moment I face in life—and for always being ready to help me in my times of trouble!

In the name of Jesus, Amen.

Embracing Truth and Rejecting Myths

For a time is coming when people will no longer listen to sound and wholesome teaching. They will follow their own desires and will look for teachers who will tell them whatever their itching ears want to hear. They will reject the truth and chase after myths. But you should keep a clear mind in every situation. Don't be afraid of suffering for the Lord. Work at telling others the Good News, and fully carry out the ministry God has given you.

— 2 TIMOTHY 4:3–5 (NLT)

Heavenly Father,

Give me a listening and discerning heart—so that I can hear the Truth of Your Word, eagerly receive and embrace the Truth that I hear, and then willingly apply that Truth to my life in every circumstance and situation that I face.

Don't ever let me turn away from those who teach the Truth of Your Word and go in search of teachers who twist Truth into something less—thinking that by doing so I can satisfy my own selfish desires or justify a lifestyle that is not pleasing to You.

Keep me from falling for the half-truths that false teachers would have me believe—lies that lead me away from the Truth that sets me free and put me in bondage to my sin once again—and help me reject the paths of evil others may choose.

Help me to keep my head straight and my discernment keen in every situation that You lead me through—so that no matter what it looks like, feels like, or smells like to my natural senses, I choose to trust the Truth of Your Word to carry me.

Help me to have the courage to suffer for You in order to hold onto the Truth—and to never give up as I work to spread the Gospel of Jesus Christ and seek to do all that You have given me to do.

Give me a listening and discerning heart—so that I can hear the Truth of Your Word, eagerly receive and embrace the Truth that I hear, and then willingly apply that Truth to my life in every circumstance and situation that I face.

In the name of Jesus, Amen.

To Grow into a Full Experience of Salvation

So get rid of all evil behavior. Be done with all deceit, hypocrisy, jealousy, and all unkind speech. Like newborn babies, you must crave pure spiritual milk so that you will grow into a full experience of salvation. Cry out for this nourishment, now that you have had a taste of the Lord's kindness.

— 1 Peter 2:1–3 (NLT)

Father God,

Make me like a hungry newborn baby who—having tasted that which is good—cries for more nourishment! Let me always crave the life-giving spiritual milk I find in Your Word, so I can grow into a full experience of the sweet salvation that You have provided for us all in Christ.

Save me from any trace of wickedness and every desire there may be within me to cause pain, injury, or distress to others—that I might learn to be kind.

Save me from any tendency to try to deceive others—so that my true intentions will always be understood and my actions will always reflect my words.

Save me from each temptation that comes to entice me to pretend to be someone who I am not. And help me to be—vulnerably and sincerely—just who I am, just who You created me to be.

Save me from any envy for, or resentment toward, the blessings I see in the lives of others—so I might be content and secure in Your generous blessing upon my own life.

Save me from ever using my words to slander another person's reputation or to hurt or offend others—so that every word I speak would be kind and honor You.

Make me like a hungry newborn baby who—having tasted that which is good—cries for more nourishment! Let me always crave the life-giving spiritual milk I find in Your Word, so I can grow into a full experience of the sweet salvation that You have provided for us all in Christ.

In the name of Jesus, Amen.

Open My Eyes to See and Understand

Open my eyes to see
the wonderful truths in your instructions.
I am only a foreigner in the land.
Don't hide your commands from me!

— PSALM 119:18–19 (NLT)

Loving LORD,

Do not hide Your commands from me, but rather open my eyes and let
me see and understand the wonderful truths in your instructions—so
that I may find my way through this foreign land, down the path that
leads me safely home to You.

Do not ever let me forget that Your Word contains every instruction that I need to navigate this evil world through which I now pass—that Your Word shows me how to live protected by Your peace, filled with Your joy, and strengthened by Your presence in me—as You make provision for every need, situation, or circumstance that I will ever face.

So help me faithfully search Your Word and be filled with wonder at the truths for life that You have waiting there for me. Then help me to apply each truth to my life—that I might better honor You with my life and bring glory to Your Holy Name.

Command me in the way that I should go! Never withhold Your instructions from me and grant that I would willingly submit to Your Word and Your Spirit—for You are the only One who knows the good plans You have for me.

Do not hide Your commands from me, but rather open my eyes and let
me see and understand the wonderful truths in your instructions—so
that I may find my way through this foreign land down the path that
leads me safely home to You.

In the name of Jesus, Amen.

The Greater One in Me

You are from God, little children, and have overcome them; because greater is He who is in you than he who is in the world.

— 1 John 4:4 (NASB)

All-Powerful God,

Help me not to be moved when I see the evil that surrounds me and let me never be afraid—but rather, let me stand firm in the assurance that Your power to overcome the evil of this world resides in me, by Your Spirit and Your Word!

Thank You that I am one of Your children—that I come from You, that I am made in Your image, and that I am chosen by You to be the focus of Your unending and unfailing love and affection.

Thank You for the Christ-raising power of Your Spirit—that greater power that lives within me—that broke the grip of sin in my life and allows me the freedom to choose to walk in the victory that Christ won for me over evil.

Thank You for the Truth-giving power of Your Word—that power that reveals to me who You are and lets me understand who I am in Christ—so that I can exercise the authority given to me, in the Name of Jesus, to counter all the lies of the enemy.

Thank You for being the Greater One—the great "I AM"—the only One who is worthy to be praised and worshiped forever! Let Your glory be seen in my life as You demonstrate Your power over the evil of this world—even through me!

Help me not to be moved when I see the evil that surrounds me and let me never be afraid—but rather, let me stand firm in the assurance that Your power to overcome the evil of this world resides in me, by Your Spirit and Your Word!

In the name of Jesus, Amen.

The Ultimate Healing

And God will wipe away every tear from their eyes; there shall be no more death, nor sorrow, nor crying. There shall be no more pain, for the former things have passed away.

— REVELATION 21:4 (NKJV)

Heavenly Father,

Thank You for the ultimate and final healing that belongs to those who have gone home to be with You—and that I get to join them there when my work here in this place is done.

Thank You for showing me that this is the place I work—and that it is not my home.

Thank You for giving me a home to look forward to—so that I don't become discouraged by the place I find myself in now.

Thank You that when I get home, I will be home forever—where there will be no more physical or emotional pain to endure, no sorrow to suffer through, and where Death can no longer hold me in his grip.

Thank You that when I get home, You will gently and lovingly wipe every tear from my eyes as You heal me completely—and there will be no more crying ever again.

Thank You for the ultimate and final healing that belongs to those who have gone home to be with You—and that I get to join them there when my work here in this place is done.

In the name of Jesus, Amen.

Constant and Unchanging

Jesus Christ is the same yesterday, today, and forever.

— HEBREWS 13:8 (NLT)

Unchanging Lord,

I want to be more like You, Jesus!

It is so wonderful that I don't have to wonder what to expect from You—that just as Your Word declares, You are always the same.

Your unchanging love and faithfulness to me in every yesterday of my life leads me to trust You—with every moment of today and with every hope for all of my tomorrows.

Help me to become more like You—to more perfectly reflect Your consistent love and faithfulness—so that others don't have to wonder what to expect from me with each new time that they encounter me.

By Your Spirit within me, shine Your unchanging love through me to everyone around me—so that those who don't yet know Your love might see Your love in me.

I want to be more like You, Jesus!

In Your Name, Lord Jesus, Amen.

Just as I Am

When the cool evening breezes were blowing, the man and his wife heard
the LORD God walking about in the garden. So they hid from the LORD
God among the trees. Then the LORD God called to the man, "Where
are you?"

He replied, "I heard you walking in the garden, so I hid. I was afraid
because I was naked."

— GENESIS 3:8–10 (NLT)

LORD God,

May I always run to You regardless of all my faults, as I sense You seeking
after me daily.

You are the all-seeing and all-knowing God. How foolishly I pretend to hide
my thoughts and actions from You, when in fact I stand nakedly exposed—in
every way—before You.

Help me to understand Your great desire to have fellowship with each one
of us—for it is the reason You created the heavens and the earth and placed
man here and the same reason You sent Your Son, Jesus, to save us from our sin
and to make a way for us to have renewed fellowship with You.

Thank You that You continually reach out to me with Your unconditional
love—despite the wrong that I have done—and that Your desire to have fellowship with me is for my own good, so I can remain under Your protection,
provision, and peace.

Help me to respond to that love not with fear at having not lived up to Your
standards but in confident faith in the One who covered my sin, and in the
truth of Your immeasurable love for me.

May I always run to You regardless of all my faults, as I sense You seeking
after me daily.

In the name of Jesus, Amen.

To Answer the Call and Go

Then Jesus came to them and said, "All authority in heaven and on earth has been given to me. Therefore go and make disciples of all nations, baptizing them in the name of the Father and of the Son and of the Holy Spirit, and teaching them to obey everything I have commanded you. And surely I am with you always, to the very end of the age."

— MATTHEW 28:18–20 (NIV)

Heavenly Father,

Thank You that it is not by my own authority or power that I am sent out to make disciples. It is according to the command of Jesus Christ and by the power and authority given to me in His Name!

Help me to answer this call and go—following the example of Your Son, Jesus.

Help me pour myself into the lives of others around me in order to help them grow in faith and become mature followers of Christ—so they, too, can then pour their lives into the lives of others and continue the work of making disciples.

Help me to teach them to obey Your commandments—so they can walk in the blessings that come from obedience, so the Good News of Jesus can be spread throughout the world, and so our whole world can be changed one life at a time.

Thank You for Your promise to be with me always, even to the end of the age.

Thank You that it is not by my own authority or power that I am sent out to make disciples. It is according to the command of Jesus Christ and by the power and authority given to me in His Name!

In the name of Jesus, Amen.

Being Quick and Slow

Understand this, my dear brothers and sisters: You must all be quick to listen, slow to speak, and slow to get angry. Human anger does not produce the righteousness God desires.

— JAMES 1:19–20 (NLT)

Heavenly Father,

Help me to be quick to choose to listen—that I might truly understand others—slow to speak—that I may not harm anyone with my words—and slow to get angry—that I might not lose control of my emotions and disappoint You.

In every conversation I have, let me listen first to what Your Spirit would have to say to me—that I might know, speak, and do only that which is pleasing to You.

Before every opportunity I have to speak, let me always make sure that I have sought to hear and understand others—more than I have sought to speak and advise.

In every situation I find myself, help me to control my emotions—so that I don't become foolishly angry and fail to produce the righteousness that You desire.

Help me to be quick to choose to listen—that I might truly understand— slow to speak—that I may not harm anyone with my words—and slow to get angry—that I might not lose control of my emotions and disappoint You.

In the name of Jesus, Amen.

AUGUST 5TH

Called Out of Darkness
into His Wonderful Light

But you are a chosen people, a royal priesthood, a holy nation, God's special possession, that you may declare the praises of him who called you out of darkness into his wonderful light.

— 1 PETER 2:9 (NIV)

Heavenly Father,

Help me to walk fully in the truth of who I am in Christ—so that I will never cease to declare the praises of the One who called me out of darkness into His wonderful light!

Thank You that You chose me—that You wanted me even before You created me—and that by Your grace, You gave me the privilege of choosing You back.

Thank You that You called me to be a part of a chosen people—the family of believers and followers of the Lord Jesus Christ—set apart to be distinctly different from this world in which we live.

Thank You that You invited me to be a part of a royal priesthood—a royalty that flows from my adoption into Your family—and that my justification, by the blood of Christ, and my sanctification, by the power of the Holy Spirit at work in me, make my service to You holy and acceptable in Your sight.

Thank You that I am privileged to be a part of a holy nation—joined with other believers committed to following Your commandments, and consecrated to You under the Lordship of Christ Jesus.

Thank You that I am included as part of Your special possession—and that as such, I am given the privilege of declaring Your story of salvation, as told through my life, by both my words and my actions, to a lost and dying world.

Help me to walk fully in the truth of who I am in Christ—so that I will never cease to declare the praises of the One who called me out of darkness into His wonderful light!

In the name of Jesus, Amen.

Feeding on Your Faithfulness

Do not fret because of evildoers,
Nor be envious of the workers of iniquity.
For they shall soon be cut down like the grass,
And wither as the green herb.
Trust in the LORD, and do good;
Dwell in the land, and feed on His faithfulness.

— PSALM 37:1–3 (NKJV)

Faithful LORD,

May I always place my trust in You, purpose in my heart to do good, live
my life here on earth to serve You, and feed my spirit on Your faithfulness
to me.

Help me not to allow my thoughts to be consumed with the evil that is being committed all around me and against me, or ever allow myself to become envious of those who seem to get away with doing wrong.

For when I do so, I allow that same evil to corrode my spirit and contaminate my witness to others. I become conformed to this world and end up looking no different than the wrongdoers themselves.

Show me the futility of their ways, which drive them ever closer to destruction, so that I might see them through Your eyes—eyes of compassion and love—and pray for them as I ought, so they might repent of their sin and find their salvation in You.

May I always place my trust in You, purpose in my heart to do good, live
my life here on earth to serve You, and feed my spirit on Your faithfulness
to me.

In the name of Jesus, Amen.

No Darkness in Him at All

This is the message we heard from Jesus and now declare to you: God is light, and there is no darkness in him at all. So we are lying if we say we have fellowship with God but go on living in spiritual darkness; we are not practicing the truth. But if we are living in the light, as God is in the light, then we have fellowship with each other, and the blood of Jesus, his Son, cleanses us from all sin.

— 1 JOHN 1:5–7 (NLT)

Holy God, Father of Light,

Draw me into ever-deeper fellowship with You—and also with my brothers and sisters in Christ. Help me resist any temptation to continue to live in spiritual darkness—but rather, let the passion of my heart be to live in the Truth of Your Word.

Don't allow my life to be a lie, but continue to lead me toward that life of Truth that You desire for me to live—toward that light of Your perfection.

For You are light and in You there is no darkness at all—for You are a Holy God, perfect in all Your attributes and actions.

And though I am made in Your image, there is yet darkness that remains within me—that keeps me from perfect fellowship with You.

So help me to live in the fullness of Your light by allowing the light of Christ to live in me—to dispel any darkness in my heart and to cleanse me of all my sin.

Let my uninterrupted fellowship with You perfect my fellowship with my brothers and sisters in Christ—and be the evidence that I am walking in the light of Truth.

Draw me into ever-deeper fellowship with You—and also with my brothers and sisters in Christ. Help me resist any temptation to continue to live in spiritual darkness—but rather, let the passion of my heart be to live in the Truth of Your Word.

In the name of Jesus, Amen.

The Full Light of Day

The way of the righteous is like the first gleam of dawn,
which shines ever brighter until the full light of day.
But the way of the wicked is like total darkness.
They have no idea what they are stumbling over.

— PROVERBS 4:18–19 (NLT)

Father of Light,

Thank You that the path that You have set me on grows brighter with
each step I take, driving the darkness away until that moment I join You
in Heaven … and darkness is no more.

Just as the light of a new day gradually overtakes the darkness of night, so
Your love overtakes the darkness of my soul as I continue to purpose to walk
the path You set before me.

And as I walk that path, You continue to brighten the way before me, so
that I am increasingly sure of the direction You are leading me and more confident of Your power at work in me along the way.

Keep me far from the way of the wicked, who—because of the darkness
they walk in—cannot even see the sin that trips them up.

Thank You that the path that You have set me on grows brighter with
each step I take, driving the darkness away until that moment I join You
in Heaven … and darkness is no more.

In the name of Jesus, Amen.

The Greater Benefits of Training for Godliness

"Physical training is good, but training for godliness is much better, promising benefits in this life and in the life to come."

— 1 TIMOTHY 4:8 (NLT)

Heavenly Father,

Help me to keep my priorities in order, so that I might enjoy the greater benefits You have promised—both in this life and in the life to come— and bring You glory with my life.

Don't allow me to neglect my physical body but give me the wisdom to know how best to take care of it as You grant me the discipline to do so—so that I will be physically able to accomplish the work that You call me to do.

But beyond physical training, let my heart be all the more devoted to the training and development of my spiritual life—knowing that it is with spiritual strength and faith that the true battles of this life are waged and won.

And help me to remember that in training for godliness, I must not only set aside that which is evil but also choose to do that which is good—so that in obedience to You I will find peace and joy, and by godly living I might bring You glory.

Help me to keep my priorities in order, so that I might enjoy the greater benefits You have promised—both in this life and in the life to come— and bring You glory with my life.

In the name of Jesus, Amen.

The Way that is Not Steep and Rough

But for those who are righteous,
the way is not steep and rough.
You are a God who does what is right,
and you smooth out the path ahead of them.
LORD, we show our trust in you by obeying your laws;
our heart's desire is to glorify your name.

— Isaiah 26:7–8 (NLT)

Gracious and Loving LORD,

Help me to walk in right standing with You—exemplifying both moral
and spiritual integrity in all I do—so that my path will not be steep and
rough but be smoothed out before me by Your hand.

You have called me to obedience for my own good—so my way will not be rough and steep. Help me to obey both Your Word and Your Spirit as I follow after You!

You are the upright God—the One who does what is right—and You smooth out the path of those who are righteous—of those who are in right standing with You—because they have put their trust in You.

We show our love and trust for You when we obey Your laws—when the deepest desire of our hearts is to glorify Your name!

Help me to walk in right standing with You—exemplifying both moral
and spiritual integrity in all I do—so that my path will not be steep and
rough but be smoothed out before me by Your hand.

In the name of Jesus, Amen.

To Love Others like Jesus Loves Me

This is my commandment: Love each other in the same way I have loved you. There is no greater love than to lay down one's life for one's friends.

— JOHN 15:12–13 (NLT)

My Lord Jesus,

Help me to love others as You have loved me ... to lay down my life for my friends.

Help me more fully understand and more completely receive Your love for me—so that I can be a channel of that love in my thoughts, words, and actions toward others.

Your love for me is not dependent on my love for You—for Your love continues constant, unchanging, and unfailing regardless of my faults and failures.

Your love for me is demonstrated in Your compassion for me—and poured out over me with mercy and grace by Your goodness and kindness toward me.

Your love for me is evidenced in Your patience and gentleness with me—for Your love for me is perfectly genuine and never superficial.

Your love for me changes me and always points me to my Heavenly Father—back to the love relationship I was made to have with Him.

Your love for me is sacrificial—You laid down Your life for me so that I could have life, so I could then follow Your example by setting aside my will, so that the Father's will would be done through me.

Help me to love others as You have loved me—to lay down my life for my friends.

In Your glorious Name, Lord Jesus, Amen.

Life or Death Decisions

For the wages of sin is death, but the free gift of God is eternal life through Christ Jesus our Lord.

— ROMANS 6:23 (NLT)

Gracious God,

Thank You for this choice that You set before me—and for making it so easy for me to choose life.

Your Word tells me I can work the works of evil and, for my sin, I will be paid with death. Or I can accept the free gift of salvation and receive, from You, eternal life through Christ.

If I choose my first option, there is payment made for the work of sin that I do in the form of a fleetingly temporary gratification of my flesh—but I become a slave to my evil master, with no power in myself to escape until he drives me to death.

If I choose my second option, You save me from my sin and give me eternal life with You, not because I have earned it but because You love me—and all You require me to do is to reach out and take it from You, just as I would receive any gift that was freely given to me.

In my first option, I work and receive just what I deserve—eternal death.

In my second option, I don't work and I receive what I don't deserve—eternal life.

May my life be a constant outpouring of gratitude for Your mercy in allowing me to choose life forever with You, through Christ.

Thank You for this choice that You set before me—and for making it so easy for me to choose life.

In the name of Jesus, Amen.

As for Me and My House...

"Now therefore, fear the LORD, serve Him in sincerity and in truth, and put away the gods which your fathers served on the other side of the River and in Egypt. Serve the LORD! And if it seems evil to you to serve the LORD, choose for yourselves this day whom you will serve, whether the gods which your fathers served that were on the other side of the River, or the gods of the Amorites, in whose land you dwell. But as for me and my house, we will serve the LORD."

— JOSHUA 24:14–15 (NKJV)

LORD God Almighty,

May the only fear I have this day be a reverential fear of You, LORD. As I seek to serve You in sincerity and in truth, let me put no other gods before You!

Multiple times within each new day, I am faced with making the same decision that Joshua told the children of Israel they must make. Because I have freewill, I get to choose whom I will serve, but I still must make that choice. Help me to choose You.

Help me to understand and remember that it is impossible for me *not* to worship—whether it is some *thing* or someone—and that whatever I give my time, talents, and money to has the potential to be my god.

So help me to reject any of the false gods that others, who came before me, may have served—gods of success, money, power, possessions, or even other people.

Help me also reject the false gods of this present world in which I must dwell—paying close attention not to allow any of the so-called "good things of this life" to become gods that I place before You.

Help me to repeatedly make the right choice for me and my house, as to whom we will serve. Help us always to choose You, LORD.

May the only fear I have this day be a reverential fear of You, LORD. As I seek to serve You in sincerity and in truth, let me put no other gods before You!

In the name of Jesus, Amen.

The Road That Leads to Life

"Enter through the narrow gate. For wide is the gate and broad is the road that leads to destruction, and many enter through it. But small is the gate and narrow the road that leads to life, and only a few find it."

— MATTHEW 7:13–14 (NIV)

Loving Father God,

Help me to seek out the narrow road and the small gate that usher me into the abundant life that You intended for me to experience both here and into eternity.

Keep me from allowing myself to be enticed, by my own evil desires, through the wide gate along the broad road that leads to only pain, misery, and destruction.

Keep me from getting swept along with the crowd of people who look for the easy way, only to find that it is, in reality, the hardest way of all.

Keep my heart from settling for anything less than Your best life for me— and help me to tell others of both the joy of the journey, and of the rich treasures that lie beyond the narrow gate that they might enter there, too.

Help me to seek out the narrow road and the small gate that usher me into the abundant life that You intended for me to experience both here and into eternity.

In the name of Jesus, Amen.

Not Just a Lot of Talk

For the Kingdom of God is not just a lot of talk; it is living by God's power.
— 1 Corinthians 4:20 (NLT)

Heavenly Father,

Let Your Kingdom be seen in me not just by the words that I say but even more so in the way I live—according to Your life-giving power at work within me.

By the power of Your Holy Spirit within me, continue to change my heart so that my walk—the evidence that proves what I truly believe—more perfectly reflects my talk—those things I claim to believe.

Help me to see that my understanding of the spiritual realm, over which You are sovereign, is not realized merely by knowing the right words to say— but that it is revealed and made alive by my personal experience of the power of Your Holy Spirit working in me, through me, and all around me.

Help me to live by submitting my will, my wants, and my desires more completely to Your authority over me, so that I might experience truly living by Your power—and so that Your Kingdom authority would be fully established both in my life and here upon the earth.

Let Your Kingdom be seen in me not just by the words that I say but even more so in the way I live—according to Your life-giving power at work within me.

In the name of Jesus, Amen.

My Confidence in You Alone

This is what the LORD says:
"Don't let the wise boast in their wisdom,
or the powerful boast in their power,
or the rich boast in their riches.
But those who wish to boast
should boast in this alone:
that they truly know me and understand that I am the LORD
who demonstrates unfailing love
and who brings justice and righteousness to the earth,
and that I delight in these things.
I, the LORD, have spoken!"

— JEREMIAH 9:23–24 (NLT)

Heavenly Father,

In times of trouble, may I never set my confidence in my own wisdom, power,
or riches, but rather put my confidence in knowing You personally—in know-
ing Your unfailing love and the justice and righteousness that You bring.

Help me when troubles come my way, not to depend on my own wisdom to get me safely through to the other side—but rather help me depend on the wisdom I find in Your Word to guide me in paths of peace and safety.

Help me not to depend on my own strength—but rather help me to find my strength in the power of Your righteous right hand to hold me up so that, though I may stumble, I will not fall.

Help me not to depend on my own riches, which are here today and gone tomorrow, to sustain my needs—but rather help me to depend on Your unending provision for every need that I have by Your immeasurable riches in glory.

Help me to seek to know You more intimately—so that my understanding of the truth of who You are and who I am in You will always carry me through anything I may face.

In times of trouble, may I never set my confidence in my own wisdom, power,
or riches but rather put my confidence in knowing You personally—in know-
ing Your unfailing love and the justice and righteousness that You bring.

In the name of Jesus, Amen.

Planting the Seeds that Lead to Life

Don't be misled—you cannot mock the justice of God. You will always harvest what you plant. Those who live only to satisfy their own sinful nature will harvest decay and death from that sinful nature. But those who live to please the Spirit will harvest everlasting life from the Spirit.

— GALATIANS 6:7–8 (NLT)

Heavenly Father,

Help me live to please Your Spirit—planting only good seeds and harvesting the best that You have for me here in this world—as I look forward with confidence to that time when You call me home to be forever there with You.

Don't allow me to forget that there are either good consequences or bad consequences associated with everything that I think, say, and do—for You are a Holy and Just God.

Remind me that when I live for myself—living only to satisfy my own sinful nature—only death and decay can come as a result. But when I live in faithful obedience to Your Spirit, I get to enjoy a harvest of abundant and everlasting life.

Keep me mindful that while You will show me mercy, completely forgive me, and even extend to me Your grace when I repent of my bad choices, there will always be consequences of my sin which still remain—consequences that hurt both myself and others.

Show me how the choices I make—that is, the seeds that I plant by my thoughts, words, and actions—will determine the kind of harvest that I will reap. And help me to choose wisely to plant the seeds that lead to life.

Help me live to please Your Spirit—planting only good seeds and harvesting the best that You have for me here in this world—as I look forward with confidence to that time when You call me home to be forever there with You.

In the name of Jesus, Amen.

God is Working in You

For God is working in you, giving you the desire and the power to do what pleases him.

— PHILIPPIANS 2:13 (NLT)

Gracious God,

I know that it is not by my own power that Your will is accomplished in my life but it is You who works within me—not only creating in me the longing desire to do what pleases You but also giving me the strength, energy, and ability to carry out that plan and purpose!

So I invite You to work within me, by Your Holy Spirit, to change the self-centered, self-serving desires of my heart, so that I will become more Christlike—that the power and peace of His presence in me would be revealed in my words and by my actions.

Help me to listen for You to speak to me through Your Spirit—as I read and study Your Word, find fellowship with other faithful Christians, and offer myself sacrificially in service to those you place before me.

And as I listen, help me be willing and eagerly obedient to act on what You ask of me—so that as I continue in that obedience, You will cause my desires to become what You desire and will give me the power to do all things that please You.

I know that it is not by my own power that Your will is accomplished in my life, but it is You who works within me—not only creating in me the longing desire to do what pleases You, but also giving me the strength, energy and ability to carry out that plan and purpose!

In the name of Jesus, Amen.

AUGUST 19TH

The One Who Sings Over Me with Joy

"For the LORD your God is living among you.
He is a mighty savior.
He will take delight in you with gladness.
With his love, he will calm all your fears.
He will rejoice over you with joyful songs."

— Zephaniah 3:17 (NLT)

O LORD my God,

You are the God who lives among His people, the God who is a mighty
Savior! Help me to make my heart a place reserved for You, and then
take delight in me—filling me with Your love and Your peace—as You
sing over me with joy!

You are a mighty Savior—the Almighty Prevailing God—who redeems me from the power of sin over me, from the guilt which weighs upon my heart, and from the pollution that defiles me as a result of my sin.

As I repent of my sin and accept so great a salvation, You help me to live in willing obedience to You—that You might gladly delight in me.

Because of Your great love, my fears are calmed and I am kept safe in every way. You sing over me with joyful songs—remembering my sin no more and counting me righteous in Your sight.

You are the God who lives among His people, the God who is a mighty
Savior! Help me to make my heart a place reserved for You, and then
take delight in me—filling me with Your love and Your peace—as You
sing over me with joy!

In the name of Jesus, Amen.

Waiting for My Lord to Answer for Me

But I am deaf to all their threats.
I am silent before them as one who cannot speak.
I choose to hear nothing,
and I make no reply.
For I am waiting for you, O LORD.
You must answer for me, O Lord my God.

— PSALM 38:13–15 (NLT)

O Lord my God,

When I feel threatened by others, when they offend me or I am falsely
accused, help me not to be provoked into sin but help me keep control of
my mind, will, and emotions—so that I might please You as I look to You
in faith to answer for me.

Make me as if I were deaf to all the threats of others as You remind me who
I am in Christ—as You remind me that You have called me *Your dearly loved*
child and that You have carefully and uniquely crafted who I am, according to
Your perfect plans and purposes for me, that I might bring You glory.

By Your mercy and grace, let my mouth remain closed and my heart
remain at peace—as if I cannot speak at all—unless *Your words* fill my mouth
with *truth and grace* … and *love requires* that they be spoken.

Help me to choose not to hear their unjustified attacks against me, knowing that their accusations are not about me but come from the brokenness of
their own hearts—that they are born out of their own hurts and not out of their
hatred for me.

Help me to make no reply on my own but wait for You, trusting You to
answer and set all things right according to Your perfect timing and purpose—
as I remain surrendered and submitted to Your will for my life.

When I feel threatened by others, when they offend me or I am falsely
accused, help me not to be provoked into sin but help me keep control of
my mind, will, and emotions—so that I might please You as I look to You
in faith to answer for me.

In the name of Jesus, Amen.

Fully Convinced That God Is Able

Abraham never wavered in believing God's promise. In fact, his faith grew stronger, and in this he brought glory to God. He was fully convinced that God is able to do whatever he promises.

— Romans 4:20–21 (NLT)

Heavenly Father,

Let me never waver but let my faith grow ever stronger, so that I will bring glory to You—being fully convinced that You are able to do everything that You have promised and will do so at just the right time, according to Your perfect plan.

Remind me that—though my life has been filled with many mistakes, much sin, and multiple failures of my faith—You have always remained faithful to love and forgive me, and to use every circumstance I find myself in to call me to a deeper faith in You.

So give the wisdom to seek out Your promises to me within the pages of Your Word, so I might, by faith, remain obedient to You in all things—and learn, from my experience of Your faithfulness to Your promises, to trust You even more.

With strengthened faith, let me never again allow any doubt or unbelief to cause me to question Your faithfulness or Your ability to carry out that which You have promised—but let me remain fully convinced that You are able!

Let me never waver but let my faith grow ever stronger, so that I will bring glory to You—being fully convinced that You are able to do everything that You have promised and will do so at just the right time, according to Your perfect plan.

In the name of Jesus, Amen.

Loving in the Same Way
Christ has Loved Me

"A new commandment I give to you, that you love one another, even as I have loved you, that you also love one another."

— John 13:34 (NASB)

Heavenly Father,

Help me to be willing and obedient to love—in the same way that Christ has loved me.

Christ's command is that I love others as He has loved me—so that the world can see His love demonstrated through me and so You would be revealed in that love.

Christ loved through service—in humility, setting aside His divine nature. So I must also be willing to humble myself to serve others.

Christ loved through sacrifice—making the needs of others more important than His own life and death. So I must sacrifice my selfish desires to meet the needs of others.

Christ loved through instructing others with Truth and Grace—wrapping every lesson He gave to them in Your love. So I must walk that fine line of teaching Truth and showing Grace—at the same time—with Love as my only motivation.

Christ loved by bearing the pain of being misunderstood, reviled, falsely accused, and abused both verbally and physically—so that the greatest act of Love could be realized. So I must be willing to endure suffering when Christ's law of love requires it—as it leads to the greater good that comes when I have loved the way Christ loves.

Help me to be willing and obedient to love—in the same way that Christ has loved me.

In the name of Jesus, Amen.

Into the Stillness and
Peace of Your Presence

Be still in the presence of the LORD,
and wait patiently for him to act.
Don't worry about evil people who prosper
or fret about their wicked schemes.

— Psalm 37:7 (NLT)

Loving LORD,

Bring me into the stillness and peace of Your presence and help me wait patiently for You to act—as You work in me, through me, and all around me. Don't allow me to worry or fret over evil people or their wicked schemes—but keep my eyes fixed on You.

Help me rest confidently in Your loving presence—far from the restless anxiousness that this life brings—content to be where You have me now and assured that You never stop working, never stop unfolding Your perfect plan.

Help me not to get caught up in fretting over those who seem to be getting away with their evil schemes—who make a game of life and appear to be winning as they play that game by their own set of rules and leave the truth behind to chase after lies.

Help me be still in Your presence and live out my life within the protection that Your instructions promise without compromising the truth, knowing that as I trust You, You will set all things right—every hurt, every offense, every injustice—according to Your perfect timing, plan, and purpose, and for Your greatest glory.

Bring me into the stillness and peace of Your presence and help me wait patiently for You to act—as You work in me, through me, and all around me. Don't allow me to worry or fret over evil people or their wicked schemes—but keep my eyes fixed on You.

In the name of Jesus, Amen.

That Deep and Abiding Joy

Our hearts ache, but we always have joy. We are poor, but we give spiritual riches to others. We own nothing, and yet we have everything.

— 2 CORINTHIANS 6:10 (NLT)

Heavenly Father,

Thank You for making it possible for me to experience a deep and abiding joy in You—a joy that is not dependent on my circumstances and is mine to keep—as I fix my eyes on Christ and look to Him to be everything I need and more.

There will always be times when my heart will ache—because of the loss, disappointments, and injustices that I experience personally, or that I may observe in the world around me.

But You came to give me hope, that my heart would rejoice in You—as I trust in Your sovereignty, mercy, grace, and love, as I watch for You to work all things together for my good, and as I trust You to guide me to my forever home with You.

Help me to remember that You have given me this hope-filled joy so that I will always have something to give to others—no matter how poor I might be—that their joy might also be full.

What joy is mine to know that—even though I own nothing in this world, because everything I have belongs to You—I have everything I need and more in Christ!

Thank You for making it possible for me to experience a deep and abiding joy in You—a joy that is not dependent on my circumstances and is mine to keep—as I fix my eyes on Christ and look to Him to be everything I need and more.

In the name of Jesus, Amen.

Loving Others God's Way

Always be humble and gentle. Be patient with each other, making allowance for each other's faults because of your love.

— EPHESIANS 4:2 (NLT)

Heavenly Father,

Teach me to love others with humility, gentleness, patience, and compassion, and with great mercy, forgiveness, and grace—out of a deep gratitude for how You love me and in willing obedience to the commands of Your Word.

Grant me a humble heart—that I might not think more highly of myself than I ought to think—as I acknowledge that any good thing that may be found in me comes only by Your hand.

Help me to be lovingly gentle in all of my dealings with others—offering them truth and grace, delivered with love—remembering at all times that Christ died for every one of us out of His immeasurable love for us all.

Remind me of the patience, mercy, forgiveness, and grace that You show me—every moment of each day—so that I might be a living offering of Christ's patient and compassionate love to others at all times.

Help me to make allowances for the faults of others by the way that I love them—as I remember that all of us are broken in some way. And help me see that You may want to use me in the work You are doing to heal their brokenness and make them whole again in You.

Teach me to love others with humility, gentleness, patience, and compassion, and with great mercy, forgiveness, and grace—out of a deep gratitude for how You love me and in willing obedience to the commands of Your Word.

In the name of Jesus, Amen.

To Be a Child Who Listens and Watches

The heavens proclaim the glory of God.
The skies display his craftsmanship.
Day after day they continue to speak;
night after night they make him known.

— PSALM 19:1–2 (NLT)

God of All Creation,

Make me like a child who listens and watches, so that my ears will hear
and my eyes will see—as the heavens declare Your glory and the skies
display Your craftsmanship.

Teach me to consider the evidence of Your existence—that proclamation of Your power and presence—which surrounds me day and night and continuously speaks to make You known.

Help me to understand the extent Your greatness—as demonstrated by the limitlessness of the heavens that You created by Your Word alone—that my faith in Your Word might soar.

Show me the wonder of the innumerable multitude of stars You placed in the skies—galaxies that You effortlessly breathed into existence—and help me know that there is nothing too difficult for You.

Help me to take comfort within the harmony and order with which You choreographed everything You created—those purposeful and perfect balances and intricacies by which the parts of Your creation interdependently exist.

Teach me to see Your love and care reflected in all that You have made and to realize that all this was made for us—so we might see You and believe.

And most of all, never let me fail to see Your divine signature written on the deepest parts of who I am—because You have made me in Your very own image.

Make me like a child who listens and watches, so that my ears will hear
and my eyes will see—as the heavens declare Your glory and the skies
display Your craftsmanship.

In the name of Jesus, Amen.

New Life with Christ

Since you have been raised to new life with Christ, set your sights on the realities of heaven, where Christ sits in the place of honor at God's right hand. Think about the things of heaven, not the things of earth. For you died to this life, and your real life is hidden with Christ in God.

— Colossians 3:1–3 (NLT)

Heavenly Father,

Since I have decided to make Christ the Lord of my life and have chosen this new life with Him, help me to seek after eternal realities and find that my real life is hidden—concealed and kept safe—with Christ in You.

Help me to flee from earthly temptations and put to death my desires for the things of this world—things which lead me to be self-focused, materialistic, pleasure-seeking, and superficial.

Help me to search out Your eternal perspective, die to self, and allow the life of Christ to live in me and change me into the person I should be—one who truly loves You and loves others with the love of Christ.

Help me to fill my thoughts with Your thoughts—in order to see things as You do—so that my desires become those things that You desire and my thoughts, words, and actions become an outflow of my love for You.

Since I have decided to make Christ the Lord of my life and have chosen this new life with Him, help me to seek after eternal realities—and find that my real life is hidden—concealed and kept safe—with Christ in You.

In the name of Jesus, Amen.

No Room for Pride

Pride goes before destruction,
a haughty spirit before a fall.

— PROVERBS 16:18 (NIV)

Heavenly Father,

Help me to truly know my heart—and drive out any pride by replacing
it with Your perfect love.

Show me those places in my heart where the ugliness of pride is hiding and
remove it far from me, so that my words and actions would not bring injury
and destruction to others and my "better-than-you" attitude would not lead to
my own collapse and destruction.

I don't want to think more highly of myself than I ought to—nor do I want
to think of someone else as less than me just because they have demonstrated
their need for a Savior just as I do daily.

Help me to see others through Your eyes and with the same love and compassion You pour out on me.

Help me to truly know my heart—and drive out any pride by replacing
it with Your perfect love.

In the name of Jesus, Amen.

Trusting My Life to the God Who Created Me

So if you are suffering in a manner that pleases God, keep on doing what is right, and trust your lives to the God who created you, for he will never fail you.

— 1 PETER 4:19 (NLT)

Heavenly Father,

Help me to keep doing what is right and to trust You with my life—regardless of any momentary suffering I may be called on to endure—because You are always faithful to ultimately work all things together for my good.

Through the repeated accounts of Your unfailing love and faithfulness found in the Holy Scriptures, You have shown me that You—the giver and sustainer of my life—can be completely trusted to order each and every step of my way.

Through the experiences of my own life, You have repeatedly proven that my trust in You is not misplaced—for You have turned every time of suffering that I have experienced to my ultimate good.

So help me not to allow my faith and trust in You to waver when I suffer—when life gets tough—and help me to continue doing that which is right and good regardless of my circumstances.

For I know that if I am truly trusting You I will not be anxious or afraid, I will not be overwhelmed with sadness or defeated by depression, and I will not be ruled by hatred, anger, or vengefulness.

If I trust You, You will sustain me in every way—no matter what I am facing—according to Your faithful promises, with unimaginable peace and unquenchable joy, and within Your unfailing and never-ending love for me.

Help me to keep doing what is right and to trust You with my life—regardless of any momentary suffering I may be called on to endure—because You are always faithful to ultimately work all things together for my good.

In the name of Jesus, Amen.

Speaking Truth, Doing Good, Chasing Peace

Whoever of you loves life
and desires to see many good days,
keep your tongue from evil
and your lips from telling lies.
Turn from evil and do good;
seek peace and pursue it.

— PSALM 34:12–14 (NIV)

Heavenly Father,

Let every word I speak be virtuous and true, let every action I take be kind and good, and let me have a heart that searches for peace and works to maintain it, down every path You have me walk.

Help me not to speak evil things—words that hurt rather than heal; words that tear down rather than build up; words that bring despair rather than hope.

And keep me from telling lies—words that deceive rather than reveal; words that slander rather than commend; words that omit rather than declare the whole truth.

Help me to remember that while it is good for me to turn away from evil, You desire so much more of me—that to be truly obedient to You, I must also do good things for others.

Help me to understand that in order for me to live in the peace that You want me to enjoy, I must never stop searching for that peace and working to maintain it through all of my thoughts, words, and actions.

Help me to do all these things as a testimony to Your power at work in me, so that I may live long enough in this world to accomplish Your plan and purpose for me here before I join You there for eternity.

Let every word I speak be virtuous and true, let every action I take be kind and good, and let me have a heart that searches for peace and works to maintain it down every path You have me walk.

In the name of Jesus, Amen.

The Things You Find in Me

There are six things the LORD hates—
no, seven things he detests:
haughty eyes,
a lying tongue,
hands that kill the innocent,
a heart that plots evil,
feet that race to do wrong,
a false witness who pours out lies,
a person who sows discord in a family.

— PROVERBS 6:16–19 (NLT)

LORD of my Heart,

Help me to surrender all of my heart and life to You—so You would have
no reason to detest the things that You find in me.

Remove any haughtiness or conceitedness from within me—especially when my eyes show contempt for others. Keep me from sinning by thinking more highly of myself than I ought to while undervaluing others.

Check me by Your Spirit should any lie be formed in my heart—before it spills across my tongue—that my words would always reflect that I hold Truth as sacred in my life.

Purge from me any desire for the shedding of innocent blood—for cruelty or blood-thirstiness—but help me to have precious reverence for the sanctity of life.

Expose any tendency to devise wickedness in my heart or to entertain or rehearse evil plans in my mind—that I might choose to meditate only on what is good and right.

Make my feet quick to run to do what is good, so that my feet will be kept from that which is evil.

Let me only speak the truth about others—and let those words be pleasing to You—so that I cannot be used as a tool of the enemy for his purposes.

And stop me from sowing any seeds of discord among my family—whether my natural family or my brothers and sisters in Christ—that unity would be preserved.

Help me to surrender all of my heart and life to You—so You would have no reason to detest the things that You find in me.

In the name of Jesus, Amen.

Being Dead to be Truly Alive

I have been crucified with Christ; it is no longer I who live, but Christ lives in me; and the life which I now live in the flesh I live by faith in the Son of God, who loved me and gave Himself for me.

— GALATIANS 2:20 (NKJV)

Heavenly Father,

Help me remember that the old me has been crucified with Christ—that the old me is dead and I don't need to go trying to resurrect him!

Help me to let what has died be dead—that is my old nature—so that, by faith, Christ may be made fully alive in the life that I now live in the flesh.

Show me that just like dead people are no longer anxious, no longer get worried, no longer can be insulted, hurt, or offended by others, I, too, should not allow anything of these things to bother me—if I am truly crucified with Christ.

When the old me tries to raise its ugly head and cause me to be held captive by my past or by the uncertainty over things yet to come, or to lust after the things of this world, remind me that I live by faith in the One who lives in me—that my life, my joy, and my peace is found in Christ alone.

Don't allow me to forget that Christ cannot be made fully alive in me when I continue to go back and try to revive my old self—when I forget that I was bought with a very high price and the life that I now live is not mine to live but His.

Help me remember that the old me has been crucified with Christ—that the old me is dead and I don't need to go trying to resurrect him!

In the name of Jesus, Amen.

Ever-Existing Creator God

In the beginning the Word already existed.
The Word was with God,
and the Word was God.
He existed in the beginning with God.
God created everything through him,
and nothing was created except through him.

— JOHN 1:1–3 (NLT)

Ever-Existing Creator God,

Help me to understand that through Christ, You created all that there is
from nothing, my existence is only thanks to Christ, and that any gifts
within me are there because You put them there—to accomplish Your
plans and purposes in me through Christ.

Help me to understand that You have always been there—that You were
there before You set time into motion—"In the beginning."

Help me to understand that Your Son, Jesus, has always been right there
with You and that everything You did in creating, You did through Him.

Help me to understand that Jesus is, and always has been, fully God—that
even though He fully took humanity upon himself, He never ceased to be
fully God.

Help me to understand that when I look to Jesus, I am looking to the
Creator of the universe, the highest revelation of God to man, the living example to me of perfect and complete holiness, and the One Who holds everything
together by the power of His might.

Help me to understand that, through Christ, You created all that there
is from nothing, my existence is only thanks to Christ, and that any gifts
within me are there because You put them there—to accomplish Your
plans and purposes in me through Christ.

In the name of Jesus, Amen.

I Have All That I Need

The LORD is my shepherd, I lack nothing.
He makes me lie down in green pastures,
he leads me beside quiet waters,
he refreshes my soul.
He guides me along the right paths
for his name's sake.
Even though I walk
through the darkest valley,
I will fear no evil,
for you are with me;
your rod and your staff,
they comfort me.
You prepare a table before me
in the presence of my enemies.
You anoint my head with oil;
my cup overflows.
Surely your goodness and love will follow me
all the days of my life,
and I will dwell in the house of the LORD
forever.

— PSALM 23:1–6 (NIV)

Gracious and Loving LORD,

You are my Shepherd. I have all that I need because I have You.

As long as I follow after You, You refresh me along my journey with rest, peace, and strength, and You guide me along right paths—so that my life might bring honor to You.

Even when I have to go through the darkest of valleys, I don't have to fear because You never leave my side. You are right here to protect and comfort me—as You guide me safely through all of my trials and struggles in unexplainable peace.

Even though I am pressed by evil on every side, when I come into Your presence I find that You have already prepared a feast of blessing for me, and You treat me as Your honored guest—so much so that the blessings You pour over me overflow from me to bless others.

Because You are my shepherd, I can have the confident hope that Your goodness to me and the mercy of Your unfailing love will follow after me—persistently and passionately pursuing my heart—all the rest of my days here on earth, until that time comes when You take me home to be with You there, forever.

You are my Shepherd. I have all I need because I have You.

In the name of Jesus, Amen.

To Be Counted Among the Wise

"Therefore everyone who hears these words of mine and puts them into practice is like a wise man who built his house on the rock. The rain came down, the streams rose, and the winds blew and beat against that house; yet it did not fall, because it had its foundation on the rock. But everyone who hears these words of mine and does not put them into practice is like a foolish man who built his house on sand. The rain came down, the streams rose, and the winds blew and beat against that house, and it fell with a great crash."

— MATTHEW 7:24–27 (NIV)

Dear God,

I want to be counted among the wise—as one who has built my house on solid rock.

Keep me far from sin—both the sin of doing what I know is wrong and the sin of not being obedient to do what You have taught me is good and right.

Help me to build my life on the rock of things eternal—on the revealed truth of Your Word—so I can stand against any storm that the enemy sends to try to destroy me.

Keep me from the self-deception that comes from building my life on the temporal things of this world—things that will cause me to fall and be completely destroyed.

Don't let me be like the foolish man who thinks all he has built will continue to stand, only to find one day that it has been completely destroyed and, just like himself, is lost forever.

I want to be counted among the wise—as one who has built my house on solid rock.

In the name of Jesus, Amen.

LORD Over All Things

Yours, O LORD, is the greatness, the power, the glory, the victory, and the majesty. Everything in the heavens and on earth is yours, O LORD, and this is your kingdom. We adore you as the one who is over all things.

— 1 CHRONICLES 29:11 (NLT)

O LORD My God,

Grant that I would always adore You as the One who is over all things—the only One worthy to receive the worship of my heart!

Capture my thoughts this day with Your unsurpassed greatness—that I would ponder the limitlessness of the great God I serve and find comfort in Your unfailing love for me.

Help me to tap into Your power—that same power that raised Christ from the dead which lives in me—so that I can do all things that You require, in Christ.

Show me Your glory all around me, that I would find comfort for my weary soul in Your presence with me—knowing that You will never leave me nor forsake me.

Strengthen me to walk in victory over all my sin—victory which You bought for me, through the redeeming sacrifice of Your Son, Jesus.

And let me worship You in all Your majesty—making much of You, so that my troubles here on earth fade from sight, in the light of who You are and of all that You have done.

Give me Your peace today, as I offer You all my adoration—knowing all things are Yours and under Your control as You hold it all in the palm of Your hand.

Grant that I would always adore You as the One who is over all things—the only One worthy to receive the worship of my heart!

In the name of Jesus, Amen.

Living Honestly with Myself

Don't think you are better than you really are. Be honest in your evaluation of yourselves, measuring yourselves by the faith God has given us.

— ROMANS 12:3B (NLT)

Heavenly Father,

Help me to live honestly with myself as I measure myself only by the faith I have been given to believe that all good things I have within me—and any good that I might do—comes by Your hand alone.

Don't allow me to become puffed up—thinking that I am something *in myself*—but help me to evaluate myself honestly and accurately, realizing that You are the author of all things good.

Help me escape the danger of judging my worth by any of the world's standards—which lead me to think too much about how much I am worth in the eyes of others and cause me to miss discovering my true value in Your eyes.

Help me properly judge my value based on who You have shown me that I am in Christ, as I use the gifts You have given me for Your glory only—rather than to promote my own self-worth in the eyes of others.

Increase my faith to be able to operate in that place into which You have called me, gifted me, and equipped me, so that I might boldly serve You—while I remain totally dependent on You and walk humbly before You.

Help me to live honestly with myself as I measure myself only by the faith I have been given to believe that all good things I have within me—and any good that I might do—comes by Your hand alone.

In the name of Jesus, Amen.

That Once Dark Place of My Heart

For God, who said, "Let there be light in the darkness," has made this light shine in our hearts so we could know the glory of God that is seen in the face of Jesus Christ. We now have this light shining in our hearts, but we ourselves are like fragile clay jars containing this great treasure. This makes it clear that our great power is from God, not from ourselves.

— 2 CORINTHIANS 4:6–7 (NLT)

Heavenly Father,

Thank You for making Your light shine in that once dark place of my heart.

Thank You for the light of the Good News of Jesus Christ which shines brightly within me, giving me knowledge of Your glory through Him—knowledge which is given to me so I can give You all the glory, honor, and praise that is due You.

Thank You that even though I am frail, fragile, and fallible, You entrusted this infinitely priceless message of salvation to me, so that Your glory would be fully seen in me—that others would be able to see and know that my life is empowered by Your presence in me and that I do not stand in my own power.

May my understanding of my total dependence on You work in me to keep me from the foolishness of pride—and may that knowledge motivate me to stay in continuous contact with You as my only source of strength.

May I take seriously my responsibility to allow others to see You in me, by being open and transparent about my powerlessness aside from You.

Thank You for making Your light shine in that once dark place of my heart.

In the name of Jesus, Amen.

Answering Softly

A soft answer turns away wrath,
But a harsh word stirs up anger.

— PROVERBS 15:1 (NKJV)

LORD of Love,

Help me to be ever mindful that my words have the power to build up or
to tear down my relationships with others.

When someone comes against me with strong and vengeful anger, remind me that their passion is driven by their need to be listened to and understood.

Remind me that how I respond to that anger is critical in helping diffuse their anger and in preventing damage to our relationship.

Remind me that by listening first, I can begin to understand their complaint and that if I purpose to continue to hear them out, they will begin to realize that I truly want to understand what has them upset.

Help me then with calm and quiet words restate my understanding of their complaint back to them, so that they are assured that their complaint has been heard and so that I will be able to constructively respond.

Only then give me soft words to say in love to explain those things that the other person might not have been aware of which led to their wrath against me.

Or, if their anger against me is justified, give me the grace to openly confess any wrongdoing on my part, ask for forgiveness, and seek to set things right so that our relationship might be not only restored but strengthened.

Help me to be ever mindful that my words have the power to build up or
to tear down my relationships with others.

In the name of Jesus, Amen.

You, LORD, are My Strength

I love you, LORD;
you are my strength.
The LORD is my rock, my fortress, and my savior;
my God is my rock, in whom I find protection.
He is my shield, the power that saves me,
and my place of safety.

— Psalm 18:1–2 (NLT)

Loving LORD GOD,

I love you, LORD—for You alone are my strength!

You are my Rock—the solid foundation beneath my feet upon which I can firmly stand and not be moved.

You are my Fortress—a strong and impenetrable place of safety from my enemies where I can confidently remain.

You are my Savior—the One who rescues me from evil, from all my trials and troubles, and gives me eternal life.

Yes, You alone, my God, are my Rock—the One in whom I find my protection.

You are my Shield—You block the accusing arrows of the devil and silence the lies of my enemies as I abide and trust in You.

As I remain in You, I do not fear—for You steadfastly continue to be my place of safety.

I love you, LORD—for You alone are my strength!

In the name of Jesus, Amen.

The Peace that Comes from Christ

And let the peace that comes from Christ rule in your hearts. For as members of one body you are called to live in peace. And always be thankful.

— COLOSSIANS 3:15 (NLT)

Heavenly Father,

Help me to answer Your call to live in the peace that comes when I allow Christ to rule my heart. And let me be forever thankful.

Though the storms of life in this fallen world rage all around me and the cold winds of change blow against me, You have given me the amazing privilege of allowing Your peace—the peace that comes from Christ—to rule and reign in me.

It is not a peace that anyone or anything in this world could ever give, but it is a peace that transcends all circumstances or situations I may face, and is a measure of my faith—a direct reflection of whether I truly believe You and the promises I find in Your Word.

Only as I allow Your peace to live in my heart can I take up my responsibility to live at peace with others in the body of Christ and do my part to bring unity within the church, so that together, we can be a beacon of hope to a lost and dying world.

So let my heart become so saturated with the peace of Christ that it flows from me, bringing peace to all those around me—that You might be glorified in my life.

Help me to answer Your call to live in the peace that comes when I allow Christ to rule my heart. And let me be forever thankful.

In the name of Jesus, Amen.

What Does My Conduct Show?

For I have told you often before, and I say it again with tears in my eyes, that there are many whose conduct shows they are really enemies of the cross of Christ. They are headed for destruction. Their god is their appetite, they brag about shameful things, and they think only about this life here on earth.

— PHILIPPIANS 3:18–19 (NLT)

Heavenly Father,

Help me to consider the way I conduct myself in life here on earth—that I might not ever be found to be an enemy of the cross of Christ.

You have given me the opportunity to embrace everything that the cross of Christ has purchased for me—so keep me from foolishly or thoughtlessly turning down a path that brings sure destruction to my joy, my peace, my purpose, and ultimately my life.

Never allow me to develop an appetite for any of the deceitful pleasures of this world—to allow my fleshly desires to become idol that I choose to worship.

Keep me from being so deceived that I would speak about my sin as if it were something to brag about, as if it were not sin at all—or to admit there is sin in my life but make light of that sin as if it were not a stench in the nostrils of a Holy God.

Help me control my thoughts so that they are not consumed with the pursuit of the ultimately empty and unsatisfying things of this life—but keep me spiritually minded so I don't miss the fullness of life that is mine in Christ.

Help me to be continually conscious of how I am living, so I might submit my will to Your will, resist temptation, flee from sin, and seek—with my whole heart—that life which is hidden in Christ.

Help me to consider the way I conduct myself in life here on earth—that I might not ever be found to be an enemy of the cross of Christ.

In the name of Jesus, Amen.

Fervent, Joyful, Patient, Faithful

Never be lacking in zeal, but keep your spiritual fervor, serving the Lord.
Be joyful in hope, patient in affliction, faithful in prayer.

— ROMANS 12:11–12 (NIV)

Heavenly Father,

Let everything I do be done out of my desire to earnestly and enthusias-
tically serve You.

Cause Your Spirit to burn within my spirit so that I won't fall into laziness and complacency about serving You, but rather find all my joy in my whole-hearted obedience to Your will for my life.

In whatever situation I may find myself, may I always express that confident joy that lives in me because of the great hope that I have found in Your saving power to carry me through, and deliver me from every circumstance that I face until I finally come to You to live forever there with You.

Help me to wait patiently for You to lift me out of my troubles and trials as I remain in total faith and trust in Your perfect plan for me.

Keep me connected with You in prayer at all times, so that my communication with You will be uninterrupted, as I place my concerns before You, wait in Your presence to hear what You would say to me, act on what You show me to do, and rest with confidence in Your promises to me.

Let everything I do be done out of my desire to earnestly and enthusias-
tically serve You.

In the name of Jesus, Amen.

With Me Always

My Spirit remains in your midst. Fear not.

— HAGGAI 2:5B (ESV)

"And be sure of this: I am with you always, even to the end of the age."

— MATTHEW 28:20B (NLT)

Ever-present LORD,

Thank You that Your Spirit remains with me always and I have no reason to fear.

Help me *never* to stop believing Your promise that You are always with me—even when I cannot sense You at work; even when I am feeling frustrated, confused, and alone in the work that I believe You have given me to do.

When the problems I face become overwhelming—because I have allowed them to become larger in my eyes than You, the Almighty God that I serve—refocus my heart on You and remind me not to be afraid, because Your Spirit fills me and surrounds me always.

When the world doesn't make sense and I begin to lose all hope that things will ever be made right, help me find my hope in the truth that You are ever-present—with me always even to the end of the age.

Thank You that Your Spirit remains with me always and I have no reason to fear.

In the name of Jesus, Amen.

The Right to Become Your Child

He came into the very world he created, but the world didn't recognize him. He came to his own people, and even they rejected him. But to all who believed him and accepted him, he gave the right to become children of God. They are reborn—not with a physical birth resulting from human passion or plan, but a birth that comes from God.

— JOHN 1:10–13 (NLT)

Heavenly Father,

Thank You for revealing Yourself to me and giving me the right to become Your child.

Thank You that because I believe in Your Son, Jesus, and have accepted the free gift of salvation that His coming into the world affords everyone who believes, I have been given this opportunity to be reborn.

Reborn—not by means of a natural, physical rebirth, but reborn by a spiritual recreation of my heart.

And just as by my physical birth I was granted the right to be called the child of my father and mother, thank You that it is through that spiritual rebirth that I was given the right to be called a child of my Heavenly Father.

Help me to live my life in devotion to those who gave me life—both by means of my physical birth but even more so through my spiritual rebirth in Christ.

Thank You for revealing Yourself to me and giving me the right to become Your child.

In the name of Jesus, Amen.

In the Temple of the Holy Spirit

Don't you realize that your body is the temple of the Holy Spirit, who lives in you and was given to you by God? You do not belong to yourself, for God bought you with a high price. So you must honor God with your body.

— 1 CORINTHIANS 6:19–20 (NLT)

Loving God,

Thank You for willingly paying the high price You did for my sin, so that there would be room made in my heart for Your Spirit to come and live in me.

Help me to remain conscious of Your ever-constant presence in me, through the gift of Your Holy Spirit to me.

Help me to be sensitive to what Your Holy Spirit would say to my spirit, as I allow You to guide all of my thoughts, words, and actions.

Help me to realize that because I gave up my rights to myself—when I accepted the price that was freely paid for my salvation and surrendered myself to Your control—I am truly set free.

Help me keep my body as a holy temple which honors, respects, and shows forth the glory of the One who lives on the inside me.

Thank You for willingly paying the high price You did for my sin, so that there would be room made in my heart for Your Spirit to come and live in me.

In the name of Jesus, Amen.

At Your Word

By the word of the LORD the heavens were made,
their starry host by the breath of his mouth.
He gathers the waters of the sea into jars;
he puts the deep into storehouses.
Let all the earth fear the LORD;
let all the people of the world revere him.
For he spoke, and it came to be;
he commanded, and it stood firm.

— PSALM 33:6–9 (NIV)

Omnipotent and Loving LORD,

How can I not revere and worship You? How can I not stand in awe of You? For You merely spoke and it all began! It all appeared at Your command!

By *Your Word* and by the *Breath of Your Mouth*—by Your Son and by the Holy Spirit—You made all things! And it is by Christ and by the Spirit that You rule and redeem this fallen world.

You spoke and *it was!* Nothing else was necessary because as You commanded, it was done and forever stands fast.

Your creation came ordered—bound by Your command to function according to Your plans and purposes and set in motion by Your unlimited faith—so that the whole world would fear You, stand in awe of Your majesty and power, and know that You are God!

How can I not revere and worship You? How can I not stand in awe of You? For You merely spoke and it all began! It all appeared at Your command!

In the name of Jesus, Amen.

Worrying Does Not Lead to Life

"Can any one of you by worrying add a single hour to your life?"
— Matthew 6:27 (NIV)

All Wise God,

Help me to remember that I never lengthen or add value to my life by worrying.

Help me to understand that when I worry I am allowing the enemy to steal from me—to steal my peace and my joy, and the time that You have given to me to praise, honor, and glorify You with my life.

Help me to understand that when I worry I am inviting the enemy to come and kill me—because worry chokes the life from me and draws me physically, intellectually, emotionally, and worst of all, spiritually closer to death.

Help me to understand that when I worry I open myself up for the enemy to come and destroy me—that worry leaves me powerless to carry out the plan of God for my life and makes me ineffective in my battle against the enemy.

Help me to understand that worrying is sin. It is in direct opposition to Christ's command not to worry—a command that is intended to protect and keep me in every way. So help me to feel the conviction of Your Spirit when I worry—and repent of my sin.

Help me to understand that worry is the opposite of faith—and that without faith it is impossible to please You. So give me a heart to seek out the Truth of Your Word, that I would strengthen my faith and leave all my worries in Your loving and capable hands.

Help me to remember that I never lengthen or add value to my life by worrying.

In the name of Jesus, Amen.

With Every Word I Say

Don't use foul or abusive language. Let everything you say be good and helpful, so that your words will be an encouragement to those who hear them.

— EPHESIANS 4:29 (NLT)

Father God,

Let every word I say be lovingly truthful and purely motivated by Your Spirit within me—so that the only words I speak will be those which edify, encourage, and give grace to those who might be listening.

Help me never speak words that are slanderous, foul, corrupt, polluting, hurtful or abusive—words that poison the minds and infect the hearts of those who hear them with the evil that they carry.

Instead, help me only speak words that are wholesome, helpful, truthful, and that encourage the spiritual growth of others—always spoken in love and at the right time—which are appropriate for the occasion and for the need of the moment.

Help me also to remember that there may be those to whom I am not directly speaking, who may overhear my words—so let me always be intentional about representing my Lord and Savior well with every word I say.

Let every word I say be lovingly truthful and purely motivated by Your Spirit within me—so that the only words I speak will be those which edify, encourage, and give grace to those who might be listening.

In the name of Jesus, Amen.

Boasting Only in Him

I will praise the LORD at all times.
I will constantly speak his praises.
I will boast only in the LORD;
let all who are helpless take heart.
Come, let us tell of the LORD's greatness;
let us exalt his name together.

— PSALM 34:1–3 (NLT)

LORD of All,

May I never cease to give You praise!

Whether I find myself alone or in a crowd of humanity, may the praise in my heart burst forth through my mouth in honor of all that You are!

Whether I am joyful or troubled, walking in victory or feeling defeated, may my greatest desire be to praise You in every situation and circumstance!

Let all of my boasting be boasting about You—and never out of pride in myself—so the helpless will see that they can find their hope in Your strength and Your power!

May my praise for Your greatness be an invitation—to all who will hear—to join me in forever exalting Your name!

May I never cease to give You praise!

In the name of Jesus, Amen.

Not Worthy of My Love

But people who long to be rich fall into temptation and are trapped by many foolish and harmful desires that plunge them into ruin and destruction. For the love of money is the root of all kinds of evil. And some people, craving money, have wandered from the true faith and pierced themselves with many sorrows.

— 1 TIMOTHY 6:9–10 (NLT)

God, My Provider,

I don't want to foolishly let a desire for money cause me to fall into temptations that would ultimately destroy me. Instead, I want to recognize that the love of money gives life to all kinds of evil, and thus save myself the anguish and sorrows that would come from wandering from faith and trust in You as my Provider.

I always want to realize that the riches of this world cannot be held and can easily slip from my grasp at any moment of time.

I always want to be content with whatever You choose to bless me with as I move through this short life here on earth.

I always want to remain conscious and mindful of the evil places the love of money will take me—so that my heart will remain pure and my integrity will stand intact at all times.

I always want to reserve "love" for my relationships with others rather than loving money or possessions.

I always want to love a life of obedience to Your Word, above any temporary gain I might receive through disobedience.

I never want to have anything that I am not willing to freely give up for Your purposes.

I don't want to foolishly let a desire for money cause me to fall into temptations that would ultimately destroy me. Instead, I want to recognize that the love of money gives life to all kinds of evil, and thus save myself the anguish and sorrows that would come from wandering from faith and trust in You as my Provider.

In the name of Jesus, Amen.

A New Grip and Renewed Strength for a Straight Path

So take a new grip with your tired hands and strengthen your weak knees. Mark out a straight path for your feet so that those who are weak and lame will not fall but become strong.

— HEBREWS 12:12–13 (NLT)

Heavenly Father,

Grant me the wisdom to grasp Your plans for me—and the strength, courage, and resolve to renew my commitment to that calling with each new day that comes—for the sake of those that are weak and lame who are on this journey with me.

When I find myself weakened—whether physically or emotionally or spiritually—help me to take a new grip on that to which You have called me and draw on the strength of Christ in me to help me be obedient to the straight path that Your call requires.

Help me daily to take a fresh hold on Your plan for my life, with deeper strength and purpose, and move forward through those fears that would weaken my knees and immobilize me—by courageously facing the unknown with the confidence that Your Spirit abides in me, to uphold me in Your strength.

Help me to follow after that straight path of willing obedience to You in all things, so that those who are weak and have been injured in this good fight of faith will see You at work—both in me and through me—and be encouraged, strengthened, healed, and made whole again in You and for Your glory!

Grant me the wisdom to grasp Your plans for me—and the renewed strength, courage, and resolve to take a new grip on that calling with each new day that comes—as I submit my will to Yours and put all of my trust in You.

In the name of Jesus, Amen.

The Sin that Pollutes
the Course of My Life

*Indeed, we all make many mistakes. For if we could control our tongues,
we would be perfect and could also control ourselves in every other way.*
— JAMES 3:2 (NLT)

Heavenly Father,

*Save me from the many mistakes I make when I open my mouth—from
the sin that pollutes the course of my life—that I might be made perfect
in You.*

Keep me from gossiping. Help me to speak only positive things about others, so that when I talk about someone, I don't cause negative feelings about them in the hearts of those who may hear me. Help me build others up, not tear them down.

Keep me from using my tongue to exaggerate, flatter, or exchange the truth for a lie—knowing that the motive behind each of these is manipulation. And help me to speak the truth in love—from a pure motive of reflecting Christ's love for us all.

Keep me from complaining—since complaining drives gratefulness and joy out of my heart and robs me of my very life. And help me to be thankful—in all situations—for the blessings You so richly pour out on my life.

Keep me from boasting—except when I testify to what You have done in my life. Help me to be humble—since I know any good thing found in me is all because of You, and is only seen in order to bring You glory.

Remind me that in order to bring You glory, I must know when to speak, where to speak, how to speak, and understand why I should speak—just as much as I need to know what to speak.

*Save me from the many mistakes I make when I open my mouth—from
the sin that pollutes the course of my life—that I might be made perfect
in You.*

In the name of Jesus, Amen.

Where Wisdom and Soundness of Mind Are Found

When pride comes [boiling up with an arrogant attitude of self-importance], then come dishonor and shame,

    But with the humble [the teachable who have been chiseled by trial and who have learned to walk humbly with God] there is wisdom and soundness of mind.

                    — PROVERBS 11:2 (AMP)

Heavenly Father,

Help me to keep a genuinely humble heart—so that in my humility I would find wisdom and live my life with soundness of mind in Christ.

Save me from any hint of pride that would boil up from within me, out of an arrogant attitude of self-importance—so that I would not bring dishonor to You while heaping shame upon myself.

Keep me mindful that any good that is in me is not by my own design or effort, but rather by Your grace and gifting—and is intended to empower me to do good works that would bring You glory, honor, and praise.

Remind me that You didn't grant me gifts and talents to make me look good—but rather that others might see Christ in me and be drawn into an intimate, personal relationship with You.

Continue to teach me to put all my trust in You as You carry me through the trials that You allow me to face—that in all things I would make very little of myself and very much of You, and find all of my value revealed in Christ alone.

Help me to keep a genuinely humble heart—so that in my humility I would find wisdom and live my life with soundness of mind in Christ.

In the name of Jesus, Amen.

Let Your Heart Take Courage

Wait for the LORD;
Be strong and let your heart take courage;
Yes, wait for the LORD.

— PSALM 27:14 (NASB)

Loving and Compassionate LORD,

Grant me the wisdom and strength to wait on You—as I let my heart take courage in Your faithfulness and stand unshaken, regardless of what troubles may come my way.

Help me to be patient in my waiting—with great faith and confident expectation—believing I will see Your hand at work on my behalf as You work all things together for my good.

As I wait on You, help me purpose to draw ever closer to You and remain faithful to do that which I already know that I should do—knowing that waiting doesn't mean that I should be idle.

Keep me busy in prayer, in searching Your Word and in listening for Your Spirit—as I humbly submit my will to Yours in obedience to all that You have asked of me.

Teach me to be courageous as I encourage myself with Your Truth—standing firm, with my mind fixed on You, unmoved by what I see in the natural—confident that my only Hope is found in You.

Grant me the wisdom and strength to wait on You—as I let my heart take courage in Your faithfulness and stand unshaken, regardless of what troubles may come my way.

In the name of Jesus, Amen.

I Don't Want to Be a Liar!

If someone says, "I love God," and hates his brother, he is a liar; for the one who does not love his brother whom he has seen, cannot love God whom he has not seen.

— 1 JOHN 4:20 (NASB)

Heavenly Father,

Show me my heart—and help me to consider the truth of my claim that I love You.

Let my love for You be demonstrated in my love for others—and especially my brothers and sisters in Christ.

Help me to see You in others—for they have been made in Your image—and help me love them as You do, with an unconditional love.

For how can I choose to hate the visible image of God who stands before me within my brothers and sisters and still claim that I love You—having never seen You?

Show me my heart—and help me to consider the truth of my claim that I love You.

In the name of Jesus, Amen.

To Worship You in Spirit and in Truth

And so the LORD says,
"These people say they are mine.
They honor me with their lips,
but their hearts are far from me.
And their worship of me
is nothing but man-made rules learned by rote."

— Isaiah 29:13 (NLT)

"For God is Spirit, so those who worship him must worship in spirit and in truth."

— John 4:24 (NLT)

Loving LORD God,

Let all that I am worship You in spirit and in truth!

Don't allow me just to claim that I am Yours—to honor You with my lips while my heart is far from You. And keep me from becoming disobedient—whether it is through my careless neglect of my relationship with You or by my willful and conscious disregard of Your commands.

Don't allow my worship of You to become mechanical or to be something I do by rote, or to flow from impure motives—which make my worship of You more about me instead of all about You. Keep me from becoming a hypocrite—from allowing my life and my worship to become a lie, told by both my words and my actions.

But rather, let me always worship You from a pure and right heart—motivated only by my love for who You are and for all that You have done—so that all of my thoughts, words, and actions at all times and in all places would bring You glory, honor, and praise.

Let Your Spirit be so fully alive on the inside of me that my life cannot help but be one continuous and unbroken act of honest, sincere, and truthful worship of You.

Let all that I am worship You in spirit and in truth!

In the name of Jesus, Amen.

To Be a Follower of Jesus Christ

Then he said to the crowd, "If any of you wants to be my follower, you must give up your own way, take up your cross daily, and follow me.

— LUKE 9:23 (NLT)

Heavenly Father,

Grant me the strength to turn away from my selfish ways and to embrace with courage and patient endurance any challenge I may face—as I daily commit to follow after Christ, wherever He may lead me, that I might represent Him well.

Help me always remember that my life is found in Christ—that I belong to Him and that the life I am called to live serves Your plans and purposes and not my own.

Give me a heart that is willing to deny myself in order to accomplish that which has been placed before me to do—and hands and feet that move quickly and willingly toward the work at hand.

Help me not to merely serve You with my mouth but rather demonstrate my love and gratitude for all that You have done for me by truly living out my life—moment by moment—for Your glory, honor, and praise.

Grant me the strength to turn away from my selfish ways and to embrace with courage and patient endurance any challenge I may face—as I daily commit to follow after Christ, wherever He may lead me, that I might represent Him well.

In the name of Jesus, Amen.

Like an Ever-Flowing Spring of Worship

The LORD will guide you continually,
giving you water when you are dry
and restoring your strength.
You will be like a well-watered garden,
like an ever-flowing spring.

— ISAIAH 58:11 (NLT)

Loving LORD,

Thank You for guiding me in every decision I make, both today and always—so that my life can be like an ever-flowing spring of worship offered up to You for Your glory, honor, and praise alone!

You are the One who guides me on the right path—that path that leads me to a more abundant life in You—to that place where You take care of all of my needs and offer me the privilege of taking part in what You are doing in the world around me.

You are the One who gives me Your life-giving water when I become dry—physically, emotionally, or spiritually—seeing to it that I have everything I need to restore my strength for the journey forward.

You are the One who causes my life to abound with good things, like a well-watered garden, for the benefit and encouragement of others—so that Your Kingdom would be fully established here on earth according to Your will.

Thank You for guiding me in every decision I make, both today and always—so that my life can be like an ever-flowing spring of worship offered up to You for Your glory, honor, and praise alone!

In the name of Jesus, Amen.

The One Who Cares About Me

Give all your worries and cares to God, for he cares about you.

— 1 PETER 5:7 (NLT)

Loving and Compassionate Heavenly Father,

Nothing more deeply demonstrates how much You care about me than the truth that You sent Jesus to die in my place—and then conquered sin and death through His resurrection, so that I could find life forever through Him!

Remind me to look at what Jesus endured on the cross to help me to better understand the depth of Your love and care for me—so I might more fully trust You with my life and so any sin of unbelief left in my heart would have to go.

Show me that when I anxiously try to carry my own worries and concerns—rather than giving them over to You and trusting You to take care of them all—I am rejecting Your love, walking away from Your care and discounting what Christ did for me.

Let me never allow my circumstances to have control over me—never believe the lie that any particular circumstance that I may find myself in cannot be overcome—and keep me on the path of life, joy, and peace that You have set before me, so I can become everything You have called me to be.

May I always look to You in faith—the One who cares for me and controls all circumstances—as I patiently wait for the good plans that You have made for me to unfold before me, as You work all things together for my good.

Nothing more deeply demonstrates how much You care about me than the truth that You sent Jesus to die in my place—and then conquered sin and death through His resurrection so that I could find life forever through Him!

In the name of Jesus, Amen.

Just a Moment to You

"LORD, remind me how brief my time on earth will be.
Remind me that my days are numbered—
how fleeting my life is.
*   You have made my life no longer than the width of my hand. My*
entire lifetime is just a moment to you;
at best, each of us is but a breath."

— PSALM 39:4–5 (NLT)

Infinite LORD,

Help me to watch for—and willingly and obediently respond to—every
invitation that You extend to me to be a part of what You are doing in the
lives of those around me, so that my brief life here—while little more than
a single breath—will shout to Your glory, honor, and praise!

Help me to use the time that has been given to me in a way that honors You! Don't allow my apathy, complacency, or fear—which comes from my failure to believe that You keep Your promises—hold me back from moving boldly forward with the things that You have given me to do.

And, at the same time, help me to remember to wait for You—to not run ahead of You—since everything good thing I do demands that I remain completely dependent on You, walking every step of the way with You.

Help me to live each moment that You give me by faith enjoying Your presence and resting in Your peace—unencumbered by my past failures or the uncertainty of my future—so that my brief life here might be used for Your glorious purposes.

Help me to watch for—and willingly and obediently respond to—every
invitation that You extend to me to be a part of what You are doing in the
lives of those around me, so that my brief life here—while little more than
a single breath—will shout to Your glory, honor, and praise!

In the name of Jesus, Amen.

The Path of Life in the Calm of God's Presence

"The LORD himself will fight for you. Just stay calm."
— Exodus 14:14 (NLT)

The LORD replied, "My Presence will go with you, and I will give you rest."
— Exodus 33:14 (NIV)

You will make known to me the path of life;
In Your presence is fullness of joy;
In Your right hand there are pleasures forever.
— Psalm 16:11 (NASB)

LORD of Life,

When I grow weary of the fight, when I long for peace and rest, when I don't know what to do, remind me to remain calm—to remain in Your Presence.

Keep me from the insanity of trying to fight on my own—when if I will be still in Your Presence, You will show me how You already are, and always have been, fighting for me.

Keep me from the insanity of trying to find rest anywhere other than in Your Presence—for only there can my mind be quieted, my will become submitted to Your will, and my emotions find the serenity I long for.

Keep me from the insanity of trying to find my way outside of Your Presence—for only You can light the path of life for me and show me the joys of obediently living in Your Presence here on earth.

And grant that I would experience all of the fullness of joy and the pleasures that are mine as You hold me in Your everlasting arms—and fight all my battles for me.

When I grow weary of the fight, when I long for peace and rest, when I don't know what to do, remind me that You are waiting for me to be still in Your Presence.

In the name of Jesus, Amen.

The Cloud of Your Glorious Presence

The trumpeters and singers performed together in unison to praise and give thanks to the LORD. Accompanied by trumpets, cymbals, and other instruments, they raised their voices and praised the LORD with these words:
*   "He is good!*
*   His faithful love endures forever!"*
At that moment a thick cloud filled the Temple of the LORD. The priests could not continue their service because of the cloud, for the glorious presence of the LORD filled the Temple of God.

— 2 CHRONICLES 5:13–14 (NLT)

Gracious LORD,

May the thick cloud of Your glorious presence fill the temple of my spirit as I raise my voice in praise and thanks to You! By the power of Your Spirit, blend the voice of my spirit with every other follower of Christ in perfect unity, so that all we know is You!

Let there be such a spirit of unity between my own heart and the hearts of all my brothers and sisters in Christ, that we would all come together as one voice lifted high to give all our praise and thanks to You.

Then let Your Spirit overwhelm us as Your presence fill our hearts, our homes, our churches, our nation, and even the whole world with Your Glory!

For it is in Your presence we find everything that we need—healing for our hurts, strength for our weakness, forgiveness for our sin, humility for our pride, comfort for our sorrows, peace for our turmoil, joy for our sadness, understanding for our confusion, courage for our fear, freedom from our bondage, hope for our future, and wisdom to live obediently in the love of Christ.

May the thick cloud of Your glorious presence fill the temple of my spirit as I raise my voice in praise and thanks to You! By the power of Your Spirit, blend the voice of my spirit with every other follower of Christ in perfect unity, so that all we know is You!

In the name of Jesus, Amen.

The Only Treasures that Satisfy

"Don't store up treasures here on earth, where moths eat them and rust destroys them, and where thieves break in and steal. Store your treasures in heaven, where moths and rust cannot destroy, and thieves do not break in and steal. Wherever your treasure is, there the desires of your heart will also be."

— MATTHEW 6:19–21 (NLT)

Heavenly Father,

Help me never to forget that the only treasures that will ever truly satisfy the longing desires of my heart are found in Jesus Christ.

Don't let me allow the distractions and attractions of this world to become a quickly vanishing treasure that I get lost in seeking after—when such a greater treasure is made available to me in Christ.

Help me remember that only the treasures that I lay up for myself in heaven are truly mine to keep—and are the only treasures which can never be taken away from me.

So, help me to keep my heart set on things eternal—things that cannot be destroyed and cannot be taken from me—holding what You bless me with in the here and now in open hands surrendered up to You to be used for Your Glory.

Help me never to forget that the only treasures that will ever truly satisfy the longing desires of my heart are found in Jesus Christ.

In the name of Jesus, Amen.

To Work the Works of God

Therefore they said to Him, "What shall we do, so that we may work the works of God?" Jesus answered and said to them, "This is the work of God, that you believe in Him whom He has sent."

— JOHN 6:28–29 (NASB)

Father God,

Help me remember that my part in the work of God is to believe in Jesus—to trust Him, to rely on Him, to faithfully cling to Him, and to place all my faith in Him.

Let my knowledge about Jesus be ever increasing—so my understanding of who He is will always be growing more and more.

Let my understanding of who He is become the foundation of wisdom that leads me into an ever-deepening relationship in which I live for Him—and by which He is made fully alive in me.

Let the *living of my life in relationship with Him* strengthen my faith in Him, as His faithfulness is shown forth through my experience of Him in my life—and as He allows me the privilege of joining Him in what He is doing in the lives of those around me.

Help me remember that my part in the work of God is to believe in Jesus—to trust in Him, to rely on Him, to faithfully cling to Him, and to place all my faith in Him.

In the name of Jesus, Amen.

Just Like You

Follow God's example, therefore, as dearly loved children and walk in the way of love, just as Christ loved us and gave himself up for us as a fragrant offering and sacrifice to God.

— EPHESIANS 5:1–2 (NIV)

Father God,

Help me learn to imitate You in love.

Just like a child who is truly loved experiences that love demonstrated for him by his father and follows after his father's example and teachings of how to love, help me to walk in the ways of Your love.

Help me to love without caution or hesitation, but rather generously and extravagantly. Help me to love others that way—not to receive something from them but only to bring glory to You.

Teach me how to give all of myself to others just as Your Son did when He came and died for us to give us life eternal in Him.

Help me learn to imitate You in love.

In the name of Jesus, Amen.

Relying on Your Unfailing Love

The best-equipped army cannot save a king,
nor is great strength enough to save a warrior.
Don't count on your warhorse to give you victory—
for all its strength, it cannot save you.
But the LORD watches over those who fear him,
those who rely on his unfailing love.

— Psalm 33:16–18 (NLT)

Almighty God, My Father,

Watch over me today. Help me to fear nothing and no one but You. Help me to rely completely on You—and the mighty saving and delivering power of Your unfailing love for me!

You teach me through Your Word that a king should not count on a great army to be able to protect and save him, nor should a warrior believe that his great strength is enough to deliver him—nor that his warhorse will bring him victory.

So help me to examine my heart and remove those things that I may have allowed to become my "warhorse"—those things in which I have foolishly placed my trust and hope for my safety, salvation, and deliverance.

Keep me from the false hope that comes from allowing anything to remain in my heart that would try to take Your rightful place—and let true hope fill my heart until all that is left in my heart is my complete faith and trust in You alone.

Watch over me today. Help me to fear nothing and no one but You. Help me to rely completely on You—and the mighty saving and delivering power of Your unfailing love for me!

In the name of Jesus, Amen.

Living in Freedom, Serving in Love

For you have been called to live in freedom, my brothers and sisters. But don't use your freedom to satisfy your sinful nature. Instead, use your freedom to serve one another in love.

— GALATIANS 5:13 (NLT)

Heavenly Father,

Thank You for calling me to live in the freedom that was bought for me by the redeeming sacrifice of Your Son, Jesus, for my sin.

Help me never forget that the freedom that was purchased with the blood of Christ was not freedom to sin but a freedom from sin's power to control my life.

Help me to understand that there is no "freedom" in the suggestion that I have freedom to sin. It is a lie from Satan designed to enslave me to himself, to others, and to my own sinful nature—making me a participant in his plans to kill, steal, and destroy.

Therefore, help me glorify You and the work of Christ in me before others—by exercising my freedom to do what is right in loving service to both my brothers and sisters in Christ and to those who are lost and enslaved by their sin.

Thank You for calling me to live in the freedom that was bought for me by the redeeming sacrifice of Your Son, Jesus, for my sin.

In the name of Jesus, Amen.

Power to the Weak, Strength to the Powerless

He gives strength to the weary
and increases the power of the weak.
Even youths grow tired and weary,
and young men stumble and fall;
but those who hope in the LORD
will renew their strength.
They will soar on wings like eagles;
they will run and not grow weary,
they will walk and not be faint.

— ISAIAH 40:29–31 (NIV)

LORD of All Power and Strength,

When I feel weak and powerless, fill me with Your power and strength!
As I patiently wait for You—putting all my trust in Your unfailing love
for me—cause me to rise up high on wings like an eagle who soars into
Your wondrous presence, where I will find the strength I need for my
journey forward with You.

You alone are the source of my strength! When I am weak, You give me power to keep going! When I feel powerless, You renew my strength by reminding me that You are all powerful!

Even the youngest and strongest of men grow weak and tired. Only those who trust in You completely find that new strength—a strength that continually sustains them and doesn't allow them to stumble and fall in exhaustion.

Only by Your power and strength can we run toward You and not grow weary—walk with You and not faint!

When I feel weak and powerless, fill me with Your power and strength!
As I patiently wait for You—putting all my trust in Your unfailing love
for me—cause me to rise up high on wings like an eagle who soars into
Your wondrous presence, where I will find the strength I need for my
journey forward with You.

In the name of Jesus, Amen.

Practicing True Hospitality

When God's people are in need, be ready to help them. Always be eager to practice hospitality.

— ROMANS 12:13 (NLT)

Generous God,

Help me to be not only ready but eager to help my brothers and sisters who are in need.

Make me into the kind of person who actively looks for opportunities to meet the needs of others—whether they are material, physical, emotional, or spiritual in nature—and willingly jumps in to help.

Help me to stay sensitive to Your Spirit as You show me ways that I can be used by You in the lives of others.

Help me to remember that practicing hospitality is not about entertaining someone to make *myself* look good, as if it was all about *me*.

Make me into the kind of person who keeps his focus on *others* and their real needs and does what he can to help.

Help me to be not only ready but eager to help my brothers and sisters who are in need.

In the name of Jesus, Amen.

His Words of Wisdom
to Comfort the Weary

The Sovereign LORD has given me his words of wisdom,
so that I know how to comfort the weary.
Morning by morning he wakens me
and opens my understanding to his will.

— Isaiah 50:4 (NLT)

Sovereign LORD,

Thank You that morning by morning You awaken me and open my understanding to Your will—giving me Your words of wisdom so that I know how to comfort the weary.

With each new day that comes, You are always faithful to reveal to me a deeper understanding of Your will—as I spend time prayerfully searching for those ever richer revelations from Your Word.

As I abide in Your Presence, You show me how to use the words of wisdom that You have revealed to comfort those who are struggling around me—so that when prompted by Your Holy Spirit, I will be ready to accept Your invitation to be a part of the work that You are doing in others to draw them to Yourself.

Never let me stop seeking You—through Your Word and through prayer— as You reveal Your character and Your will to me. And make me a vessel that Your words of wisdom can overflow from, so that all those around me can be comforted by the richness of Christ's love for us all.

Thank You that morning by morning You awaken me and open my understanding to Your will—giving me Your words of wisdom so that I know how to comfort the weary.

In the name of Jesus, Amen.

A Way Out

*The temptations in your life are no different from what others experience.
And God is faithful. He will not allow the temptation to be more than
you can stand. When you are tempted, he will show you a way out so that
you can endure.*

— 1 CORINTHIANS 10:13 (NLT)

Faithful God,

*Thank You for being faithful—and for showing me a way out of every
temptation that I face.*

Thank You for showing me that I am not alone in temptation—that everyone is tempted and that to be tempted is *not* sin.

Thank You that You do not allow me to be tempted beyond what I am able
to stand—that You are always ready to show me a way of escape so that I can
endure.

So help me to avoid people or situations that might cause me to be
tempted—and help me to run from that which I know is wrong.

Help me to pray for strength in the midst of any temptation that I encounter—that I might make choices that are good and right.

Help me to remember that You set me free from sin so that I *could* make
the right choice—so that I *could* resist the temptation and choose the abundant
life I find in You.

Help me to live in Your Presence seeking Your will—by spending time in
prayer, in reading and studying Your Word, and in quietly listening for Your
voice to speak to my heart—so that when temptation comes, I will be prepared
to resist it and do what is pleasing to You.

*Thank You for being faithful—and for showing me a way out of every
temptation that I face.*

In the name of Jesus, Amen.

My Joy and My Heart's Delight

When I discovered your words, I devoured them.
They are my joy and my heart's delight,
for I bear your name,
O LORD God of Heaven's Armies.

— JEREMIAH 15:16 (NLT)

Dear LORD,

Keep me hungry—eager to receive and ready to apply every word that You would speak into my life. Let my joy and my heart's delight be in discovering the Truth that is found in Your Word, which is revealed by Your Spirit and proven through my personal experience of relationship with You.

Continue to speak to me through Your Holy Spirit, and by that same Spirit reveal and illuminate the words of the Bible to my spirit—that I might devour the fresh Truth that You have waiting there for me to discover.

Use that Truth to help me grow in obedience and faithfulness to You, so that I can live my life submitted to Truth and can become all that You have planned for me to be in Christ—for Your own glory and honor and praise.

For it is in Your words that I find my strength and hope! And in them I discover the responsibilities of obedience that I carry, because I have been chosen—and I have chosen—to bear Your name, O LORD God of Heaven's Armies!

Keep me hungry—eager to receive and ready to apply every word that You would speak into my life. Let my joy and my heart's delight be in discovering the Truth that is found in Your Word, which is revealed by Your Spirit and proven through my personal experience of relationship with You.

In the name of Jesus, Amen.

The Flavor That My Life Brings to the World

"You are the salt of the earth. But what good is salt if it has lost its flavor? Can you make it salty again? It will be thrown out and trampled underfoot as worthless."

— MATTHEW 5:13 (NLT)

Taste and see that the LORD is good.
Oh, the joys of those who take refuge in him!

— PSALM 34:8 (NLT)

Heavenly Father,

Do not let me ever forget the calling that Christ placed on my life to be the salt of the earth—so that others may taste and see that You are good and find the joy that comes when they take their refuge in You.

Help me to guard against losing my saltiness—the flavor that my life brings to the world—for to do so would leave me in a most miserable state, good for nothing and left to be trampled under the feet of a carelessly bustling world.

Help me to remember that in order to remain salty, I desperately need to invest my time in being in Your Presence, learning from Your Word and being taught by Your Spirit—as I pray, search the Bible, and sit quietly before You to hear what the Spirit would have to say to my life and circumstances—so that when You add me into the mix of this day, I will be in a position to improve its flavor.

So fill me with the deep and unfailing love of Christ, until it overflows from within me by the power of the Holy Spirit—so that the flavor of every thought that I have, of every word that I speak, and of every action I take will be made alive—having been seasoned with genuine compassion, patient kindness, fresh and daily-renewed mercy, freely-offered forgiveness, and abundant grace.

Do not let me ever forget the calling that Christ placed on my life to be the salt of the earth—so that others may taste and see that You are good and find the joy that comes when they take their refuge in You.

In the name of Jesus, Amen.

That Which Will Define My Future

"Forget the former things;
do not dwell on the past.
See, I am doing a new thing!
Now it springs up; do you not perceive it?
I am making a way in the wilderness
and streams in the wasteland."

— ISAIAH 43:18–19 (NIV)

Almighty God,

Help me not to dwell so much on the past—even on those great and won-drous miracles that have marked my life thus far—that I end up missing out on the new things—those even far greater things—which will define my future with You.

Teach me to see—to stop, look, and perceive Your will for me—as You work in me, through me, and all around me in new and fresh ways to bring glory to Yourself!

Make me open to receive all that this ever-changing gift of life You have given me has to offer—as You unfold before me the newness of the perfect path that You have for me to walk.

Grant me the faith to believe that You are able—and You certainly will—make a road for me in the wilderness and cause life-giving rivers to flow in any desert that lies before me, both now and forevermore.

Help me not to dwell so much on the past—even on those great and won-drous miracles that have marked my life thus far—that I end up missing out on the new things—those even far greater things—which will define my future with You.

In the name of Jesus, Amen.

The Weapons We Fight With

For though we live in the world, we do not wage war as the world does. The weapons we fight with are not the weapons of the world. On the contrary, they have divine power to demolish strongholds. We demolish arguments and every pretension that sets itself up against the knowledge of God, and we take captive every thought to make it obedient to Christ.

— 2 CORINTHIANS 10:3–5 (NIV)

Heavenly Father,

Help me always to remember this: the real battles I must fight in this life are spiritual battles against anything that challenges Truth—that is the knowledge of God—for the control of my heart.

Thank You that my battles are not like those of the world which—when waged in the flesh—only bring misery and destruction to all who fight them. Thank You there is victory in Christ for every battle I face!

Remind me that You have given me divinely powerful weapons—to use in the spiritual battles I must fight for the control of my heart, soul, and spirit—weapons that are able to demolish any strongholds of the enemy, every argument he may make and each lie that he spews which contradicts the Truth I find in Your Word.

Grant me the wisdom to use these weapons—the weapons of prayer, the power of Truth of Your Word proclaimed, the witness of Your Holy Spirit within my spirit, and my authority in Christ as Your child—to enforce Your victory over the enemy in my life.

Help me to examine carefully every thought or argument that enters my mind and hold it captive and isolated—unable to escape, deceive, or influence me in any way—until such time as it conforms to, agrees with, and is obedient to Truth as measured by Christ.

Help me always to remember this: the real battles I must fight in this life are spiritual battles against anything that challenges Truth—that is the knowledge of God—for the control of my heart.

In the name of Jesus, Amen.

Like a Bright Light of Hope

Do everything without complaining and arguing, so that no one can criticize you. Live clean, innocent lives as children of God, shining like bright lights in a world full of crooked and perverse people.

— PHILIPPIANS 2:14–15 (NLT)

Heavenly Father,

Help me to live a life free from complaining and arguing, so others would not have reason to criticize me. Let my life be clean and innocent—like a bright light of hope in a world that is darkened by crooked and perverse people.

Help me never to complain about anything, but choose a life full of gratefulness and thanksgiving—knowing that Your plan for me is always good and that You use everything that I experience to draw me to Yourself, turning all of it to my benefit and for Your glory.

Help me not to needlessly stir up strife between myself and others with petty arguments, when You want me to walk humbly before others, full of truth and grace, as expressed in the perfect love of Christ—leaving to You the work of changing hearts.

As Your very own child, let my response to the Truth of Your Word and the promptings of Your Spirit always be one of willing obedience, so others will have no room to criticize me and so they might be drawn to the light of Christ at work in me.

Help me to live a life free from complaining and arguing, so others would not have reason to criticize me. Let my life be clean and innocent—like a bright light of hope, in a world that is darkened by crooked and perverse people.

In the name of Jesus, Amen.

The Word of the LORD Holds True

For the word of the LORD holds true,
and we can trust everything he does.
He loves whatever is just and good;
the unfailing love of the LORD fills the earth.

— PSALM 33:4–5 (NLT)

Faithful LORD,

Thank You that every word You have ever spoken to us holds true—and
we can trust everything that You do because it flows out of Your unfailing
love for us.

Thank You that we can take comfort and find peace in You—because You
are always Holy, Just, and Good.

For You are the ever-true, all-knowing, never-changing, ever-constant,
always-trustworthy, Almighty God of all creation. Your Word always reflects
Your character perfectly—as it goes forth in power to accomplish Your
purposes.

Help us to submit to the working of Your Spirit within us so that the character of Christ would be established in our lives—in order to bring You glory,
honor, and praise.

Thank You for loving all things that are just and good and for dealing with
us according to Your never-failing love—which ever surrounds us as it fills the
whole earth with Your glory.

Thank You that every word You have ever spoken to us holds true—and
we can trust everything that You do because it flows out of Your unfailing
love for us.

In the name of Jesus, Amen.

The Richness of the Message of Christ

Let the message about Christ, in all its richness, fill your lives. Teach and counsel each other with all the wisdom he gives. Sing psalms and hymns and spiritual songs to God with thankful hearts. And whatever you do or say, do it as a representative of the Lord Jesus, giving thanks through him to God the Father.

— Colossians 3:16–17 (NLT)

Heavenly Father,

Thank You for the rich message of Christ—and the example that He gave us to follow. Help me to represent Him well today.

I know that if I ever hope to represent Christ well, I must allow the truth of the message of Christ in all of its richness to fill every part of my life

Help to understand fully that this means that every thought that I allow to remain within my mind, every word that I speak, every action that I take, and every motive of my heart must be a reflection of Christ in me.

Help me to teach and counsel others with all the wisdom that He gives—speaking only words of truth and grace in love—as I spend time in His Word and allow its rich message to fill me so completely that it can't help but overflow to others.

Bring up from within me psalms, hymns, and spiritual songs of praise and worship that I might sing for You—from a heart that is filled with gratitude—giving thanks, through Christ, to You.

Thank You for the message of Christ—and the example that He gave us to follow. Help me to represent Him well today.

In the name of Jesus, Amen.

Forgiven: Cleared of Guilt

Oh, what joy for those
whose disobedience is forgiven,
whose sin is put out of sight!
Yes, what joy for those
whose record the LORD has cleared of guilt,
whose lives are lived in complete honesty!
When I refused to confess my sin,
my body wasted away,
and I groaned all day long.
Day and night your hand of discipline was heavy on me.
My strength evaporated like water in the summer heat.
Finally, I confessed all my sins to you
and stopped trying to hide my guilt.
I said to myself, "I will confess my rebellion to the LORD."
And you forgave me! All my guilt is gone.

— PSALM 32:1–5 (NLT)

Dear LORD,

Thank You for such an amazing love as this.

Help me never to lose sight of the truth that You want to forgive me of my sins—that because of Your love for me, this has always been Your great desire—so I can fully and freely live with joy in Your presence.

When I begin to question whether You would *want* to forgive me, help me to look back to the cross and see the great price You already paid to make my forgiveness possible—and there discover my value to You.

Help me to understand that when I try in vain to hide my sins from You—refusing to honestly and completely confess them before You—I am only inviting You to extend Your hand of discipline and I am opening up myself to the destruction of my body, soul, and spirit.

Help me always to hurry to lay myself bare before You in repentance of my sin—knowing that You forgive my disobedience, You put my sin out of Your sight, and You clear my record of all guilt, making me as righteous in Your eyes as Christ Himself.

Thank You for such an amazing love as this.

In the name of Jesus, Amen.

To Speak the Truth in Love

And we urge you, brothers and sisters, warn those who are idle and disruptive, encourage the disheartened, help the weak, be patient with everyone.

— 1 THESSALONIANS 5:14 (NIV)

Heavenly Father,

Help me to be the kind of person who always speaks the Truth—that Truth which is found in Your Word and revealed to us by Your Spirit—out of obedience to Your instruction and motivated only by a deep and compassionate love for others.

Your Word instructs us to warn those who are idle and disruptive. So grant me the courage to warn them with the Truth in love—as You place those opportunities before me—so that they can become productive and unifying forces for good.

But keep me from appearing to speak down to them—as if I was in any way spiritually superior. Help me only admonish them as equals, as brothers and sisters in this same good fight of faith.

When someone has become disheartened, grant me the privilege of coming beside them to encourage them with what You say about their situation and circumstances—offering them Truth in love so that they would not give up the fight.

Place before me opportunities to help those who are weak—that by the power of the Truth of Your Word, they would be made strong in Christ and in His love as seen through me.

At all times, let me demonstrate the kind of patience for others that can only come from an overflow of my heart in response to Christ's love for me.

Help me to be the kind of person who always speaks the Truth—that Truth which is found in Your Word and revealed to us by Your Spirit—out of obedience to Your instruction and motivated only by a deep and compassionate love for others.

In the name of Jesus, Amen.

My Life Is Not My Own!

LORD, I know that people's lives are not their own;
it is not for them to direct their steps.
Discipline me, LORD, but only in due measure—
not in your anger,
or you will reduce me to nothing.

— JEREMIAH 10:23–24 (NIV)

Sovereign LORD,

Let me always trust that You will direct my steps according to Your
plans and purposes for me, and will discipline me with mercy, grace,
and justice—according to Your unfailing love for me—that I might live
for You.

Keep me mindful that my life is not my own but belongs to Jesus Christ—
the One who died for me that I might live for Him—and that I was not put
here to direct my own steps and carry out my own plans, because my plans are
shortsighted and impurely motivated.

For I know that when I wander off and try to go my own way, my feet
always seem to travel to those places that hold darkness, death, and destruction
rather than the life, joy, and peace I find along the path You have for me.

So correct me when I behave as if I know better than You what is best for me,
disciplining me as You must—not out of Your anger but rather patiently, gently,
and justly in order to set me on the right course once again.

Thank You that any anger You have with me will never exceed Your unfailing love for me—nor will it surpass the mercy and grace that that You pour
over me each and every day—for I know that if it did, I would be reduced to
nothing. I would surely die.

Let me always trust that You will direct my steps according to Your
plans and purposes for me, and will discipline me with mercy, grace,
and justice—according to Your unfailing love for me—that I might live
for You.

In the name of Jesus, Amen.

To Become the Servant of Everyone Else

After they arrived at Capernaum and settled in a house, Jesus asked his disciples, "What were you discussing out on the road?" But they didn't answer, because they had been arguing about which of them was the greatest. He sat down, called the twelve disciples over to him, and said, "Whoever wants to be first must take last place and be the servant of everyone else."

— MARK 9:33–35 (NLT)

Heavenly Father,

Let everything that I say and do, the deepest thoughts of my mind, and every hidden motive of my heart always be pleasing to You—so that I never have to be ashamed when I am asked to account for them.

Help me to guard against being caught up in chasing after any man-made ideas of what success or achievement might be—only to find that my own self-promotion has kept me from Your higher plans and better purposes for my life.

Help me to watch that I don't allow my own deep-rooted insecurities or foolish pride to cause me to put too much stock in the power of a position, or the amount of prestige it might happen to carry—but humbly remember that I am nothing without You.

Help me to fully understand that all of my energy, time, and talents should be directed to knowing Christ for myself and making Him known to others—by following His example of leadership and reflecting His love—as I become a servant of all.

Let everything that I say and do, the deepest thoughts of my mind and every hidden motive of my heart always be pleasing to You—so that I never have to be ashamed when I am asked to account for them.

In the name of Jesus, Amen.

Walking Closely After You

You shall walk after the LORD your God and you shall fear [and wor-ship] Him [with awe-filled reverence and profound respect], and you shall keep His commandments and you shall listen to His voice, and you shall serve Him, and cling to Him.

— DEUTERONOMY 13:4 (AMP)

O LORD My God,

Let me walk after You all the days of my life! Be for me the only God I fear and worship—the God I obey, the God I listen to, the God I serve, and the God I cling to always!

Help me only go down paths that You lead me down—as I walk closely after You—and not go wandering off on my own.

Help me always worship You in reverential awe of who You are, Your infinite and delivering power, and Your unfailing love for me—and not allow myself to become afraid of anything that looms before me whether man, demon, or circumstance.

Help me to be careful to obey all Your commands and instructions—knowing that You have given them to me so I might live in the peace, provision, and protection that can only come from Your hand.

Help me to listen to Your voice alone—and silence the many "voices" of this world which would try to pull my attention away from You.

Help me to examine my thoughts, words, and actions to ensure that everything that I do is in service to You—that it is done from pure and right motives in order to bring glory to Your Name.

Help me to cling to You with all of my heart, mind, and strength—and allow no temptation to overcome me and separate me from You.

Let me walk after You all the days of my life! Be for me the only God I fear and worship—the God I obey, the God I listen to, the God I serve, and the God I cling to always!

In the name of Jesus, Amen.

Inspired by God and Useful to Teach Us

All Scripture is inspired by God and is useful to teach us what is true and to make us realize what is wrong in our lives. It corrects us when we are wrong and teaches us to do what is right. God uses it to prepare and equip his people to do every good work.

— 2 Timothy 3:16–17 (NLT)

God of Truth,

Thank You for the Holy Scriptures—words of truth—which were inspired by You and written for us, so that we—Your people—would be prepared and equipped to do every good work.

Draw us to the Scriptures so we can learn what is true and come to realize what is wrong in our lives—as the life by which You breathed the Scriptures breathes life into our spirits through Your Holy Spirit.

Humble us so we will be receptive and responsive when Your Word corrects us—teachable and willingly obedient as You help us learn to do what is right.

Grant that we would become thoroughly prepared and equipped to do every good work that You have planned for us to do—having been made full of Truth and Grace, and abounding in Your love for all.

Thank You for the Holy Scriptures—words of truth—which were inspired by You and written for us, so that we—Your people—would be prepared and equipped to do every good work.

In the Name of Jesus, Amen.

To Give and to Receive God's Mercy

So whatever you say or whatever you do, remember that you will be judged by the law that sets you free. There will be no mercy for those who have not shown mercy to others. But if you have been merciful, God will be merciful when he judges you.

— JAMES 2:12–13 (NLT)

Just and Merciful God,

Let all of my thoughts, words, and actions be evidence that I have truly understood the depths of the mercy that has been offered to me—for I know that I will receive Your mercy according to my willing obedience to extend that same mercy to others.

Help me remember that the same law that sets me free—that moral law that sets all obedient followers of Christ free from the bondage of sin—is the law by which I will be judged.

For while I have been saved by grace through faith, the evidence of my having received that salvation is my obedience to Christ—which is the path upon which perfect freedom is found—and my ability to extend mercy to others is a proof that I am walking out that salvation which the Gospel of Christ has provided.

Let the mercy that You have poured over me be reflected in me, to all those around me, through my willing obedience to Christ's command to love You with all my heart, soul, mind, and strength—for therein lies the power to love my neighbor as myself.

Let all of my thoughts, words, and actions be evidence that I have truly understood the depths of the mercy that has been offered to me—for I know that I will receive Your mercy according to my willing obedience to extend that same mercy to others.

In the name of Jesus, Amen.

To Be Glad and Rejoice

I will be glad and rejoice in your unfailing love,
for you have seen my troubles,
and you care about the anguish of my soul.

— PSALM 31:7 (NLT)

Loving LORD,

How wonderful it is to be glad and rejoice in Your love—to know, in my
heart, that it's always Your unfailing love which carries me through the
hardest things that life on this earth can bring!

In the midst of my troubles, let me know Your unfailing love for me—Your
mercy and Your grace poured out over me—for only by the power of Your
caring and compassionate presence here with me can the anguish of my soul
be truly put to rest.

Don't allow my anguish to overwhelm my soul. Don't allow my troubled
heart to see the very hard but momentary struggles I face here on earth as
larger than Your capacity to bring me through them all—in unfathomable
peace and with enduring joy, because of the ultimate victory made available to
me in Christ.

Help me to run to Your love, allow You to hold me in that love, trust You to
protect me and provide for me by that love—and through that unfailing love,
show me the path of life you have for me.

How wonderful it is to be glad and rejoice in Your love—to know, in my
heart, that it's always Your unfailing love which carries me through the
hardest things that life on this earth can bring!

In the name of Jesus, Amen.

The Blessings of Living in Truth and Love

Grace, mercy, and peace, which come from God the Father and from Jesus Christ—the Son of the Father—will continue to be with us who live in truth and love.

— 2 JOHN 1:3 (NLT)

Heavenly Father,

Thank You for the way that Your Word assures me that grace, mercy, and peace will continue to be with me if I live in truth and love.

Thank You for revealing to all those who choose to believe You the absolute Truth and the unfailing Love found in Your written Word and in Your Word made flesh—in the person of Jesus Christ, my Lord and Savior—who is Your greatest expression of love and of truth .

Save me from the lies of the enemy which would try to convince me that there is no truth, that truth is defined by a person's personal preferences, or that somehow the lusting of my flesh is really love—and help me always look to You to guide me into all Truth that I may always walk in Love.

And should I ever find my peace disrupted, Your mercy for me in question, or feel as though Your grace to me is running low, remind me to examine my heart to see if I have walked away from truth and love—and bring me back to Your Word that I might repent and be restored.

Thank You for the way that Your Word assures me that grace, mercy, and peace will continue to be with me if I live in truth and love.

In the name of Jesus, Amen.

To Please Only You

Yet at the same time many even among the leaders believed in him. But because of the Pharisees they would not openly acknowledge their faith for fear they would be put out of the synagogue; for they loved human praise more than praise from God.

— JOHN 12:42–43 (NIV)

Heavenly Father,

Grant me the courage to boldly testify to my faith in Jesus Christ at all times.

Help me not to miss any opportunity that You place before me to acknowledge Christ—His saving power, His delivering power, and His preserving power which is mightily at work within me—so that no one would doubt the sincerity of my faith.

May my boldness to declare the marvelous goodness of my Savior encourage others who believe—and yet are somehow held back by their fears—to openly profess their belief in Him, not allowing their fears to restrain them from taking their stand in Christ.

May I never care more about what others think than I do about what You think. May I never allow Your creation to become an idol in my life—by worshiping man rather than worshiping You alone. And may I never allow my fears over what man can do to me keep me silent about the Truth.

For the greatest desire of my heart is to give all of my praise and honor and worship to You—to please only You—that any praise I might receive would come from You alone.

Grant me the courage to boldly testify to my faith in Jesus Christ at all times.

In the name of Jesus, Amen.

When I Look and See

When I look at the night sky and see the work of your fingers—
the moon and the stars you set in place—
what are mere mortals that you should think about them,
human beings that you should care for them?

— PSALM 8:3–4 (NLT)

Creator God,

As I gaze upon the night sky, as I try to take it all in, I cannot even
begin to comprehend the vastness of all that You have made. And when
I think that Your creation is no more than a mere glimpse of Your power
and glory, I am overwhelmed to think that You would choose to set Your
unfailing love and affection on one like me!

I am amazed at the intricate details with which You designed, created, set
in place, and put in perfectly synchronized motion the moon and each of the
stars in the multitude of galaxies that You spread across the vastness of an end-
less space.

I am even more amazed that You created them all and put them on display
for us—to demonstrate Your power and greatness and majesty to all of mankind—in order to reveal who You are and to draw us into relationship with You.

I am most amazed that You would make mankind the reason for, and focus
of, everything that You have created—that You not only would think about us
but would want us and truly care for us—making us the objects of Your amazing and immeasurable love.

As I gaze upon the night sky, as I try to take it all in, I cannot even
begin to comprehend the vastness of all that You have made. And when
I think that Your creation is no more than a mere glimpse of Your power
and glory, I am overwhelmed to think that You would choose to set Your
unfailing love and affection on one like me!

In the name of Jesus, Amen.

The Hope that Is in Me

But in your hearts set Christ apart as holy [and acknowledge Him] as Lord. Always be ready to give a logical defense to anyone who asks you to account for the hope that is in you, but do it courteously and respectfully.

— 1 PETER 3:15 (AMP)

Heavenly Father,

May the Holiness and Lordship of Christ be so established in my heart that it causes people to ask me about the hope that is in me—and may I always be ready to respectfully give an answer that will help them find that same hope.

May I never so fear what man might do to me that I fail to speak out about what Christ has done for me.

Let the only fear that remains in me be that reverential fear of You—my LORD GOD—as I stand humbly before You and rely solely on Your power to sustain me.

Help me to place all of my confidence in Your faithfulness to me as I submit myself to Your will—and trust in Your wisdom to direct my every thought, word, and action.

Help me as I work to reflect Christ's love in all that I do—that He alone might be glorified in my life.

Let every word that I speak be delivered respectfully—with humility, courtesy, and gentleness—so that my heart for You, and for them, may be heard above all else.

May the Holiness and Lordship of Christ be so established in my heart, that it causes people to ask me about the hope that is in me—and may I always be ready to respectfully give an answer that will help them find that same hope.

In the name of Jesus, Amen.

Those Who Have Humble and Contrite Hearts

This is what the LORD says:
"Heaven is my throne,
and the earth is my footstool.
Could you build me a temple as good as that?
Could you build me such a resting place?
My hands have made both heaven and earth;
they and everything in them are mine.
I, the LORD, have spoken!
"I will bless those who have humble and contrite hearts,
who tremble at my word."

— Isaiah 66:1–2 (NLT)

My LORD and Father,

Help me to live in this blessed truth—that the temple in which You wish
to come and remain is deep within my heart!

Human hands could never make a dwelling suitable for You, for You have made all things both in heaven and on earth. You already own everything there is, so what new thing can I give to You that isn't Yours already?

Neither are You interested in what "great things" I can do for You. You are only interested in the condition of my heart toward You. So help me to keep a humble heart—not only realizing but boldly declaring that You are the source of any good found in me.

And help me to keep a contrite spirit—deeply sorry, remorseful, and repentant for my sins, shortcomings, and failures. Shake me to my core with the magnificent power of Your Word—which is alive and able to change even the darkest reaches of the human soul.

Help me to live in this blessed truth—that the temple in which You wish
to come and remain is deep within my heart!

In the name of Jesus, Amen.

Following the Spirit's Leading in Every Part of Our Lives

Since we are living by the Spirit, let us follow the Spirit's leading in every part of our lives. Let us not become conceited, or provoke one another, or be jealous of one another.

— GALATIANS 5:25–26 (NLT)

Heavenly Father,

Let my claims that I live empowered by the Holy Spirit within me be evidenced by my humble obedience to His leading in every part of my life.

By Your Spirit, alive and active in me, You have shown me the path to eternal life—and, by that same Spirit, you give me the power to live as I should in the here and now.

So help me to live every aspect of my life in total harmony with Your Spirit—allowing You to guide my thoughts, emotions, and behaviors at all times—so that by faith my life will produce those things that please You.

Help me live out every relationship of my life reflecting the Light of Christ in me—as I give You all my praise from a grateful heart, as I encourage my brothers and sisters in Christ with joy and in strength of fellowship, and as I reach out to the lost and hurting with Christ-like compassion.

Help me to find my identity in Christ alone—so there is no room in me for conceit, no need in me to provoke others, no temptation to be envious or jealous—so that I can live my life with courage, integrity, and godly character at all times.

Let my claims that I live empowered by the Holy Spirit within me be evidenced by my humble obedience to His leading in every part of my life.

In the name of Jesus, Amen.

Don't Worry About Anything

Don't worry about anything; instead, pray about everything. Tell God what you need, and thank him for all he has done. Then you will experience God's peace, which exceeds anything we can understand. His peace will guard your hearts and minds as you live in Christ Jesus.

— PHILIPPIANS 4:6–7 (NLT)

Heavenly Father,

Thank You that I don't have to waste one more moment of time worrying—because You are the God who protects me, provides for my every need, and gives me peace beyond my own understanding as I live my life in Christ Jesus.

When the enemy does everything he can to make me worry, as he attacks me with his lies, help me to pray that I would stand against his attacks—and remember that the same Spirit that raised Christ from the dead lives in me.

Help me to run to You with whatever is bothering me—asking You for what I need—knowing that as I let my worries go, give them over to You, and leave them all in Your hands, You will do what only You can do. You will multiply Your peace back to me.

When that flood of negative thoughts assaults me, remind me to thank You for how You have always carried me through my life—providing for my every need and consistently working for my good.

Show me that You have given me a way to escape the torment, quiet the enemy, and experience Your peace—when I hold my thoughts captive until they line up with the Truth of Your Word—so that Your peace can guard my heart and mind in Christ Jesus.

Thank You that I don't have to waste one more moment of time worrying—because You are the God who protects me, provides for my every need, and gives me peace beyond my own understanding as I live my life in Christ Jesus.

In the name of Jesus, Amen.

Life as a Continual Feast of Blessing

For the despondent, every day brings trouble;
for the happy heart, life is a continual feast.

— PROVERBS 15:15 (NLT)

Good and Generous God,

Let all my thoughts be filled with hope as I give thanks for the continual feast of blessings that You have prepared for me to enjoy—so that I can keep a happy-hearted attitude no matter what comes my way.

I know that if I never miss an opportunity to dwell on every bad thing that happens—my attitude will become poisoned, my days will be filled with worry and trouble, and my hope will be lost to the lies the enemy has deceived me into accepting as truth.

I know that if I never miss an opportunity to dwell on every good thing with which You have so abundantly blessed me—my attitude will be nourished, my days will be filled with joy and happiness, and my hope will grow as You help me to live in the truth of Your love.

Let me always choose wisely those things that I allow to continue in my thoughts and influence my beliefs—so that I might fully experience the abundant life that You have invited me to live out each and every day.

Let all my thoughts be filled with hope as I give thanks for the continual feast of blessings that You have prepared for me to enjoy—so that I can keep a happy-hearted attitude no matter what comes my way.

In the name of Jesus, Amen.

The LORD Who Watches Over Me

I lay down and slept,
yet I woke up in safety,
for the LORD was watching over me.

— PSALM 3:5 (NLT)

Ever-watching LORD,

How blessed I am to be able to lie down and sleep—knowing that I am
under Your ever-watchful care!

Thank You for the comforting truth that You never take Your eyes off me—
that You are always there to keep me safe in every way.

Thank You that when the troubles and worries of this world try to steal
my peace away from me, I need only cry out to You and You are there to hear
me and to restore my peace—with the full assurance that You are in control of
whatever circumstances that I may have to face.

Help me not to forget that—because I am Your very own—You will always
use every circumstance I may have to endure for my good and will not withhold any good thing from me as long as I walk uprightly.

How blessed I am to be able to lie down and sleep—knowing that I am
under Your ever-watchful care!

In the name of Jesus, Amen.

Healthy Interdependence

Just as our bodies have many parts and each part has a special function, so it is with Christ's body. We are many parts of one body, and we all belong to each other.

— Romans 12:4–5 (NLT)

Heavenly Father,

Help me to remember that You have designed Your church to be a healthy, interdependent group of individually gifted believers unified by the Spirit of God who is alive and at work in each one of us.

When I see the interdependence of all the intricate parts of my physical body and how they must all work together to maintain the health of my life, I am reminded of my responsibility to open myself to allow You to use the gifts You have placed in me as I fulfill my role in supporting the health of the body of Christ—that is, the church.

Help me to courageously do my part with humbleness of spirit and with confidence in You alone. Help me realize that there are a variety of vital roles that we as Christian brothers and sisters have been called to do and each one is just as critical to the health of the church as is my own role.

But despite the diversity of functions within that body that we may have, remind me that it is the same Holy Spirit that holds us together in unity of purpose as we move forward, each one doing his part to carry out God's plan for His church.

Help me to understand not only that others in this body depend on me but also remind me of my dependence on others within this fellowship, as we all strive together to keep the body healthy, effective, and growing for Your glory, God.

Help me to remember that You have designed Your church to be a healthy, interdependent group of individually gifted believers unified by the Spirit of God who is alive and at work in each one of us.

In the name of Jesus, Amen.

NOVEMBER 6TH

To Hear Your Voice and Follow

The sheep that are My own hear My voice and listen to Me; I know them, and they follow Me.

— JOHN 10:27 (AMP)

Lord Jesus,

From within this noisy world in which I live, I pray that You would quiet my heart to help me hear Your voice—and not only listen to You but act upon the Truth that You reveal to me—so that I would follow You more perfectly.

Help me truly see that I am one of Your very own—that You have called me to Yourself and redeemed me from my sin, that I might follow You all the days of my life.

Help me to understand that as one of Your own, You will always speak to me, always guide me in the best way for me to go, always protect me, always provide for me, and always keep me at peace, if I will listen to hear Your voice and follow You.

Help me to grasp that You fully know me—that there is nothing about me that is hidden from You—yet You still love me, want me, and have called me to be one of Your own, so that through my relationship with You, I would bring glory to You and to my Heavenly Father.

From within this noisy world in which I live, I pray that You would quiet my heart to help me hear Your voice—and not only listen to You but act upon the Truth that You reveal to me—so that I would follow You more perfectly.

In Your glorious name I pray, Amen.

Expressing Faith through Love

Love never fails.

— 1 CORINTHIANS 13:8A (NIV)

And without faith it is impossible to please God...

— HEBREWS 11:6A (NIV)

The only thing that counts is faith expressing itself through love.

— GALATIANS 5:6B (NIV)

Heavenly Father,

With a grateful heart and in response to Your love for me, help me to do only that which pleases You—expressing my faith through love.

Fill me with the love of Christ so I might learn how to love others with the same sacrificial love with which He first loved me—not with some less-than-adequate human love which self-centeredly picks and chooses when to love and whom to love.

Help me to love in obedience to Christ's command when I don't really want to love—when I'm just not feeling it—and when I can't see any apparent return for my efforts.

Help me to love sacrificially those I may think don't deserve my love—who may act oblivious to my actions of love—and to whom my love seems to make no difference.

Help me love in faith, having faith that my expression of Christ's love always accomplishes the purpose for which You have ordained it—whether by changing the other person or by bringing about a change in myself—and that it never falls uselessly to the ground.

With a grateful heart and in response to Your love for me, help me to do only that which pleases You—expressing my faith through love.

In the name of Jesus, Amen.

Never Forget the Good Things

Let all that I am praise the LORD;
with my whole heart, I will praise his holy name.
Let all that I am praise the LORD;
may I never forget the good things he does for me.
He forgives all my sins
and heals all my diseases.
He redeems me from death
and crowns me with love and tender mercies.
He fills my life with good things.
My youth is renewed like the eagle's!

— PSALM 103:1–5 (NLT)

Heavenly Father,

Let me never forget the good things You have done for me and continually show my gratitude in wholehearted praise to You!

I don't want to be that guy who always has something to complain about. I want to live my life continually recounting the good things You have done for me—not only as an encouragement to myself, but for the benefit of others as well!

For You alone are Holy, LORD, and worthy of all praise, honor, and glory.

You forgive all my sins—past, present, and future—and You alone are the healer of my diseases.

You have redeemed me from the death I deserve, clothed me in righteousness, and granted me eternal life in Christ.

Out of the favor You have given me, You have lifted me up to live in joy and peace, have made me Your child, and have crowned me with Your love and compassionate mercy.

Oh, how You have filled my life with good things! They surround me on every side! May I never take for granted Your goodness to me!

Let my heart be filled with thanksgiving as I look to see the beauty of Your creation, listen to hear the music that it sings, breathe to smell the fragrance that it offers, taste to enjoy the pleasure of its flavor, touch to feel the wonder of it all, and know that You created all of this for me.

You continually renew my life—replacing my old ways with a fresh, new life in You—as You lift me up and carry me on the winds of Your unfailing love!

Let me never forget the good things You have done for me and continually show my gratitude in wholehearted praise to You!

In the name of Jesus, Amen.

To Be the Light of the World

"You are the light of the world—like a city on a hilltop that cannot be hidden. No one lights a lamp and then puts it under a basket. Instead, a lamp is placed on a stand, where it gives light to everyone in the house. In the same way, let your good deeds shine out for all to see, so that everyone will praise your heavenly Father."

— Matthew 5:14–16 (NLT)

Heavenly Father,

In Your Word You have called us (the followers of Jesus Christ) "the light of the world"—like a city on a hilltop that cannot be hidden, like a lamp designed and purposed to give light to everyone in the house. May the good deeds I do shine out for all to see—in such a way that You alone will get the praise!

Make me keenly aware that if I am truly a follower of Jesus—the things I say and do cannot be hidden, but will be seen by those around me. Let it be that *the light that I am* would be fueled by the power of the presence of Christ within me.

As "the light of the world," help me to embrace the opportunity that You give me to give light to everyone around me—rather than foolishly try to hide the amazing goodness of the treasure that lives in me by Your Holy Spirit.

And may any words or acts of goodness I offer to others—any patience, kindness, mercy, forgiveness, or grace I give, any truth I gently offer—be motivated by the love of Christ and bring praise to You and You alone.

In Your Word You have called us (the followers of Jesus Christ) "the light of the world"—like a city on a hilltop that cannot be hidden, like a lamp designed and purposed to give light to everyone in the house. May the good deeds I do shine out for all to see—in such a way that You alone will get the praise!

In the name of Jesus, Amen.

Ongoing Conversation

Pray in the Spirit at all times and on every occasion. Stay alert and be persistent in your prayers for all believers everywhere.

— EPHESIANS 6:18 (NLT)

Dear God,

Let my prayers be an ongoing conversation with You as I walk out Your plan for me in this new day.

I don't want to be a person who cries out to You only after they have gone their own way and made a mess of things.

I want to listen for Your Spirit to guide me in every step I take along the way, so that I can be right where Your plan for my life takes me, because I know Your plan is for my good—for my protection and provision and peace.

Help me remember to talk with You in prayer, in every moment, on every occasion—good and bad—with a grateful heart asking for Your guidance and direction so I won't get off course.

Help me be alert to the promptings of the Holy Spirit as I lift up not only my own concerns and praises but also as I persist in prayer for the needs of my brothers and sisters in Christ.

Let my prayers be an ongoing conversation with You as I walk out Your plan for me in this new day.

In the name of Jesus, Amen.

To Do All Things through Christ

I know how to live on almost nothing or with everything. I have learned the secret of living in every situation, whether it is with a full stomach or empty, with plenty or little. For I can do everything through Christ, who gives me strength.

— PHILIPPIANS 4:12–13 (NLT)

Father God,

Help me hold onto the secret of living in every situation—keeping my eyes, my mind, and my heart fixed on Jesus Christ, the One who gives me all the strength I need to do everything that You ask me to do.

Help me remember that I can remain content if I keep a heart full of gratitude and faith—gratitude expressed by continual thankfulness for all the undeserved blessings of my life, and faith demonstrated by my unwavering confidence that You will always provide everything that I need to accomplish the plans and purposes You have for me.

Help me to rest in the truth that You provide for me out of Your unlimited knowledge, wisdom, and understanding—that You completely know me and the good plans You have for me—while I have only a cloudy memory of where I have been, a partial understanding of where I am now, and by Your grace perhaps a mere glimpse of where You are taking me.

Help me remember that the power You give to me through Christ is not so that I can do whatever I please with my life—or to have anything that I think I want—but rather that I might have the strength to do whatever You would require of me whether I have little or plenty.

Help me hold onto the secret of living in every situation—keeping my eyes, my mind, and my heart fixed on Jesus Christ, the One who gives me all the strength I need to do everything that You ask me to do.

In the name of Jesus, Amen.

The Work of Your Hand

But now, O LORD, You are our Father,
We are the clay, and You our potter;
And all of us are the work of Your hand.

— Isaiah 64:8 (NASB)

Heavenly Father,

Like a skilled potter patiently fashions his lump of clay according to his plans, so continue to make me into that uniquely original vessel which is perfectly suited for Your purposes and divinely marked for all to see—a product of Your gentle loving hand, one who bears within himself the image of his Maker.

It is You, O LORD, who has created me and given me life—and it is to You that I owe my life and my existence—so mold me as You will and make me Your very own!

With gentleness and patience, remove from me that which does not reflect Your long-planned purposes for my life—and smooth away any rough edges so that I would become all that You intend for me to become according to Your perfect design.

To those areas where I am vulnerable to failure, those places where I am weak, add the strength of Your grace—as You help me to seek out and more fully depend on Your presence in my life to carry me through.

According to the marvelous grace which You pour out on me, let others see Your hand at work in me and through me—that they might see You reflected in me—and be drawn to You to bring You glory.

Like a skilled potter patiently fashions his lump of clay according to his plans, so continue to make me into that uniquely original vessel which is perfectly suited for Your purposes and divinely marked for all to see—a product of Your gentle loving hand, one who bears within himself the image of his Maker.

In the name of Jesus, Amen.

With Grace, Truth, and Unfailing Love

Live wisely among those who are not believers, and make the most of every opportunity. Let your conversation be gracious and attractive so that you will have the right response for everyone.

— COLOSSIANS 4:5–6 (NLT)

Heavenly Father,

Help me to live wisely among those who are not believers, so that I might make the most of every opportunity to offer them truth and grace spoken in love.

Help me not to act foolishly—speaking thoughtlessly or reacting rashly toward others—but rather to walk in the wisdom that comes from knowing Your Word and applying it to my life with willing obedience.

Help me to watch for how You are working in the hearts of those around me and to make the most of every opportunity to show Your love to them—especially to those who do not know You as their Savior.

When I speak, fill my mouth with Your words so my conversation would not be my own—so they would be drawn to You, not driven away.

Help me always give the right response in every interaction that I have with them—that response which is crafted with grace and truth, and wrapped in the beauty of Your unfailing love for them.

Help me to live wisely among those who are not believers, so that I might make the most of every opportunity to offer them truth and grace spoken in love.

In the name of Jesus, Amen.

For His Unfailing Love, For His Wonderful Deeds

Let them give thanks to the LORD for his unfailing love
and his wonderful deeds for mankind,
for he satisfies the thirsty
and fills the hungry with good things.

— PSALM 107:8–9 (NIV)

Loving LORD,

Help me to establish new and better ways of thinking and acting—always
expressing my heartfelt gratitude to You for Your unfailing love and the
wonderful things You have done for us all.

For too long I have continued in my sinful tendencies to whine and complain about things that are not within my control to change—things that You either allowed or caused to happen—instead praising You for Your unfailing love for us and for all the amazing things You have done, are doing, and still have yet to do.

Help me to understand the seriousness of continuing down the pathway of complaining—a pathway which can lead me to a place of turmoil, even to the point of questioning Your goodness and rejecting the truth of Your Sovereignty.

Help me to remember that You long for me to express my thanks to You at all times—not because You need my thanksgiving but because within that attitude of gratefulness You cause my faith to grow, and are able to satisfy the hunger and thirst of my soul with good things.

Work in me to keep me grateful in all situations—so that I might stay at peace and experience the joy of knowing that You are always working for my ultimate good.

Help me to establish new and better ways of thinking and acting—always
expressing my heartfelt gratitude to You for Your unfailing love and the
wonderful things You have done for us all.

In the name of Jesus, Amen.

Keep Me Always Connected

"I am the vine, you are the branches. He who abides in Me, and I in him, bears much fruit; for without Me you can do nothing."

— JOHN 15:5 (NKJV)

Giver of Life,

Help me to never choose to walk down a path that separates me from You!

You are the life-giving source of my being. As long as I continue to walk according Your Holy Spirit—immersed in Your power, strength, and guided by Your Voice alone—my life will produce those things which a godly life *should* produce.

But if I choose to take a path that leads me away from an intimate, living union with You, then I will no longer be able to produce anything good because You—the Giver of all things good—will no longer be able to flow through me.

So keep me grafted into the power of Christ in me—so that I will remain nourished by the One who is the source of my very life, in order that I would bear much fruit all to Your glory, honor, and praise!

Help me to never choose to walk down a path that separates me from You!

In the name of Jesus, Amen.

Teach Me to Overcome Evil with Good

Do not be overcome by evil, but overcome evil with good.

— ROMANS 12:21 (NIV)

Heavenly Father,

Let me never be overcome by the evil that surrounds me but teach me to overcome that evil with good!

When I feel overwhelmed by the evil that is evident all around me, remind me of the power of Christ's love which has delivered me out of the enemy's hand and help me to enforce his defeat in my life—as You lead me to do the next good and right thing which You have placed before me—so that others will see Your glory and be drawn to You.

Remind me that good will always win over evil in the end, and help me to rest in the wonderful hope that if I remain surrendered to Your will, You will set all things right—every hurt, every offense, every injustice—according to the perfect timing of the working of Your plan, in order that You will receive the most glory.

Help me not be moved by how others act—understanding that other people are broken, just as I am broken, and in need of the healing and wholeness that can only be found in our Savior, Jesus Christ. Help me to see that they are not really operating out of their hate but are operating out of their hurt—and help me respond to that hurt with the compassionate love of Christ.

Let me never be overcome by the evil that surrounds me but teach me to overcome that evil with good!

In the name of Jesus, Amen.

To Tear My Heart with Grief and Repent

That is why the LORD says,
"Turn to me now, while there is time.
Give me your hearts.
Come with fasting, weeping, and mourning.
Don't tear your clothing in your grief,
but tear your hearts instead."
Return to the LORD your God,
for he is merciful and compassionate,
slow to get angry and filled with unfailing love.
He is eager to relent and not punish.

— JOEL 2:12–13 (NLT)

Merciful and Gracious LORD God,

Fully expose my every sin and bring me to heartfelt grief, so that my grief would lead me to true, godly repentance. And in that repentance let me return to You, so You can heal me and make me whole again.

Let any outward, visible manifestation of my grief over my sin be an accurate indication of how my heart is torn with grief—as I resolve to turn from that sin, to leave it behind forever, to throw myself once again on Your mercy, to ask for Your forgiveness and return to You.

Help me to make the choice to return to You now, with the confidence that comes from believing that You truly want to be in relationship with me—and in the understanding that You are full of mercy and compassion, slow to get angry, and filled with unfailing love.

Let me run back to You quickly with the assurance that You are willing to welcome me back, ready to relent from giving me the punishment that I deserve, and are eager to bring me back to that walk of obedience into which You first called me.

Fully expose my every sin and bring me to heartfelt grief, so that my grief would lead me to true, godly repentance. And in that repentance, let me return to You so You can heal me and make me whole again.

In the name of Jesus, Amen.

NOVEMBER 18TH

Alive and Powerful, Sharp and Cutting

For the word of God is alive and powerful. It is sharper than the sharpest two-edged sword, cutting between soul and spirit, between joint and marrow. It exposes our innermost thoughts and desires.

— HEBREWS 4:12 (NLT)

Heavenly Father,

Thank You that Your Word is so much more than just words on a page. Thank You that it is alive and powerful in me!

Never let me forget that Your Word is filled with Your life and power as the Almighty God. For it tells me who You are—as my Creator, Sustainer, Redeemer, and Sanctifier—and tells me who I am as Your child in Christ—so that when I go to Your Word and allow Your Word to wash over me, it heals me and makes me whole.

Help me to hear and understand Your Word—so that I can receive all the Truth that it contains into my heart. And then help me willingly and obediently apply that Truth to my life—as my loving and grateful response for all You have done for me.

Use Your Word to plunge deeply within me, to separate and expose the innermost thoughts and desires and motives of my soul and spirit—and to bring to light anything within me that is not in line with the Truth, so that I can repent and walk in the fullness of life to which You have called me.

Thank You that Your Word is so much more than just words on a page. Thank You that it is alive and powerful in me!

In the name of Jesus, Amen.

In Your Own Image

So God created mankind in his own image,
in the image of God he created them;
male and female he created them.

— GENESIS 1:27 (NIV)

I will praise You, for I am fearfully and wonderfully made;
Marvelous are Your works,
And that my soul knows very well.

— PSALM 139:14 (NKJV)

Creator God,

I stand amazed at the intricate and marvelous ways that You have fash-
ioned me in Your own image and have uniquely crafted me for Your
particular plans and purposes for me individually—and according to the
part I play in Your great plan for humanity as well.

Help me remember not only that I am Your greatly loved creation but also
that You created me in Your own image—that I bear the mark of my Creator as
Your very special creation, and I belong to You.

Help me never to disrespect myself by believing the lies that the enemy
would try to get me to believe—lies that are devised to keep me from being all
you want me to be—but rather help me to hold onto Your Truth and what it
reveals about who I am in Christ and to whom I belong.

Help me to realize that You know me perfectly and that You have always
had a plan for me—even before You knit me together in my mother's womb—
that I might bring You glory with my life.

I stand amazed at the intricate and marvelous ways that You have fash-
ioned me in Your own image and have uniquely crafted me for Your
particular plans and purposes for me individually and according to the
part I play in Your great plan for humanity as well.

In the name of Jesus, Amen.

Seeking the Kingdom of God, Above All Else

"So don't worry about these things, saying, 'What will we eat? What will we drink? What will we wear?' These things dominate the thoughts of unbelievers, but your heavenly Father already knows all your needs. Seek the Kingdom of God above all else, and live righteously, and he will give you everything you need."

— MATTHEW 6:31–33 (NLT)

Heavenly Father,

Help me always to seek You above all else—fully believing that You will give me everything that I need as I live uprightly before You.

Keep me from wasting my time by allowing my mind to be cluttered with the anxious worries that unbelievers invite to consume them all day and all night. I believe Your Word—help me to act like I do!

Help me to fix my attention on the answer—the answer that I always find revealed in Your Word—rather than the problem, since I know that You are already aware of my every need and are always working Your plan to provide for my needs if I will just place my trust in You.

As I commit to putting You above all else in my life—and You show me Your faithfulness by supplying every spiritual, mental, emotional, and physical need I may have—don't allow me to let the "what if" lies of the enemy rob me of the privilege that You have placed before me of walking obediently and fully living out Your perfect will for me each day.

Help me always to seek You above all else—fully believing that You will give me everything that I need as I live uprightly before You.

In the name of Jesus, Amen.

God's Will for You
Who Belong to Christ Jesus

Always be joyful. Never stop praying. Be thankful in all circumstances,
for this is God's will for you who belong to Christ Jesus.

— 1 THESSALONIANS 5:16–18 (NLT)

Heavenly Father,

Let me remain in the perfect peace that You offer to all those who belong
to Christ Jesus—those who, in accord with Your will, are joyful, prayer-
ful, and thankful in all circumstances.

Regardless of how I may feel at any particular moment, may my joy—that
deep happiness that is fueled by continuing to walk with You in faith—remain
constant and unchanged.

Regardless of how busy and disordered my day might become, may I
continue unceasingly in prayerful conversation with You—the only One who
brings order to my chaos and peace to all things.

Regardless of what circumstances I may find myself in, remind me to
remain thankful—continually expressing my gratefulness to You from the
innermost parts of my heart—knowing that You are working in all things for
my good.

Let me remain in the perfect peace that You offer to all those who belong
to Christ Jesus—who, in accord with Your will, are joyful, prayerful, and
thankful in all circumstances.

In the name of Jesus, Amen.

To Look at the Heart

"The LORD doesn't see things the way you see them. People judge by outward appearance, but the LORD looks at the heart."

— 1 SAMUEL 16:7B (NLT)

O LORD, who sees each heart,

Help me not to judge others based on their outward appearance, but rather help me to take the time to see them as You see them—at the level of their hearts—and then empower me to love them as You do.

Keep me from being that person who makes snap judgments about others based on what he sees on the surface—discounting another person's value with the glance of his eye.

Rather, teach me to take the time to try to understand the heart of each person that I encounter—to search out the treasures that You have hidden there just waiting to be discovered.

Then help me to see what You see, LORD—a soul worth saving, a life worth sacrificing Your only begotten Son to redeem—and give me that kind of love for them.

Help me not to judge others based on their outward appearance, but rather help me to take the time to see them as You see them—at the level of their hearts—and then empower me to love them as You do.

In the name of Jesus, Amen.

Come Before His Presence with Thanksgiving!

Oh come, let us sing to the LORD!
Let us shout joyfully to the Rock of our salvation.
Let us come before His presence with thanksgiving;
Let us shout joyfully to Him with psalms.
For the LORD is the great God,
And the great King above all gods.

— PSALM 95:1–3 (NKJV)

My LORD and my Great King,

Establish within me new, stronger, and truer pathways of thought, word, and action—pathways that spring forth out of a heart overflowing with gratitude for who You are and for all the wondrous things You have done for me!

Let songs and shouts of joy erupt from my grateful heart and be lifted up to You in spontaneous praise and worship—for You are the Rock, the immovable and firm foundation that every aspect of my life is built upon! You are the God of my salvation—the author of my freedom over the sin of this evil world!

Let me come before You as Your beloved child—entering confidently into Your Holy Presence and remaining and abiding with You, that I might know You as You are—and continue to give my life back to You in thanksgiving!

Let me always praise You with shouts and songs of joy—for You are the Great and Sovereign God! You are far above all other so-called gods, and the Great and Almighty King of all, forever!

Thank You for choosing me to be Your very own child, for blessing my life with every good thing, and for allowing me to experience the joy and peace that comes as I choose You back—as my only God and King forevermore!

Establish within me new, stronger, and truer pathways of thought, word, and action—pathways that spring forth out of a heart overflowing with gratitude for who You are and for all the wondrous things You have done for me!

In the name of Jesus, Amen.

No Room for Divided Loyalty

Come close to God and God will come close to you. Wash your hands, you sinners; purify your hearts, for your loyalty is divided between God and the world. Let there be tears for what you have done. Let there be sorrow and deep grief. Let there be sadness instead of laughter, and gloom instead of joy. Humble yourselves before the Lord and he will lift you up in honor.

— JAMES 4:8–10 (NLT)

Heavenly Father,

Help me as I seek to come closer to You with each new day, so I might live in the blessings that come out of fully experiencing Your presence with me—seeing Your power working within me, through me, and all around me.

Grant me the courage to allow Your Spirit to reveal my own heart to me—to point out that which I must change—and then cleanse my heart, replacing my sin with the desire to live in Your purity.

Give me the strength I need to resist the temptation to compromise my loyalty to You—that draw to give into the pleasures of this world—for there is no room for divided loyalty, if I want to live in close relationship to You.

Allow me the sincerity of heart to express my shame for my sin with great sorrow before You—to deeply grieve over my disloyalty—and in repentance, to turn from my sin and to go a better way.

Help me to approach You in complete humility—recognizing the *great insignificance* of what I have to offer when compared to the *great significance* of what You offer me—trusting that You will take me as I am and lift me up in honor as Your beloved child in Your everlasting arms.

Help me as I seek to come closer to You with each new day, so I might live in the blessings that come out of fully experiencing Your presence with me—seeing Your power working within me, through me, and all around me.

In the name of Jesus, Amen.

Love, Obedience, and Victory for Those Who Believe

Loving God means keeping his commandments, and his commandments are not burdensome. For every child of God defeats this evil world, and we achieve this victory through our faith. And who can win this battle against the world? Only those who believe that Jesus is the Son of God.

— 1 JOHN 5:3–5 (NLT)

Heavenly Father,

Help me to love You ever more deeply with each new day and demonstrate my love for You through my obedience to Your commandments—as I secure my victory over this evil world as an act of my faith, because I believe that Jesus is Your Son.

I know that when my obedience to You flows from my love for You, it is not a burden for me to obey Your commands but rather a joy—which brings the blessings of peace, protection, and provision to my life.

And though I am surrounded by the evil of this fallen world, You have given me the victory over it—as Your beloved child—and I claim and enforce this victory by believing in my Lord and Savior, Jesus Christ.

So let me walk more fully in victory over this evil world—as I fight for a deeper love for You, a greater faith in You, and a more obedient heart after You.

Help me to love You ever more deeply with each new day and demonstrate my love for You through my obedience to Your commandments—as I secure my victory over this evil world as an act of my faith, because I believe that Jesus is Your Son.

In the name of Jesus, Amen.

Doing Good with Christ as My Example

For God called you to do good, even if it means suffering, just as Christ suffered for you. He is your example, and you must follow in his steps.
> *He never sinned,*
> *nor ever deceived anyone.*
> *He did not retaliate when he was insulted,*
> *nor threaten revenge when he suffered.*
> *He left his case in the hands of God,*
> *who always judges fairly.*

— 1 PETER 2:21–23 (NLT)

Dear Father God,

Help me to do good—even if it means suffering because of it, as long as I remain here on earth.

Thank You for the perfect example set by Your Son, Jesus Christ. Help me to follow in His steps.

Help me to turn my back on sin—and to be obedient to Christ in all my ways

Help me to be honest, open, and transparent in all my affairs—to live in truth and never act deceitfully.

When I am reviled or insulted, help me to control my flesh and my thoughts—as I choose not to retaliate or threaten to get even—even when I *suffer unjustly* as I follow after Christ.

Help me rest in the peace that comes as I continue to entrust my case, indeed my very life, into Your loving hands—with full confidence that You will always judge fairly.

Help me to do good—even if it means suffering because of it, as long as I remain here on earth.

In the name of Jesus, Amen.

Clothed with Joy!

You have turned my mourning into joyful dancing.
You have taken away my clothes of mourning and clothed me with joy,
that I might sing praises to you and not be silent.
O LORD my God, I will give you thanks forever!

— PSALM 30:11–12 (NLT)

Heavenly Father,

Oh that I would never stop singing Your praises and never let my thanks-
giving be silenced! For You have done great and wonderful things for me!

The path I once walked down was leading me to defeat, destruction, and death—as my sin separated me farther and farther from You. Then, at last, I heard You calling me home to You.

I mourned greatly over how I had allowed my sin to make a mess of my life and distance me from You. I acknowledged my helpless state and asked You to forgive me and save me. And You looked on me, saw my repentance, and out of Your compassionate and unfailing love for me, forgave me of my sin and saved me completely—by the blood of Your Son, Jesus.

You turned my mourning into joyful dancing—took away my clothes of mourning over my regrettable past and exchanged them for clothes of inexpressible joy for the good things You have planned for me—so that I might forever sing praises to You and not be silent.

Oh that I would never stop singing Your praises and never let my thanks-
giving be silenced! For You have done great and wonderful things for me!

In the name of Jesus, Amen.

For the LORD Is Good

Enter into His gates with thanksgiving,
And into His courts with praise.
Be thankful to Him, and bless His name.
For the LORD is good;
His mercy is everlasting,
And His truth endures to all generations.

— PSALM 100:4–5 (NKJV)

Loving and Merciful God,

May I always come to You with thanksgiving in my heart and praise on my lips for the goodness and mercy that You pour over me with each new day.

May it always be my first desire to seek You out and enter into Your presence—in good times and in bad—with gratitude for all that You have done for me and praise for who You are.

May I be encouraged by Your goodness, comforted in Your boundless mercy and never-ending love, and strengthened in my faith by Your unchanging truth which endures forever.

May I always come to You with thanksgiving in my heart and praise on my lips for the goodness and mercy that You pour over me with each new day.

In the name of Jesus, Amen.

Alert to the Threat of Attack, But at Perfect Peace in God

Be alert and of sober mind. Your enemy the devil prowls around like a roaring lion looking for someone to devour. Resist him, standing firm in the faith, because you know that the family of believers throughout the world is undergoing the same kind of sufferings.

— 1 PETER 5:8–9 (NIV)

Gracious and Merciful God,

Help me to be alert to the threat of attack from the devil, but still remain at perfect peace in You—knowing that if I stand strong in my faith, You will deliver me from all the traps he has set for me by the power of Christ in me.

Keep me on guard against his deceptions and aware of his divisive tactics. Remind me that he is battling for my soul—my mind, my will, and my emotions—and that the battle is primarily waged in my mind.

As I carefully hold and consider every thought that passes through my mind, let Your Spirit warn me when a thought does not align itself with the Truth of Your Word. And let me discard any thought that contradicts that Truth for what it is—a lie from the enemy meant to steal, kill, and destroy.

Remind me that I don't have to be afraid because he can only harm me by deceiving me into believing his lies—and while he may make a lot of noise, he is defeated and cannot have any control over me *that I don't give him.*

Help me trust, LORD, that You have already saved me from the enemy— that the victory is mine to take—as I stand firm in my faith and resist his attacks.

Keep me mindful that the whole family of believers is in this same battle with me—and that we are most effective when, in unity, we fight together against this common foe.

Help me to be alert to the threat of attack from the devil, but still remain at perfect peace in You—knowing that if I stand strong in my faith, You will deliver me from all the traps he has set for me by the power of Christ in me.

In the name of Jesus, Amen.

Weary of the Heavy Burden,
Let Me Find Your Rest

"For I have given rest to the weary and joy to the sorrowing."

— JEREMIAH 31:25 (NLT)

Then Jesus said, "Come to me, all of you who are weary and carry heavy burdens, and I will give you rest."

— MATTHEW 11:28 (NLT)

Heavenly Father,

Make me weary of the heavy burden that my sin brings upon me and sorrowful for those times when my thoughts, words, and actions do not honor You—that I might flee from the evil that keeps me bound and fully experience the rest that I can only find in Your Holy Presence.

Help me to repent—to turn my back on and walk away from anything that separates me from You—for only in repentance can I fully experience the abundance of mercy, grace, forgiveness, and love that You have for me.

Help me more fully understand Your ways and the extent of Your love for me—even though I could never fully grasp them completely—that I would respond to Your great love in grateful and willing obedience to all Your commands and instructions.

And in that obedience, help me always to be continually coming to Jesus—humbly submitting my will to His—so that I will find the peace and joy that comes only when I place all my hope in Him, and there find rest for my soul.

Make me weary of the heavy burden that my sin brings upon me and sorrowful for those times when my thoughts, words, and actions do not honor You—that I might flee from the evil that keeps me bound and fully experience the rest that I can only find in Your Holy Presence.

In the name of Jesus, Amen.

The Choice Between Life and Death, Between Blessings and Curses

"Today I have given you the choice between life and death, between blessings and curses. Now I call on heaven and earth to witness the choice you make. Oh, that you would choose life, so that you and your descendants might live! You can make this choice by loving the LORD your God, obeying him, and committing yourself firmly to him."

— DEUTERONOMY 30:19–20A (NLT)

O LORD, My God,

Thank You for setting this choice before me. Help me daily to choose the blessing of life—help me to choose You.

Each day You give me the choice over the path that I take—whether it be a path of life or a path of death, a path of blessing or a path of curses.

In Your Word I find Your encouragement to choose life—so that not only I can truly live but that my descendants might truly live as well.

You show me in Your Word that I make the right choice when I love You, when I obey You, as an outflow of that love for You, and when I commit myself firmly to You without wavering.

In choosing You I am choosing life—for You are the only One who can give me life, preserve my life, revive my life, and lengthen my life.

Thank You for setting this choice before me. Help me daily to choose the blessing of life—help me to choose You.

In the name of Jesus, Amen.

To Enter in Like a Child

"I tell you the truth, anyone who doesn't receive the Kingdom of God like a child will never enter it."

— MARK 10:15 (NLT)

Loving Father God,

Teach me how to come to You like a child, that I might enter into all that You have for me—both in the here-and-now and for eternity to come.

Teach me how to come to You with childlike humility—knowing that I have only my heart to bring to You and that I can do no good thing apart from You.

Teach me how to come to You with childlike dependence—knowing I am helpless and hopeless without You but still that I can still find my help and hope in You.

Teach me how to come to You with childlike inquisitiveness—that I might gain knowledge and grow in wisdom, and leave behind my foolish ways.

Teach me how to come to You with childlike faith—asking confidently for Your best for me and believing You will give me every good thing You have for me.

Teach me how to come to You with childlike obedience—willingly going and doing that which You require of me, knowing You always have my best interests at heart.

Teach me how to come to You with childlike gratefulness—giving thanks and rejoicing in all situations for all of Your goodness, knowing You work all things together for my good.

Teach me how to come to You with childlike love—a love that is purely motivated and freely offered, just because of who You are.

Teach me how to come to You like a child—that I might enter into all that You have for me both in the here-and-now and for eternity to come.

In the name of Jesus, Amen.

To Be Your Disciple

In the same way, those of you who do not give up everything you have cannot be my disciples.

— LUKE 14:33 (NIV)

Father God,

Move within my heart to make me a disciple of Christ Jesus!

Help me to see that all those things that I may call my own—whether they are possessions, plans that I have for my life, or even relationships with family and friends—are in truth only on loan from You and are only entrusted to me to manage according to Your will.

Help me to be *ready and willing* to surrender my *perceived* ownership of those things, so that I can fully follow You even when where You are taking me requires me to give up things I hold dear.

Help me to realize that when I demonstrate an unwillingness to release those things to You, I am practicing nothing short of idolatry.

Help me to understand that holding on to things is acting out of my fear rather than a testimony of my faith in You alone.

Help me to believe in Your teachings, to rest and take my peace in the sacrifice that You made for me, to abide with Your Spirit within me, and to imitate Your example as a true disciple.

Move within my heart to make me a disciple of Christ Jesus!

In the name of Jesus, Amen.

Blood Bought Peace

"Peace I leave with you, My peace I give to you; not as the world gives do I give to you. Let not your heart be troubled, neither let it be afraid."

— JOHN 14:27 (NKJV)

Prince of Peace,

Thank You for leaving us Your gift of peace—that gift You purchased for us with Your own blood.

Thank You that I receive Your gift of peace when—in response to Your great love for me—I truly believe that I have been completely reconciled with God by Your sacrifice on the cross.

Thank You that within this reconciliation I can find freedom from all fears—and I can live in Your peace at all times.

Thank You that it is not like the peace that the world offers—which is imperfect, untrustworthy, temporary, dependent on circumstances, and tainted by the sin of man.

Thank You that Your peace is a peace that no one else can offer—it is perfect, everlasting, not dependent on what the world does or does not do, nor on the circumstances that I may face.

Thank You that as I believe and choose to receive Your peace, it resides deep within my spirit—and it goes far beyond my ability to comprehend it.

Thank You that within the peace You give me, You have given me the power to keep my heart from being troubled—by things from my past, by any trials or struggles that I face today, or by the uncertainties of tomorrow and beyond.

Thank You for leaving us Your gift of peace—that gift You purchased for us with Your own blood.

In Your Precious and Perfect Name, Jesus, Amen.

Keep My Lamp Burning

You, LORD, keep my lamp burning;
my God turns my darkness into light.

— Psalm 18:28 (NIV)

Light of my life,

Let the oil of Your Spirit always keep the light of my lamp burning brightly
within me—illuminating the path of my heart—as You turn my darkness
into glorious light!

When troubles and trials seek to overwhelm me, I thank You that Your
great love for me continually brings light into my heart—to comfort my spirit
with hope.

Thank You that when I find it hard to see the way which You would have
me go, if I step out in faith and believe that You will lead me, You make my way
plain before me and order my steps—lighting each next step along the way.

Thank You that Your Holy Spirit is always at work within my heart—to
drive out my darkness and to make more space for Christ—so I can live in that
place of peace, provision, protection, and sustaining joy that I can only find
in Him.

Cause the light of Christ to shine through me so that others will be drawn
to Christ in me—and may experience for themselves the joy of Your Presence
and the depth of Your love for them.

Let the oil of Your Spirit always keep the light of my lamp burning brightly
within me—illuminating the path of my heart—as You turn my darkness
into glorious light!

In the name of Jesus, Amen.

No Purpose of Yours Can Be Thwarted

"I know that You can do all things,
And that no purpose of Yours can be thwarted."

— JOB 42:2 (NASB)

Almighty God,

Expand the limits of my heart, my mind, and my faith, so that I might
more fully embrace the Truth of Your unlimited strength and power,
unlimited knowledge and wisdom, unlimited authority and dominion,
and unlimited love for me as Your child.

Help me to repent of all the times when, by my thoughts, words, or actions, I have shown a lack of faith in the Truth of Your greatness, glory, and perfection—times when I have put limits on what I believed that You were able or were willing to do.

Help me to see, believe, and take comfort in the Truth that Your purposes cannot be thwarted—cannot be restrained or prevented—even by the mistakes and misjudgments I make in my life. You work all things—good and bad—together for my good and interweave them all into the perfection of Your plan!

So help me to move boldly forward with my life, trusting that You will guide my every step and position me in the place that You want me to be, so that You can receive the greatest glory—because of Your unfailing love for us all.

Expand the limits of my heart, my mind, and my faith, so that I might
more fully embrace the Truth of Your unlimited strength and power,
unlimited knowledge and wisdom, unlimited authority and dominion,
and unlimited love for me as Your child.

In the name of Jesus, Amen.

Fully Armed

Therefore put on the full armor of God, so that when the day of evil comes, you may be able to stand your ground, and after you have done everything, to stand.

Stand firm then, with the belt of truth buckled around your waist, with the breastplate of righteousness in place, and with your feet fitted with the readiness that comes from the gospel of peace. In addition to all this, take up the shield of faith, with which you can extinguish all the flaming arrows of the evil one. Take the helmet of salvation and the sword of the Spirit, which is the word of God.

— EPHESIANS 6:13–17 (NIV)

Heavenly Father,

Thank You for supplying me with all the armor that I need to stand firmly against the attacks of the enemy.

Help me to remember that in this spiritual battle that is raging all around me, the enemy will try to disarm me by speaking lies to my mind in repeated attempts to deceive me into believing that he has power to harm me—to persuade me to loosen the belt of Your truth that holds me together, and allow his lies to cause me to fall apart.

Help me to be ready for his attacks against my heart—for those times when he attacks my emotions to say I am not worthy—by remembering my righteousness comes from Christ and by His sacrifice for my sin I am made worthy—spotlessly clean before You.

Help me to stand against his attempts to quiet my declaration of the peace that comes to all who will accept the Good News of Jesus Christ—and stand ready to run to the battle, allowing the great hope of Your salvation through Christ to cause me to carry this truth to others.

Help me to hold the shield of my faith in You before me so that the enemy's flaming arrows of insults, setbacks, and temptations are extinguished before they can reach me.

Help me to protect my mind from his attempts to get me to doubt You and to doubt my salvation by blocking his lies with helmet of my knowledge of the truth of Your Word.

Help me to use the Sword of the Spirit—by speaking the truth of the Bible—to turn back the attacks and send the enemy fleeing from me.

Thank You for supplying me with all the armor that I need to stand firmly against the attacks of the enemy.

In the name of Jesus, Amen.

Clothed in His Presence

The night is almost gone; the day of salvation will soon be here. So remove your dark deeds like dirty clothes, and put on the shining armor of right living. Because we belong to the day, we must live decent lives for all to see. Don't participate in the darkness of wild parties and drunkenness, or in sexual promiscuity and immoral living, or in quarreling and jealousy. Instead, clothe yourself with the presence of the Lord Jesus Christ. And don't let yourself think about ways to indulge your evil desires.

— ROMANS 13:12–14 (NLT)

Awesome LORD God,

Thank You for the hope that is mine—because the evil age in which we now live is coming to an end and the day of salvation is nearly upon us.

In the time that I have left, before You call me home, help me to remove any dark deeds with which I have clothed myself and put on the shining armor of right living—that the example of my repentance would be a testimony to the power of Christ at work within me, which brings light out of such darkness.

Help me to live a decent life—at all times and in all situations—so that others might see that I don't belong to the night and would be drawn to the light of presence of the Lord Jesus Christ in me.

Help me to guard my heart and resist those temptations that would draw me again into the works of darkness—that would try to pollute my thoughts, words, and actions.

And help me to make my identity the very presence of Christ within me—as I make His love my own, follow in the footsteps of His wisdom, find my strength in His power, and walk in His peace and grace toward all those around me.

Thank You for the hope that is mine—because the evil age in which we now live is coming to an end and the day of salvation is nearly upon us.

In the name of Jesus, Amen.

The LORD's Purpose Prevails

Many are the plans in a person's heart,
but it is the LORD's purpose that prevails.

— PROVERBS 19:21 (NIV)

Sovereign LORD,

Help me always to lift up my plans before You—with my palms wide
open—as I submit my will to Your will, my plan to Your plan, and give
my life over to Your perfect purpose.

You know every plan of my heart—before it is ever formed in my thoughts.

You know when I make my plans in perfect concert with Your will for me.
And You know when I make my plans without first considering or consulting
You at all.

You know when I make my plans after much prayer and meditation on
Your Word. And You know when I make my plans in spite of what I have heard
from You, in great foolishness and selfishness.

Yet despite all my plans, it is always Your purpose that prevails.

So mold my plans to accomplish Your purposes and help me to have faith to
believe that Your plans are always best—and that Your plans cannot be stopped.

And help me to remember that Your plans are always crafted with my best
interest at heart—and for my ultimate good—a reflection of Your perfect and
unfailing love for me.

Help me always to lift up my plans before You—with my palms wide
open—as I submit my will to Your will, my plan to Your plan, and give
my life over to Your perfect purpose.

In the name of Jesus, Amen.

The Joy I Find Down the Path of Life

You will make known to me the path of life;
In Your presence is fullness of joy;
In Your right hand there are pleasures forever.

— Psalm 16:11 (NASB)

Heavenly Father,

It is in You that I have placed all of my trust, for I know that You will
always lead me down the path of life—to that place of joy and peace that
is found only in Your Presence.

Thank You that as I consistently seek to hear Your voice, as I listen for Your
Holy Spirit within me to speak to every decision I make, You are always faithful
to lead me down paths that bring me life—life that is full, rich, and free; life that
fulfills Your will for me.

Thank You that as I remain in Your Presence and allow the power of Christ
in me to carry me through every hardship I face, the weight of the cares of
this world is lifted from my shoulders—and my joy is made complete in serving You.

Thank You that Your invitation—to me and to all believers—is that I remain
at Your right hand and enjoy the pleasure of living in the protection, provision,
and peace of Your Presence with me, forever and ever.

It is in You that I have placed all of my trust, for I know that You will
always lead me down the path of life—to that place of joy and peace that
is found only in Your Presence.

In the name of Jesus, Amen.

Faith, Love, and Hope

We remember before our God and Father your work produced by faith, your labor prompted by love, and your endurance inspired by hope in our Lord Jesus Christ.

— 1 Thessalonians 1:3 (NIV)

My God and Father,

Make me ever mindful that a person's best work is produced by faith, that a person's most honest labor is prompted by love, and that a person's strength to endure all things can only be inspired by hope in our Lord Jesus Christ.

Help me to remember to give thanks for those people that You have placed in my life whose best work is produced out of their absolute faith in You—for their example of steadfast faith, which challenges me to trust You more.

And to give thanks for those who emulate well Christ's labor of love toward all those He died to save—whose example of Christ's love in action prompts me to love more deeply and express that love more completely.

And to give thanks for those whose endurance is made possible only by their hope in our Lord Jesus Christ—for their example of long-suffering, which inspires me to endure my struggles because of the hope that stands forever before me.

Let me always aspire to work by faith, labor in love, and endure through hope—as I make reflecting Your Presence within me my great obsession.

Make me ever mindful that a person's best work is produced by faith, that a person's most honest labor is prompted by love, and that a person's strength to endure all things can only be inspired by hope in our Lord Jesus Christ.

In the name of Jesus, Amen.

Submit to God, Resist the Devil

Submit yourselves, then, to God. Resist the devil, and he will flee from you.

— JAMES 4:7 (NIV)

Heavenly Father,

Help me not to forget that as I humbly submit myself in obedience to You in all things, You give me the power to resist the attacks of the enemy so that he has no choice but to run from me in fear.

Help me always humbly and willingly acknowledge Your authority over me, Your power at work in me through Your Holy Spirit, and the authority that is given to me in the name of Jesus as a follower of Christ.

Help me to remember that the only power the enemy has to use against me is that which I give him—when because of his lies, I begin to doubt the Truth of Your Word.

Don't let me forget that You alone have the authority over me, and it is Your Word that gives me the authority to act on Your command to resist the attacks of the devil, with the full confidence that he must flee from me.

Help me not to forget that as I humbly submit myself in obedience to You in all things, You give me the power to resist the attacks of the enemy so that he has no choice but to run from me in fear.

In the name of Jesus, Amen.

Nothing Too Hard

"I am the LORD, the God of all mankind. Is anything too hard for me?"
— JEREMIAH 32:27 (NIV)

Dear LORD,

You ask if there is anything too hard for You? And I would be quick to say, "Nothing is too hard for my God!"

But far too often my twisted thoughts, my careless words, and my foolish actions betray me for having put the difficulties I face above Your power to handle them.

How is it that I can stand before You—the Creator of all that there is, the One who put it all in order and set it all in motion—and declare to Your face, by my behavior, that You are too weak to handle the particulars of my circumstances?

How can I stand before You and build a case against Your claim of absolute power based on the wisdom of this world—when You are not dependent on this world for Your wisdom, Your power, or Your absolute authority?

How can I stand here anxiously before You, worried about what might happen next, when by doing so I am in effect saying to Your face, "I don't trust You!"? Why can't I see that You are the only One worthy of my complete and total trust?

Forgive me, LORD, for losing faith and taking up my fears! Have mercy on me and help me always remember who You are—the self-sufficient and self-existent God of all mankind!

You ask if there is anything too hard for You? And I would be quick to say, "Nothing is too hard for my God!"

In the name of Jesus, Amen.

God's Rightful Place in My Heart

Dear children, keep away from anything that might take God's place in your hearts.

— 1 JOHN 5:21 (NLT)

Heavenly Father,

Help me to keep away from anything that might take Your place in my heart—from any false god that I might put before You.

Don't ever allow me to idolize a person—to allow my relationship with them to become more important to me than my relationship with You. But rather, help me to keep my relationship with You in proper order, so that all of my other relationships will fall in order as well and bring You glory.

Don't ever allow me to idolize a place—to make where I am now more important than my obedience to Your calling to stretch myself to go somewhere new, or to do something different. Make me willing and obedient to go wherever You call me—knowing You will never leave me, so I have nothing to fear.

Don't ever allow me to idolize a thing—to believe that I need some "thing" more than I need to believe that You are the source of everything I need, the giver of all good things. Let me realize, instead, that everything I have is Yours and is only placed temporarily in my hands for me to use for Your glory, honor, and praise.

Don't ever allow me to idolize an idea—substituting it for Truth. But rather, help me walk in the freedom, the joy, and the peace that comes from knowing the Truth of Your Word and walking in faithful obedience to it.

Don't ever allow me to idolize myself—thinking that it is somehow by my own power that I live, or claiming that I have some right to live as I choose—as if I were wiser, higher, or more powerful than the One who made me and orders my every step according to His will and purpose.

Help me to keep away from anything that might take Your place in my heart—from any false god that I might put before You.

In the name of Jesus, Amen.

Fearing People Is not Trusting the LORD

Fearing people is a dangerous trap,
but trusting the LORD means safety.

— Proverbs 29:25 (NLT)

Loving and Caring LORD,

Keep me far from the dangerous trap of fearing people—whether it is a
fear of what they may think of me, fear of what they might try to do to
me, or even a fear of what they might choose to do to themselves—and
help me find my safety and rest in trusting You.

Don't allow me to let my fear of people keep me from doing that which You
have called me to do, or from being who You have called me to be—but help
me keep my eyes focused on You, so that I won't be enslaved by the power that
the fear of others can hold over me.

Let me fear You only—to respect, reverence, and honor You with wholehearted trust—knowing that You are well able to turn what others intend for
evil, into great good, and so protect me and provide for my every need, through
Christ Jesus.

And let me fully experience the liberating freedom of rejoicing in all things
by placing them and leaving them all—both the overwhelmingly big and the
seemingly small—in Your hands for safe keeping, with the absolute assured-
ness that You are always in control and want the very best for us all.

Keep me far from the dangerous trap of fearing people—whether it is a
fear of what they may think of me, fear of what they might try to do to
me, or even fear of what they might choose to do to themselves—and help
me find my safety and rest in trusting You.

In the name of Jesus, Amen.

Knowing What I Ought to Do

Remember, it is sin to know what you ought to do and then not do it.

— JAMES 4:17 (NLT)

Heavenly Father,

All my sin is found in my disobedience.

Help me to see how foolishly I see the sin of my *actions* as being of greater consequence than the sin of my *inaction*.

I know that You have given me instructions on what I *should not* do, in order to protect me from those paths that lead to destruction and death.

But help me not to forget that You have also instructed me in things that I *should do*, in order to bring me joy and peace—so that I might live life more abundantly.

Help me to see the foolishness in having been given the light of life but not walking in the fullness of that light in total obedience—doing both those things that You have told me to do, as well as fleeing from that which You have warned me against.

All my sin is found in my disobedience.

In the name of Jesus, Amen.

DECEMBER 17TH

A Shield Around Me

But you, O LORD, are a shield around me;
you are my glory, the one who holds my head high.

— PSALM 3:3 (NLT)

O LORD my God,

Even when I am surrounded by troubles on every side, remind me that
You are a shield around me, You are my Glory, You are the One who
holds my head high—giving me the victory!

You are not a shield *that I must carry and direct* toward the attacks that come against me—as if its usefulness was up to my own strength, skill, or ability.

But rather, You are a shield that *continually and completely* surrounds me on every side, in total protection against the attacks of the enemy—as I place all my hope and trust in You.

You are all that I glory in and all of my worship and praise goes to You alone! For You are the one who carries me through every trial or trouble I face. You hold my head high—not allowing me to fall—so my victory is made complete in You!

Even when I am surrounded by troubles on every side, remind me that
You are a shield around me, You are my Glory, You are the One who
holds my head high—giving me the victory!

In the name of Jesus, Amen.

Using the Gifting of God

God has given each of you a gift from his great variety of spiritual gifts. Use them well to serve one another. Do you have the gift of speaking? Then speak as though God himself were speaking through you. Do you have the gift of helping others? Do it with all the strength and energy that God supplies. Then everything you do will bring glory to God through Jesus Christ. All glory and power to him forever and ever! Amen.

—1 PETER 4:10–11 (NLT)

Heavenly Father,

Help me to use well the particular spiritual gifts that You have graciously given to me—that I might serve others by Your power and bring You glory as I live my life through Christ.

Help me not to compare my gifts to the gifts that others may have received—but rather help me to understand that what You have granted to me uniquely enables me to fulfill Your perfect plans and purposes for me.

Help me never forget that the working of these gifts within me requires me to be willing and obedient and submitted to the Holy Spirit at work in me and through me—so that whatever I do in service to others is not done with my own words or in my own strength but is done with the words, strength, and energy that You supply.

In everything I do to help others, let my thoughts, words, and actions bring Glory to You through Christ—to whom belongs all glory and power, forever and ever!

Help me to use well the particular spiritual gifts that You have graciously given to me—that I might serve others by Your power and bring You glory as I live my life through Christ.

In the name of Jesus, Amen.

Offering a Continual Sacrifice of Praise

For this world is not our permanent home; we are looking forward to a home yet to come. Therefore, let us offer through Jesus a continual sacrifice of praise to God, proclaiming our allegiance to his name. And don't forget to do good and to share with those in need. These are the sacrifices that please God.

— HEBREWS 13:14–16 (NLT)

Heavenly Father,

Let my life be a continual sacrifice of praise to You! Help me submit my every thought, word, and action to the power of Christ in me—as I proclaim my allegiance to His name and journey on toward my forever home with You.

Help me to see this world for what it truly is and not lose sight of the fact that this world is not my permanent home but is just a part of the journey that I am taking to get to that place which Christ has prepared for me.

As I move through the troubles of this life, make me bold to proclaim my allegiance to Christ—as I joyfully and continually give a sacrifice of praise to You with a grateful heart.

Remind me that whatever I gather here on earth must remain here, and only what I give away here on earth—both things tangible and intangible—can be measured for eternity.

Help me with willing obedience to do good at all times and freely share with those in need—those gifts and blessings You have entrusted to me for the time I remain here on earth—so that I might please You and so my time spent here on earth might count for eternity.

Let my life be a continual sacrifice of praise to You! Help me submit my every thought, word, and action, to the power of Christ in me—as I proclaim my allegiance to His name and journey on toward my forever home with You.

In the name of Jesus, Amen.

A New Heart and a New Spirit Within

"Then I will sprinkle clean water on you, and you will be clean. Your filth will be washed away, and you will no longer worship idols.

And I will give you a new heart, and I will put a new spirit in you. I will take out your stony, stubborn heart and give you a tender, responsive heart.

And I will put my Spirit in you so that you will follow my decrees and be careful to obey my regulations."

— EZEKIEL 36:25–27 (NLT)

Gracious Heavenly Father,

Let that new heart that You placed within me—when You first made me clean in Your sight—always remain tender and responsive to Your Spirit, so that the paths I travel down would be paths of obedience for Your glory, honor, and praise.

Through the sacrifice of Your Son, Jesus Christ, for my sins, You have pardoned me from all guilt and have placed Your Spirit within me to sanctify my corrupt nature—to wash away my filth and to remove from within me anything that I might have allowed to come before You in my life.

You removed my cold, hard, self-centered, stubborn heart of stone and gave me a heart that longs to follow Your will—a heart tender and responsive to Your Spirit—so that I now not only have the desire to do what is right but I have within me the power to carry it out.

Grant me the wisdom to make good choices—choices that are pleasing to You—that will guard my heart and keep it from ever becoming hard and unresponsive to Your Spirit.

Let that new heart that You placed within me—when You first made me clean in Your sight—always remain tender and responsive to Your Spirit, so that the paths I travel down would be paths of obedience for Your glory, honor, and praise.

In the name of Jesus, Amen.

Great Joy, Deep Peace

You have given me greater joy
than those who have abundant harvests of grain and new wine.
In peace I will lie down and sleep,
for you alone, O LORD, will keep me safe.

— PSALM 4:7–8 (NLT)

Gracious LORD,

Thank You that there is no greater joy—nor any deeper peace—than that
which is given by Your hand to those who fully trust in You.

When I see others reaping a harvest of momentary happiest from an abundance of material gains, help me remember that only You can give the lasting rewards of joy and peace—rewards which are far beyond anything this world has to offer.

Comfort me with the assurance that I can overcome every discouragement and disappointment that I face—when my faith is strong, steady, and unchanging—knowing that You love me, that You are always in control, and that You are working in every situation for my good.

Help me to learn to trust You more each day, so I can lie down and sleep in perfect peace, knowing that You alone, O LORD, are able and will keep me safe in every way—mentally, emotionally, physically and spiritually.

Thank You that there is no greater joy—nor any deeper peace—than that
which is given by Your hand to those who fully trust in You.

In the name of Jesus, Amen.

Our Great and Faithful Shepherd

He will feed his flock like a shepherd.
He will carry the lambs in his arms,
holding them close to his heart.
He will gently lead the mother sheep with their young.

— ISAIAH 40:11 (NLT)

O LORD, My Shepherd,

Thank You for the intimate and loving relationship with You that is ours to enjoy, when we trust You to be our Shepherd—to look after us in every way just as a good shepherd watches over and cares for his sheep.

Help us always to trust You as the Great Shepherd—the One who will see to it that His flock is fed in every way, with food and water for their bodies and Your Word and Your Spirit for their souls, so that they will not lack any good thing.

Help us to see how You gather in Your lambs—those most dependent on You for protection and provision—with Your mighty yet gentle and loving arms, and how You carry them close to Your heart, never letting them slip from Your grasp.

Help us to believe that You gently and compassionately lead those who are with young—carefully showing them the way they should go and guiding them and empowering them for every step of their journey—as they put their trust in Your strength, wisdom, and love.

Thank You for the intimate and loving relationship with You that is ours to enjoy, when we trust You to be our Shepherd—to look after us in every way just as a good shepherd watches over and cares for his sheep.

In the name of Jesus, Amen.

God with Us

Behold, a virgin shall be with child, and shall bring forth a son, and they shall call his name Emmanuel, which being interpreted is, God with us.

— MATTHEW 1:23 (KJV)

Heavenly Father,

Thank You for sending Your Son, Jesus, into our world, to be for us, Emmanuel, God with us—forevermore!

Help me fully grasp this Truth: that just like we could not *truly love You* until You showed us what love is *by first loving us*, we also could not freely come into Your presence until You revealed Yourself to us by coming to live with us.

So thank You for coming—as a baby born to a virgin, who lived as a perfect man, who died in our place as a payment for our sin, that we might find our life in Him and be restored to a right relationship with You both now and forevermore.

Help me daily to take advantage of this invitation *to live in Your presence*—in direct and continually uninterrupted fellowship with You—that I might experience *all* of the blessings of peace, protection, provision, and purpose that You have waiting there for me with You.

Thank You for sending Your Son, Jesus, into our world, to be for us Emmanuel, God with us—forevermore!

In the name of Jesus, Amen.

For unto Us a Child Is Born!

For unto us a Child is born,
Unto us a Son is given;
And the government will be upon His shoulder.
And His name will be called
Wonderful, Counselor, Mighty God,
Everlasting Father, Prince of Peace.

— Isaiah 9:6 (NKJV)

Immanuel, God with Us,

Thank You for coming into our world as a baby, living a sinless life, taking
our sin on Yourself, and dying in our place to gain for us the victory over
sin and death—so that we could find our life in You!

You were born into the world through a virgin girl—to be fully human—
and You were conceived in her womb by the Holy Spirit as the Son of God—to
be fully God—and sent to a world in desperate need of a Savior.

You brought a new government, a new covenant—perfect and just in all
its ways—that would rest on Your shoulders and not our own, so that it would
never end.

You are my Wonderful Counselor—awesomely wonderful in all Your ways
and perfectly wise in all Your counsel.

You are my Mighty God—strong and powerful on my behalf, protecting
me from my enemies, preserving me with Your mighty right hand and never
letting me slip from Your loving grip.

You are my Everlasting Father—the One who gave life *itself* in the beginning, the One who gave life *to me* when I was conceived in my mother's womb,
and the One Who gives me life *forevermore* in You.

You are my Prince of Peace—as in You alone do I find that peace that is far
greater than I can understand when I humbly submit myself to Your will for me.

Thank You for coming into our world as a baby, living a sinless life, taking
our sin on Yourself, and dying in our place to gain for us the victory over
sin and death—so that we could find our life in You!

In Your Most Holy and Glorious Name, Amen.

Come with Haste, Then Go and Tell

And there were in the same country shepherds abiding in the field, keeping watch over their flock by night. And, lo, the angel of the Lord came upon them, and the glory of the Lord shone round about them: and they were sore afraid. And the angel said unto them, Fear not: for, behold, I bring you good tidings of great joy, which shall be to all people. For unto you is born this day in the city of David a Saviour, which is Christ the Lord. And this shall be a sign unto you; Ye shall find the babe wrapped in swaddling clothes, lying in a manger.

And suddenly there was with the angel a multitude of the heavenly host praising God, and saying, Glory to God in the highest, and on earth peace, good will toward men.

And it came to pass, as the angels were gone away from them into heaven, the shepherds said one to another, Let us now go even unto Bethlehem, and see this thing which is come to pass, which the Lord hath made known unto us. And they came with haste, and found Mary, and Joseph, and the babe lying in a manger.

And when they had seen it, they made known abroad the saying which was told them concerning this child.

— LUKE 2:8–17 (KJV)

Heavenly Father,

Just like the shepherds on that night long ago, may I come with haste to find my Savior waiting for me, then go and tell the story of His great love for me.

Thank you for choosing to reveal this good news to shepherds, to show me that Jesus is a King for every man—so I would know that He was sent for me.

Thank You that just like You did for the shepherds, You meet me where I am—and surround me with Your Glory.

Thank You that I don't have to fear—because what You have to tell me is always for my good.

Thank You that the "good tidings of great joy" which You brought that night continue in the good news You bring to me today.

Thank You that when I seek Jesus today—through prayer and through Your Word—He shows Himself to me and I learn to experience for myself His great love for me.

Thank You that I, too, am invited to join with the angels and sing praises to You for all the wondrous things You have done for me.

Help me not only to continue to seek Jesus for myself but also to tell the story of my experience of His love for me—so that others might come to know Him, too.

Just like the shepherds on that night long ago, may I come with haste to find my Savior waiting for me, then go and tell the story of His great love for me.

In the name of Jesus, Amen.

Wise Enough to Seek a Worship-Worthy King

Now after Jesus was born in Bethlehem of Judea in the days of Herod the king, behold, wise men from the East came to Jerusalem, saying, "Where is He who has been born King of the Jews? For we have seen His star in the East and have come to worship Him."

— MATTHEW 2:1–2 (NKJV)

Dear LORD,

Help me to be wise enough to seek You and to worship You just for who You are.

I don't want to be a man who foolishly sits back and waits for You to seek me out—like I am the one who is worthy to be sought after.

I don't want to be a man who foolishly acts like You should be held accountable to me for Your actions—as if I were a judge over You.

I don't want to be a man who foolishly demands that You prove that You are who You say You are—refusing to submit to You by faith.

I don't want to be a man who foolishly looks to You for what I can get from You—as if You owed me something.

Rather, help me to be a wise man who goes to great lengths to find You even if it means the journey is long, difficult, and filled with danger—because You are worthy to be sought after.

Help me to be a wise man who seeks after You from my heart—knowing that it is by faith that You will be found when I seek You with all that I am.

Help me to be a wise man who recognizes and worships You for Who You are—the Sovereign Almighty God, Creator of all there is.

Help me to be a wise man, who looks to see what I can give back to You from the great blessings that I have been given—and be that man who does so as an act of worship to You.

Help me to be wise enough to seek You and to worship You just for who You are.

In the name of Jesus, Amen.

Brotherly Affection

Be kindly affectionate to one another with brotherly love, in honor giving preference to one another.

— Romans 12:10 (NKJV)

Loving Lord,

Help me to check my motives, making sure they are pure, so that when I show honor to someone else, I do it with kind affection out of a heart of brotherly love.

I *don't* want to be that guy who is only kind to others in order to gain some benefit for himself.

Instead, I want to be that guy who is kind to others because his heart is overflowing with gratefulness for the love and affectionate kindness that has been shown to him by His Heavenly Father through Jesus Christ.

I want to honor others because they have been created in Your image and given life in order to become Your children—and as such are my brothers and sisters in Christ.

I want to honor the unique gifts You have given each one so that they might live for You and fulfill the plan You have for them.

I want to lay aside my competitiveness and take my delight in seeing another person's efforts praised rather than my own efforts—rejoicing in Christ for them and the gifts You have specifically blessed them with for Your glory.

Help me to check my motives, making sure they are pure, so that when I show honor to someone else, I do it with kind affection, out of a heart of brotherly love.

In the name of Jesus, Amen.

The Life of Jesus Seen in Us

We are pressed on every side by troubles, but we are not crushed. We are perplexed, but not driven to despair. We are hunted down, but never abandoned by God. We get knocked down, but we are not destroyed. Through suffering, our bodies continue to share in the death of Jesus so that the life of Jesus may also be seen in our bodies.

— 2 Corinthians 4:8–10 (NLT)

Heavenly Father,

Whenever I am pressed on every side by troubles, help me hold onto this Truth: You never leave me, You never let go of my hand, and victory over this world is found in Christ—who is my strength and who has won for me eternal life.

In those times when it seems as if my world is falling in on me, remind me that as hard as it is to endure, You will not allow me to be crushed—but will strengthen me through the struggle and deliver me safely through to the other side.

When I feel confused, perplexed, or at a loss as to how to find my way, remind me that I find my way in You—that You hold all wisdom and I don't have to be driven to despair because You will always show me what to do, when I ask in faith.

If I am ever pursued or persecuted for my beliefs, remind me that it is Your right hand that protects me and Your Spirit who tells me how to answer my accusers.

When I get my feet knocked out from under me, help me trust that You will pick me up and brush me off and set me on solid ground again—that in Christ, I will not be shaken and I cannot be destroyed.

Remind me that in every situation I face, in every suffering I endure, Christ has already won the victory—that these are all opportunities for Him to demonstrate His power and presence in me and through me, to all those around me.

Whenever I am pressed on every side by troubles, help me hold onto this Truth: You never leave me, You never let go of my hand, and victory over this world is found in Christ—who is my strength and who has won for me eternal life.

In the name of Jesus, Amen.

Serving Only Him

Whatever you do, work at it with all your heart, as working for the Lord, not for human masters, since you know that you will receive an inheritance from the Lord as a reward. It is the Lord Christ you are serving.

— COLOSSIANS 3:23–24 (NIV)

Heavenly Father,

Save me from any tendency I might have to work half-heartedly, by keeping me mindful of the One that I work for—Jesus Christ, my Lord!

I truly want to please You in all things and at all times—because of my love for You.

May I always put myself wholeheartedly into everything You ask me to do—both the very big things and the very small things—in order to bring glory to You alone.

May my true purpose *not* be found in working to please man, but let it be found in my love for You and my desire to please You.

Convict my heart when I am tempted to complain about the mundane tasks of life, and give me a heart to give You the very best I have to offer—no matter what task I find before me—never forgetting the great reward You have waiting for me at the end of my labor here on Earth.

Keep me ever mindful that You see everything that I do, and help me as I purpose to always be willing and obedient as I work for You—that I might prove my love for You.

Save me from any tendency I might have to work half-heartedly, by keeping me mindful of the One that I work for—Jesus Christ, my Lord!

In the name of Jesus, Amen.

To Do Good

So let's not get tired of doing what is good. At just the right time we will reap a harvest of blessing if we don't give up. Therefore, whenever we have the opportunity, we should do good to everyone—especially to those in the family of faith.

—GALATIANS 6:9–10 (NLT)

Generous God,

Help me never to get tired of doing what is good!

I confess that sometimes when I get tired, I am tempted to buy into the lie that my continuing to try to do good towards others at all times doesn't really make that much difference.

I confess that sometimes I forget that You use and multiply that smile, encouraging word, or act of kindness which I deliver in ways that I don't always see—and could never begin to imagine.

Thank you that there will come a time if I don't give up and fall away from doing good, when I will be blessed to see how You have used me.

Help me to take every opportunity to do something good for *everyone* I meet today—but keep me especially mindful to do so for my brothers and sisters in the faith, so that they might be encouraged to continue in the good work that You have called them to.

Help me never to get tired of doing what is good!

In the name of Jesus, Amen.

Press on to Finish Strong

No, dear brothers and sisters, I have not achieved it, but I focus on this one thing: Forgetting the past and looking forward to what lies ahead, I press on to reach the end of the race and receive the heavenly prize for which God, through Christ Jesus, is calling us.

— Philippians 3:13–14 (NLT)

Heavenly Father,

Help me to remember that my past should not be a prison which holds me captive, but rather a springboard that launches me into the things that You have prepared for me today and in the days to come, as I seek to serve You with all that I am.

I don't ever want to arrogantly take up the notion that I have achieved the perfection to which You are calling me—because I haven't even come close.

Nor do I want to be trapped by the sin of my past failures and shortcomings—unable to move forward because of my guilt and shame.

Help me to realize the dangerous path that I take when I fail to walk fully in the light of Your forgiveness—because when I allow the sin of my past to cripple me, I am in effect saying that what Christ did to save me from my sin was not enough!

I want to acknowledge Christ's power to forgive me and truly receive that forgiveness of my sin—so that I am able to focus on moving on from my past and looking forward to those things that You have waiting for me with each new day that comes.

And help me to finish strong the race that You have put before me and receive the heavenly reward that You have prepared for me through Christ Jesus.

Help me to remember that my past should not be a prison which holds me captive, but rather a springboard that launches me into the things that You have prepared for me today and in the days to come, as I seek to serve You with all that I am.

In the name of Jesus, Amen.

INDEX OF VERSES USED IN THIS DEVOTIONAL

Psalm 103:13–14 (NLT): MAY 31
Psalm 104:33–34 (NLT): MAR 29
Psalm 107:8–9 (NIV): NOV 14
Psalm 112:6–8 (NIV): MAR 17
Psalm 118:24 (NLT): FEB 9
Psalm 119:1–3 (NLT): APR 18
Psalm 119:4–5 (NLT): FEB 28
Psalm 119:7–8 (NLT): MAR 18
Psalm 119:11 (NKJV): JUN 2
Psalm 119:18–19 (NLT): JUL 29
Psalm 119:59–60 (NLT): JUL 13
Psalm 119:73 (NLT): JAN 22
Psalm 119:92–93 (NLT): MAY 3
Psalm 119:105 (NLT): JAN 3
Psalm 119:165 (NLT): JUL 8
Psalm 121:1–3 (NLT): FEB 17
Psalm 126:5–6 (NLT): APR 27
Psalm 130:3–4 (NLT): FEB 18
Psalm 130:5–6 (AMP): APR 19
Psalm 135:15–18 (NLT): MAR 21
Psalm 139:1–6 (NIV): FEB 25
Psalm 139:7–10 (NIV): APR 30
Psalm 139:14 (NKJV), Genesis 1:27 (NIV): NOV 19
Psalm 139:23–24 (NLT): MAY 11
Psalm 143:8 (NLT): APR 1
Psalm 145:8–10 (NLT): FEB 4
Psalm 147:3–5 (NLT): APR 2
Proverbs 1:7 (NKJV): MAR 14
Proverbs 3:5–6 (NLT): JAN 10
Proverbs 3:7 (NLT): JUN 5
Proverbs 4:18–19 (NLT): AUG 8
Proverbs 4:20–22 (NLT): FEB 29
Proverbs 4:23 (NLT): MAY 8
Proverbs 4:26–27 (NLT): APR 10
Proverbs 6:16–19 (NLT): AUG 31
Proverbs 9:10 (NLT): JAN 23
Proverbs 11:2 (AMP): SEP 23
Proverbs 11:27 (NLT): FEB 8
Proverbs 14:10 (NLT): JUL 6
Proverbs 14:12 (NLT): FEB 12
Proverbs 15:1 (NKJV): SEP 8
Proverbs 15:14 (NLT): JAN 18
Proverbs 15:15 (NLT): NOV 3
Proverbs 16:2 (AMP): MAR 24
Proverbs 16:18 (NIV): AUG 28
Proverbs 19:11 (NIV): FEB 20
Proverbs 19:21 (NIV): DEC 9
Proverbs 26:20 (NLT): JUN 22
Proverbs 28:26 (NIV): MAR 5
Proverbs 29:25 (NLT): DEC 15
Ecclesiastes 3:11 (NLT): JAN 19
Ecclesiastes 5:1–2 (NLT): JUL 11
Isaiah 9:6 (NKJV): DEC 24
Isaiah 12:2 (NASB): JAN 17
Isaiah 26:3–4 (NLT): APR 7
Isaiah 26:7–8 (NLT): AUG 10

Isaiah 29:13 (NLT), John 4:24 (NLT): SEP 26
Isaiah 30:15, 18 (NLT): MAY 21
Isaiah 30:21 (NLT): JUN 20
Isaiah 35:4 (NLT): JUN 6
Isaiah 40:11 (NLT): DEC 22
Isaiah 40:29–31 (NIV): OCT 8
Isaiah 41:10 (NLT): JAN 24
Isaiah 43:2 (NLT): MAR 6
Isaiah 43:18–19 (NIV): OCT 14
Isaiah 44:22 (NIV): MAY 16
Isaiah 50:4 (NLT): OCT 10
Isaiah 51:15b–16a: JUN 14
Isaiah 53:6 (NLT): APR 12
Isaiah 55:2 (NKJV): JUN 16
Isaiah 55:6–7 (NLT): JUL 20
Isaiah 55:8 (NLT): JAN 31
Isaiah 55:12 (NIV): JAN 5
Isaiah 58:11 (NLT): SEP 28
Isaiah 59:1–2 (NIV): MAY 25
Isaiah 64:8 (NASB): NOV 12
Isaiah 66:1–2 (NLT): OCT 31
Jeremiah 6:16 (NLT): JAN 29
Jeremiah 9:23–24 (NLT): AUG 16
Jeremiah 10:23–24 (NIV): OCT 21
Jeremiah 15:16 (NLT): OCT 12
Jeremiah 17:7–8 (NLT): FEB 11
Jeremiah 29:11 (NLT): APR 22
Jeremiah 29:12–13 (NASB): JUL 14
Jeremiah 31:25 (NLT), Matthew 11:28 (NLT): NOV 30
Jeremiah 32:27 (NIV): DEC 13
Jeremiah 33:2–3 (NIV): JUN 11
Lamentations 3:25–26 (NLT): MAY 28
Ezekiel 34:31 (NLT): FEB 6
Ezekiel 36:25–27 (NLT): DEC 20
Hosea 14:9 (NLT): JAN 15
Joel 2:13 (NLT): NOV 17
Amos 5:6a (AMP): JUN 30
Obadiah 1:3 (NLT): MAR 20
Micah 6:8 (NLT): JAN 28
Micah 7:7 (NLT): MAY 30
Habakkuk 3:2 (NLT): APR 21
Zephaniah 3:17 (NLT): AUG 19
Haggai 2:5b (ESV), Matthew 28:20b (NLT): SEP 13
Zechariah 7:9 (NLT): FEB 3

NEW TESTAMENT

Matthew 1:23 (KJV): DEC 23
Matthew 2:1–2 (NKJV): DEC 26
Matthew 3:8 (NLT): JUL 1
Matthew 4:20 (NLT), Exodus 20:3 (NKJV): FEB 23
Matthew 5:13 (NLT), Psalm 34:8 (NLT): OCT 13
Matthew 5:14–16 (NLT): NOV 9
Matthew 6:9 (NASB): MAR 11
Matthew 6:19–21 (NLT): OCT 3
Matthew 6:27 (NIV): SEP 17

Matthew 6:31–33 (NLT): NOV 20
Matthew 7:7–8 (NLT): JAN 4
Matthew 7:13–14 (NIV): AUG 14
Matthew 7:24–27 (NIV): SEP 4
Matthew 11:28 (NLT), Jeremiah 31:25 (NLT): NOV 30
Matthew 11:28–30 (NIV): JUL 21
Matthew 13:44 (NLT): JAN 9
Matthew 22:29 (NLT): JAN 1
Matthew 22:37–40 (NIV): MAY 9
Matthew 26:39 (NLT): JUN 3
Matthew 26:41 (NKJV): APR 11
Matthew 28:18–20 (NIV): AUG 3
Matthew 28:20b (NLT), Haggai 2:5b (ESV): SEP 30
Mark 1:35 (NLT): FEB 2
Mark 4:24–25 (NLT): JUL 10
Mark 4:39–40 (NKJV): MAY 29
Mark 9:33–35 (NLT): OCT 22
Mark 10:15 (NLT): DEC 2
Mark 10:42–45 (NLT): JAN 14
Luke 2:8–17 (KJV): DEC 25
Luke 4:13 (AMP): APR 5
Luke 6:27–28, 31 (NLT): JUL 12
Luke 6:45 (NIV), Philippians 4:8 (NLT): FEB 19
Luke 6:46 (NLT): JAN 20
Luke 9:23 (NLT): SEP 27
Luke 14:33 (NIV): DEC 3
John 1:1–3 (NLT): SEP 2
John 1:10–13 (NLT): SEP 14
John 3:16–17 (NKJV): JAN 25
John 3:27 (NLT): FEB 10
John 4:24 (NLT), Isaiah 29:13 (NLT): SEP 26
John 6:28–29 (NASB): OCT 4
John 8:12 (NLT): MAY 20
John 8:31–32 (NLT): JUL 18
John 8:34–36 (NLT): FEB 27
John 10:10 (NKJV): JUL 5
John 10:27 (AMP): NOV 6
John 11:35 (NASB): MAY 14
John 12:25 (NLT): JUN 15
John 12:42–43 (NIV): OCT 28
John 13:15 (NLT): MAR 16
John 13:34 (NASB): AUG 22
John 14:15–17a (NLT): APR 14
John 14:27 (NKJV): DEC 4
John 15:5 (NKJV): NOV 15
John 15:7 (NASB): APR 29
John 15:12–13 (NLT): AUG 11
Acts 4:32 (NLT): JAN 30
Acts 20:24 (NLT): JUN 9
Romans 1:16–17 (NLT): JAN 7
Romans 1:25 (NLT): MAY 23
Romans 3:22–24 (NLT): JUN 1
Romans 4:20–21 (NLT): AUG 21
Romans 5:3–5 (NLT): JUN 17
Romans 6:16 (NLT): MAR 19
Romans 6:23 (NLT): AUG 12

Romans 8:12–14 (NLT): JUN 27
Romans 8:28 (NLT): JAN 21
Romans 8:35, 37 (NLT): APR 17
Romans 8:38–39 (NLT): JUL 19
Romans 12:1 (NIV): MAR 12
Romans 12:2 (NLT): APR 8
Romans 12:3b (NLT): SEP 6
Romans 12:4–5 (NLT): NOV 5
Romans 12:6–8 (NLT): JUN 7
Romans 12:9 (NLT): MAY 10
Romans 12:10 (NKJV): DEC 27
Romans 12:11–12 (NIV): SEP 12
Romans 12:13 (NLT): OCT 9
Romans 12:16 (NLT): MAR 4
Romans 12:17–18 (AMP): JUL 4
Romans 12:21 (NIV): NOV 16
Romans 13:12–14 (NLT): DEC 8
Romans 15:13 (NLT): APR 23
1 Corinthians 1:30–31 (NLT): MAY 2
1 Corinthians 4:20 (NLT): AUG 15
1 Corinthians 6:19–20 (NLT): SEP 15
1 Corinthians 10:13 (NLT): OCT 11
1 Corinthians 13:4–7 (NLT): FEB 14
1 Corinthians 13:8a (NIV), Hebrews 11:6a (NIV),
    Galatians 5:6b (NIV): NOV 7
1 Corinthians 16:13–14 (NLT): JUL 9
2 Corinthians 1:3–4 (NLT): MAR 22
2 Corinthians 4:6–7 (NLT): SEP 7
2 Corinthians 4:8–10 (NLT): DEC 28
2 Corinthians 4:18 (NLT): JAN 27
2 Corinthians 5:7 (NKJV): JUL 15
2 Corinthians 5:20–21 (NLT): FEB 5
2 Corinthians 6:10 (NLT): AUG 24
2 Corinthians 7:10 (NLT): JUN 19
2 Corinthians 10:3–5 (NIV): OCT 15
Galatians 1:3–5 (NLT): FEB 7
Galatians 2:20 (NKJV): SEP 1
Galatians 5:6b (NIV), 1 Corinthians 13:8a (NIV),
    Hebrews 11:6a (NIV): NOV 7
Galatians 5:13 (NLT): OCT 7
Galatians 5:16 (NLT): MAY 5
Galatians 5:22–23 (NLT): JUL 2
Galatians 5:24 (NLT): JUN 12
Galatians 5:25–26 (NLT): NOV 1
Galatians 6: 2–3 (NLT): FEB 16
Galatians 6:7–8 (NLT): AUG 17
Galatians 6:9–10 (NLT): DEC 30
Ephesians 1:4–5 (NLT): JUL 16
Ephesians 2:8–10 (NLT): FEB 24
Ephesians 4:2 (NLT): AUG 25
Ephesians 4:29 (NLT): SEP 18
Ephesians 4:30 (NLT): MAR 25
Ephesians 5:1–2 (NIV): OCT 5
Ephesians 5:15–17 (NLT): MAY 17
Ephesians 6:12 (NLT): APR 4
Ephesians 6:13–17 (NIV): DEC 7

Printed in the USA
CPSIA information can be obtained
at www.ICGtesting.com
JSHW030715020124
54381JS00008B/2